Intercultural Dialogue

'Intercultural dialogue', as a concept and ideology in the European Union, suggests a rational 21st century society where people can engage in (intercultural) communication on a global scale, and can do so openly and freely in conditions of security and mutual respect. Intercultural dialogue connotes dialogic communication that is peaceful, reconciliatory and democratic. Yet the term and its accompanying rhetoric belie the intercultural communicative undercurrents and their manifestations that people encounter in their daily lives.

The research-informed chapters in this book, which are situated in international contexts, provide more nuanced understandings, and many even challenge this non-critical ideology by suggesting that the concept of intercultural dialogue is inoperable and problematic under the present conditions of globalisation and migration, where there exists conflict, vulnerability and instability. The different theoretical perspectives and analyses presented by the authors are a reminder that researchers in the field of intercultural communication require robust and appropriate theories, methods and pedagogies in order to research these complex conditions and contexts, particularly where different languages and identities are present. The book is also a reminder of how context and power both (re)shape and contest the central tenets of intercultural dialogue – in particular, of who speaks for whom, when, how and under what circumstances and conditions.

This book was originally published as a special issue of *Language and Intercultural Communication.*

Prue Holmes is Reader in the School of Education at Durham University, UK, and Adjunct Professor at the University of Helsinki, Finland. She teaches and researches in intercultural communication and education. She has published widely in international journals, leads the AHRC-funded project 'Researching Multilingually' and holds several editorial board positions on international journals.

Melinda Dooly holds a Serra Húnter fellowship as teacher and researcher at the Education Faculty of the Universitat Autònoma de Barcelona, Spain, where she teaches English as a Foreign Language Methodology and research methods courses. Her teaching and research address technology-enhanced project-based language learning in teacher preparation as well as with very young language learners. She has been involved in several national and international projects as both team member and as principal manager.

John P. O'Regan is Senior Lecturer in Applied Linguistics at the Institute of Education, University College London, UK, where he is a doctoral supervisor and leads the MA

Applied Linguistics programme. His research interests include the political economy of global English, intercultural communication theory, identity politics and critical discourse analysis. He is the author of articles covering a wide range of topics in the fields of applied linguistics and cultural studies.

Intercultural Dialogue
Questions of research, theory and practice

Edited by
**Prue Holmes, Melinda Dooly and
John P. O'Regan**

LONDON AND NEW YORK

First published 2016
by Routledge
2 Park Square, Milton Park, Abingdon, Oxon, OX14 4RN, UK

and by Routledge
711 Third Avenue, New York, NY 10017, USA

Routledge is an imprint of the Taylor & Francis Group, an informa business

© 2016 Taylor & Francis

All rights reserved. No part of this book may be reprinted or reproduced or utilised in any form or by any electronic, mechanical, or other means, now known or hereafter invented, including photocopying and recording, or in any information storage or retrieval system, without permission in writing from the publishers.

Trademark notice: Product or corporate names may be trademarks or registered trademarks, and are used only for identification and explanation without intent to infringe.

British Library Cataloguing in Publication Data
A catalogue record for this book is available from the British Library

ISBN 13: 978-1-138-63914-0

Typeset in Times New Roman
by RefineCatch Limited, Bungay, Suffolk

Publisher's Note
The publisher accepts responsibility for any inconsistencies that may have arisen during the conversion of this book from journal articles to book chapters, namely the possible inclusion of journal terminology.

Disclaimer
Every effort has been made to contact copyright holders for their permission to reprint material in this book. The publishers would be grateful to hear from any copyright holder who is not here acknowledged and will undertake to rectify any errors or omissions in future editions of this book.

Contents

Citation Information	vii
Notes on Contributors	ix

Introduction – Intercultural dialogue: challenges to theory, practice
and research   1
Prue Holmes

1. Ethical communication and intercultural responsibility: a philosophical
perspective   7
Giuliana Ferri

2. Zones of interculturality and linguistic identity: tales of Ladino by
Sephardic Jews in Bulgaria   24
Richard Fay and Leah Davcheva

3. Cultural identities in international, interorganisational meetings:
a corpus-informed discourse analysis of indexical *we*   41
Michael Handford

4. Faithful imitator, legitimate speaker, playful creator and dialogical
communicator: shift in English learners' identity prototypes   59
Yihong Gao

5. Interreligious dialogue in schools: beyond asymmetry and
categorisation?   76
Anna-Leena Riitaoja and Fred Dervin

6. Capabilities for intercultural dialogue   91
Veronica Crosbie

7. 'They are bombing now': 'Intercultural Dialogue' in times of conflict   108
Alison Phipps

Pedagogical Forum

8. The application of general education and intercultural communication
in a 'news-listening' class   125
Tiao Wang

CONTENTS

9. How pedagogical blogging helps prepare students for intercultural communication in the global workplace   132
Radhika Jaidev

10. Intercultural education in primary school: a collaborative project   140
Marta Santos, Maria Helena Araújo e Sá and Ana Raquel Simões

Index   151

Citation Information

The chapters in this book were originally published in *Language and Intercultural Communication*, volume 14, issue 1 (February 2014). When citing this material, please use the original page numbering for each article, as follows:

Introduction
Intercultural dialogue: challenges to theory, practice and research
Prue Holmes
Language and Intercultural Communication, volume 14, issue 1 (February 2014)
pp. 1–6

Chapter 1
Ethical communication and intercultural responsibility: a philosophical perspective
Giuliana Ferri
Language and Intercultural Communication, volume 14, issue 1 (February 2014)
pp. 7–23

Chapter 2
Zones of interculturality and linguistic identity: tales of Ladino by Sephardic Jews in Bulgaria
Richard Fay and Leah Davcheva
Language and Intercultural Communication, volume 14, issue 1 (February 2014)
pp. 24–40

Chapter 3
Cultural identities in international, interorganisational meetings: a corpus-informed discourse analysis of indexical we
Michael Handford
Language and Intercultural Communication, volume 14, issue 1 (February 2014)
pp. 41–58

Chapter 4
Faithful imitator, legitimate speaker, playful creator and dialogical communicator: shift in English learners' identity prototypes
Yihong Gao
Language and Intercultural Communication, volume 14, issue 1 (February 2014)
pp. 59–75

CITATION INFORMATION

Chapter 5
Interreligious dialogue in schools: beyond asymmetry and categorisation?
Anna-Leena Riitaoja and Fred Dervin
Language and Intercultural Communication, volume 14, issue 1 (February 2014)
pp. 76–90

Chapter 6
Capabilities for intercultural dialogue
Veronica Crosbie
Language and Intercultural Communication, volume 14, issue 1 (February 2014)
pp. 91–107

Chapter 7
'They are bombing now': 'Intercultural Dialogue' in times of conflict
Alison Phipps
Language and Intercultural Communication, volume 14, issue 1 (February 2014)
pp. 108–124

Chapter 8
The application of general education and intercultural communication in a 'news-listening' class
Tiao Wang
Language and Intercultural Communication, volume 14, issue 1 (February 2014)
pp. 125–131

Chapter 9
How pedagogical blogging helps prepare students for intercultural communication in the global workplace
Radhika Jaidev
Language and Intercultural Communication, volume 14, issue 1 (February 2014)
pp. 132–139

Chapter 10
Intercultural education in primary school: a collaborative project
Marta Santos, Maria Helena Araújo e Sá and Ana Raquel Simões
Language and Intercultural Communication, volume 14, issue 1 (February 2014)
pp. 140–150

For any permission-related enquiries please visit:
http://www.tandfonline.com/page/help/permissions

Notes on Contributors

Maria Helena Araújo e Sá is a Professor in the Department of Education of the University of Aveiro, Portugal, where she teaches Language Teacher Education and coordinates the Laboratory of Research and Training in Foreign Languages. She has participated in international projects concerning intercomprehension and intercultural communication, and she runs several training courses at national and international levels. She has published extensively in the field of foreign languages teaching and plurilingual communication.

Veronica Crosbie is a Lecturer in ESOL and Intercultural Studies at Dublin City University, Ireland. Her research interests include capabilities approach, cosmopolitan citizenship, critical pedagogy and intercultural competence. She coordinated the Lingua 2-funded LOLIPOP in 2004–2007. She is currently interested in developing a capability-based curriculum for language and intercultural learning.

Leah Davcheva is an intercultural consultant and facilitator at AHA Moments, Centre for Interculturality, Solutions Focus and Host Leadership, in Sofia, Bulgaria. She works with educators, young people and business practitioners to assist them in developing routes for personal and collective achievements. She is interested in the intercultural agenda of mobility (both historically and in present day terms), linguistic and cultural diversity on the Balkans, mutuality and inclusion.

Fred Dervin is Professor of Multicultural Education at the University of Helsinki, Finland. He specialises in language and intercultural education, the sociology of multiculturalism, and linguistics for intercultural communication and education.

Melinda Dooly holds a Serra Húnter fellowship as teacher and researcher at the Education Faculty of the Universitat Autònoma de Barcelona, Spain, where she teaches English as a Foreign Language Methodology and research methods courses. Her teaching and research address technology-enhanced project-based language learning in teacher preparation as well as with very young language learners. She has been involved in several national and international projects as both team member and as principal manager.

Richard Fay is a Lecturer in Education at The University of Manchester, UK, specialising in TESOL, intercultural communication, and researcher education (including narrative research). He is an ethnomusicologist, klezmer aficionado, and leader of the university's klezmer ensemble, the *Michael Kahan Kapelye*. His intercultural interests (educational, linguistic, cultural and musical) are focused on, amongst other contexts, the Balkans.

NOTES ON CONTRIBUTORS

Giuliana Ferri is a Ph.D. student at the Institute of Education, University College London, UK. Her current research focuses on the implications of Levinasian ethics in the conceptualisation of intercultural communication studies. Her other research interests are sociolinguistics, language in education and the philosophy of education.

Yihong Gao is Professor of Linguistics and Director of the Research Institute of Linguistics and Applied Linguistics in the School of Foreign Languages at Peking University, Beijing, China. She is also Vice President of the China English Language Education Association, and served as the President of The Association of Chinese Sociolinguistics. Her publications include *Understanding and Transcending Linguistic and Cultural Differences* (2000), *Foreign Language Leaning: '1+1>2'* (2001), *The Social Psychology of English Learning by Chinese College Students Motivation and Learners' Self-Identities* (2004), and *College Students' English Learning Motivation and Self-Identity Development – A four-year longitudinal study* (2013).

Michael Handford is Professor of Applied Linguistics at Cardiff University, where he is Director of Research for the Centre for Language and Communication Research. He has published on discourse in professional settings, cultural identities at work, the application of corpus tools in discourse analysis, English as a Lingua Franca in the construction industry and language learning.

Prue Holmes is Reader in the School of Education at Durham University, UK, and Adjunct Professor at the University of Helsinki, Finland. She teaches and researches in intercultural communication and education. She has published widely in international journals, leads the AHRC-funded project 'Researching Multilingually' and holds several editorial board positions on international journals.

Radhika Jaidev is a Senior Lecturer at the Centre for English Language Communication at the National University of Singapore. She teaches Professional Communication to graduating Science and Engineering students as well as Academic English to postgraduate students. Her research is in group learning processes in higher education as well as content and language-integrated learning. She also has a keen interest in the scholarship of teaching and learning and its application to enhance her teaching in higher education.

John P. O'Regan is Senior Lecturer in Applied Linguistics at the Institute of Education, University College London, UK, where he is a doctoral supervisor and leads the MA Applied Linguistics programme. His research interests include the political economy of global English, intercultural communication theory, identity politics, and critical discourse analysis. He is the author of articles covering a wide range of topics in the fields of applied linguistics and cultural studies.

Alison Phipps is Professor of Languages and Intercultural Studies at the University of Glasgow, UK, and co-convener of Glasgow Refugee Asylum and Migration Network.

Anna-Leena Riitaoja is a Postdoctoral Researcher in the Institute of Behavioural Sciences of the University of Helsinki, Finland. She works on the project 'Perceptions and Constructions on Marginalisation and Belonging in Education', which examines exclusion and inclusion in lower secondary education through ethnographic and participatory methods. Alongside otherness, marginalisation and belonging, her research interests include intercultural education and dialogue. She is also interested in sociology, philosophy and ethics of education as well as post-colonial and post-structural feminist pedagogies.

NOTES ON CONTRIBUTORS

Marta Santos is a primary school teacher. She also holds a degree in Communication Design and a post-graduate degree in Educational Multimedia. She works as an IT (information and technology) teacher in extra-curriculum activities in two primary schools in Ílhavo, Portugal, with children aged 6–10. She is currently finishing a PhD project entitled 'Intercultural education in primary school: partnerships involving schools and the community', under the supervision of Maria Helena Araújo e Sá and Ana Raquel Simões at the Universidade de Aveiro, Portugal.

Ana Raquel Simões is a Professor in the Department of Education at the University of Aveiro, Portugal. She holds a PhD in Language Education and has published in reviewed book chapters, scientific international and national journals and proceedings. She has also taken part in the scientific commission and organisation of scientific events and is a member of international and national research projects. She is a member of the Open Laboratory for the Learning of Foreign Languages (LALE), based on CIDTFF/ UA, since January 2000, where she is responsible for activities within the fields of research, dissemination and cooperation with society.

Tiao Wang is an Associate Professor in English in the School of Foreign Languages at Harbin Institute of Technology, China. She visited the Department of English Studies at Durham University, UK, in 2012 for a year as a visiting scholar. Her academic interests include Teaching English as a Foreign Language, intercultural communication and English literatures.

INTRODUCTION

Intercultural dialogue: challenges to theory, practice and research

Prue Holmes

School of Education, Durham University, Durham, UK

This special issue showcases papers presented at the International Association of Languages and Intercultural Communication (IALIC) conference in Durham in December 2012. The conference, similarly entitled 'Intercultural dialogue: Current challenges; future directions', invited presenters to critically examine the concept of intercultural dialogue and its implications for researching and learning about intercultural communication in the increasingly intercultural communities in which people now live.

The term 'intercultural dialogue' is now in wide currency and offers much hope to peace and harmony among nations. Officially inaugurated in 2008, via the Council of Europe's White Paper and promulgated by the European Union's declaration in the same year, the concept suggests a social and political response to the need for intercultural communication and understanding in what was then a rapidly expanding European Union. (Currently, there are 28 nations encompassing a mix of languages, ethnicities, religions, histories, geographical complexities, etc., including emergent transcultural landscapes brought about by migration and other global flows of people.) The term engenders a rational post-war European society where people can engage in (inter) cultural communication openly and freely in conditions of security and mutual respect, thanks to the numerous institutions within the European Union, and the laws and conventions that require and condone civil communicative practices.

Other organisations, e.g., UNESCO, the British Council, have also developed their own definitions (see Phipps' paper in this issue for their description and critique) and institutional structures associated with the term. The aims and activities of these institutions within the European Union seek to advance peace, reconciliation and democracy through the principles of intercultural dialogue, earning the European Union the Nobel Peace Prize for 2012.

The concept has been taken up outside of Europe, too, through the National Communication Association's Summer Conference on Intercultural Dialogue in 2009 at Maltepe University, Istanbul, Turkey, resulting in the establishment of the Center for Intercultural Dialogue (http://www.centerforinterculturaldialogue.org/) by Wendy Leeds-Hurwitz and supported by the Council of Communication Associations in the USA. And there are many other institutions, too numerous to mention here, in support of the cause of intercultural dialogue, and much associated research activity.

However, the term, its accompanying rhetoric, and the institutions that have emerged in its name, belie the intercultural communicative undercurrents and their manifestations people encounter in their daily lives. Within context of the European Union, Näss (2010) noted that policy documents were both ambiguous and indistinct in their understanding of the term both as a concept to guide policy construction and as a political instrument to manage cultural diversity and variation. Most noticeably, the absence of dialogue is apparent where the Roma in Europe are concerned. Herakova (2009) argues that the Roma people's 'inarticulateness and nondominant worldview (because of difference experiences) prevent them from participation in the public sphere' (p. 294); they are a socially excluded group, muted by the voices of the majority. Similarly, Witteborn (2011) illustrated the limits of intercultural dialogue on the Internet, e.g., as Uighur calls for democracy in Xinjiang on a multilingual Uighur pro-independence website were subverted and reinterpreted by Chinese nationalist voices. And Anoush Ehteshami (School of Government and International Affairs, Durham University), in his opening address at the Durham conference, reminded us that the concept is full of optimism in a world where challenges for resources, power and ownership are often accompanied by an unwillingness to relinquish them; the result is often intractable conflict. In such contexts, the aims of intercultural dialogue are unrecognisable and meaningless.

Yet many intercultural communication scholars remind us that conflict is a normal and evolving state in building intercultural alliances and relationships (e.g., Collier, 2003; Oetzel & Ting-Toomey, 2006). What then is the scope – and hope – for intercultural dialogue? Indeed, intercultural communicative processes are essentially dialogic, and involve recognising and negotiating points of sameness as well as difference. Yet, it is often at the points of difference – the scope of dialogue – where communicators focus on the linguistic, political, religious, historical, economic, etc., positioning and identities of each communicator. Through dialogue individuals have the possibility to (re)negotiate and (re)construct their positions and identities within and across groups (Collier, 2003), to acknowledge the complexity and diversity of relationships, and to work towards solutions to seemingly intractable divergences and unrelenting postures in situations of conflict. This is the hope of intercultural dialogue.

The authors of the papers in this special issue offer new and fresh ways of theorising and researching intercultural dialogue – its potential for development, and its limits and qualifications. They do this through their critical examination of the concept, its meaning in practice, and its implications for intercultural communication, intercultural education, language teaching and improving people's lives.

The special issue papers

The special issue leads with Ferri's theoretical analysis of Levinas's understanding of the nature of language which she draws on to illustrate the limitations of current conceptualisations of intercultural communication competence and responsibility. In her analysis, Ferri highlights the importance of the interdependence of Self and Other, the role of power, and an awareness of the position of the self as a potential all-knowing subject capable of silencing others. She concludes:

> [an] ethical approach to IC [intercultural communication] entails taking the risk of meeting the other qua other, without the safety net of cultural categorisation, and at the same time being aware that the encounter with the other does not occur in a vacuum, because we are always positioned within networks of power.

Dacheva and Fay's study of Bulgarian Ladino speakers' narratives reminds us that intercultural dialogue is not a new phenomenon. Drawing on Brunner's narrative construction of reality and theories of interculturality, they reveal, through (re)storied narratives, the highly situated complexities of language-based identity performances of Ladino speakers in Bulgaria. Their analysis uncovers five zones of interculturality (intrapersonal, domestic, local, diasporic, international) as a framework for appreciating and exploring how languages, cultures, affiliations, identities are in constant interaction with one another.

Handford's paper draws on a corpus-informed discourse analysis of the indexical *we* to show how speakers signal different identities at different moments in the unfolding discourse in international, inter-organisational meetings. Handford concludes that the ubiquitous use of *we* – as a cultural as well as statistical keyword – 'constitutes the collaborative tenor of much professional discourse'. However, he suggests that further research is required to understand how cultural as well as organisational identities are indexed beyond this specific use of *we*.

Gao Yihong explores how intercultural dialogue is played out in Chinese youths' linguistic identities through their learning of English. Through an historical examination of approaches to second language acquisition and learning, she outlines four key proto-types – faithful imitator, legitimate speaker, playful creator and dialogical communicator – of the English language learner. The fourth, the dialogical communicator, is the contemporary language learner prototype which emerges through an 'internal conversation between structure and agency, society and individual, other and self'. Gao argues that the dialogical communicator prototype relies on 'sustained personal commitment and gradual maturation in a nurtured environment', and 'does not lend itself easily to programmed training or testing'. This prototype raises questions about training and assessment found in some models of intercultural competence. Instead, the dialogical communicator prototype lends itself to approaches that encourage responsibility and civic action through intercultural citizenship, and capabilities approaches (see Crosbie's paper below).

The fifth paper, by Riitaoja and Dervin, shifts the focus to an ethnographic study of interreligious dialogue in two Finnish schools. Drawing on postcolonial, poststructural and related feminist theories, they examine constructions of self and other in the everyday encounters among teachers and students, and the resultant otherising of individuals and the religious groups to which they belong. Thus, they question whether the aims of interreligious dialogue in schools offer 'a viable way to learn about each other and to increase mutual understanding'.

Crosbie takes up Ferri's critique of intercultural competence theory and the need for an ethical approach to intercultural dialogue by drawing on Nussbaum's capabilities approach in democratic citizenship education and Sen's idea of individuals' freedom in reasoning and decision-making. Crosbie highlights the limitations of 'skills' or 'competence' based approaches in that they 'focus on the results or ends that an individual can achieve'. By contrast, the capabilities approach emphasises 'the freedom and agency that an individual has to be and to act', requiring people to make ethically informed choices. Crosbie's paper provides a pedagogic direction for building capability in language learners, by foregrounding social justice and agency through a content and language integrated learning approach in the language classroom.

The final paper by Phipps completes the dis-ease, initiated by Ferri and developed further by the authors of the other papers, over the robustness of 'intercultural dialogue' to achieve its aims. Phipps questions the idealised meanings of intercultural dialogue, as promulgated by European organisations such as UNESCO, the British Council and the Council of Europe. Through an ethnographic study of peace work in Gaza, she argues that 'concepts which have arisen in contexts of relative peace and stability in Europe are not suited to conditions of conflict and siege'. She concludes that the concept 'is at best problematic and largely inoperable under present conditions of globalisation' where there is 'conflict, vulnerability, insecurity and aggression'. Instead, she argues, models that are designed for 'depoliticised and normatively conservative conditions' need to be replaced by 'models of creative practice and transformation'.

Thus, the different theoretical perspectives and analyses presented by the authors in these seven papers are a reminder that researchers in the field of intercultural communication require theories and methods that are both robust and appropriate for the complex contexts and conditions in which they are researching. Together, the papers illustrate and exemplify the need for theoretical and methodological complexity and nuance when researching people who are communicating where there are different languages and identities at play, and the need for intercultural communication researchers to be ever mindful of context and power in intercultural dialogue – who speaks for whom, when, how and under what circumstances and conditions.

The Pedagogic Forum papers

The three papers in the Pedagogic Forum provide international scenarios – in China, Singapore and Portugal – where intercultural dialogue is operationalised through intercultural pedagogies. Wang highlights how the emergence of General Education programmes in China offer the potential to develop students' intercultural communication and competence. The courses within these general education programmes, e.g., in a news listening class in an English course, enable students to develop interdisciplinary knowledge alongside intercultural perspectives and competence, seen as necessary for communication with others in an intercultural world. A corollary is that teachers, too, need to develop intercultural competence.

In the second paper, Jaidev deals with preparing international and local students in Singapore for managing intercultural dialogic encounters in increasingly globalised workplaces. Jaidev discusses how students used reflective blog posts on their own and on their peers' intercultural interactions in group learning tasks and assignments. She argues that blogs create 'a non-threatening, low stress environment' where students can openly and freely discuss and learn about intercultural communication with cultural others, in order to prepare for similar scenarios they are likely to encounter in the workplace.

Finally, Santos, Araújo e Sá and Simões, drawing on a larger collaborative project in Aveiro, Portugal, present a model for intercultural education, developed within a partnership involving two primary schools (largely monocultural), an immigrants' association, a cultural association, an institution working with disabled people, the City Hall and Library belonging to the City Hall. The model consisted of several practical activities, integrating the various partners, and thus facilitating opportunities for intercultural dialogue and the development of intercultural awareness and competence. Santos and her team report that participants demonstrated increased knowledge of different countries and cultures, and developed their critical thinking and attitudes such as increased curiosity and awareness of linguistic and cultural diversity, respect for the others and working in partnership.

An afterword...

Robi Damelin, an Israeli mother, and Basswam Aramin, a Palestinian father, are two parents who each lost a child in the Israeli–Palestinian conflict. They each interpret their

INTERCULTURAL DIALOGUE

understanding of that loss on the BBC's Radio 4 *Today* programme (7 November 2013), and how they seek a solution to the killing – through dialogue. Robi interprets the killing of her son, serving in the Reserves, by a Palestinian sniper:

> I'm sure the Palestinian did not kill him because he was David; he killed him because he was a symbol of an occupying army. That's not an easy thing to say.

Basswam interprets the killing of his 10-year old daughter by an Israeli soldier with a rubber bullet, from a distance of 15–20 m, outside her school:

> I didn't find the answer in revenge because for more than 100 years we have been killing each other, and the result will bring to ourselves more blood, and more victims, more pain.

Neither seeks revenge, but instead, dialogue. As members of the Parents' Circle, they believe that through intercultural dialogue with others, and by engaging with political figures, it is possible to stop the killing and influence the peace process. Robi states:

> We are not about rainbows and flowers and bad poetry. We are talking about really understanding the other, and we're talking about creating a framework for a reconciliation process to be an integral part of any future peace agreement.

Despite the anger and pain they feel, and the inhumanity of the other, they do not want retaliation and revenge, but dialogue with others to seek understanding, build trust, come to know the other – not as the enemy, but as a human being who wants security and peace. Bassram concludes 'our role is to convince others that peace is possible…it starts with individuals'. Their dialogic intentions and actions embody the hope of dialogue.

Together, the papers in this special issue illustrate the scope and hope of intercultural dialogue. They offer a new theoretical, methodological and pedagogic agenda for building on, and perhaps even transforming, the concept of intercultural dialogue. They open up new lines of inquiry which invite further theorising of intercultural dialogic communication and its related concepts of interculturality, capability, responsibility, ethics, interreligious dialogue and conflict transformation. They also highlight the importance of educational programmes and pedagogic methods that provide foundations of intercultural understanding among students, young people and the wider community.

References

Collier, M. J. (2003). Negotiating intercultural alliance relationships: Toward transformation. In M. J. Collier (Ed.), *Intercultural alliances: Critical transformation* (pp. 1–16). Thousand Oaks, CA: Sage.

Herakova, L. L. (2009). Identity, communication, inclusion: The Roma and (new) Europe. *Journal of International and Intercultural Communication, 2*, 279–297. doi:10.1080/1751305090 3177318

Näss, H. E. (2010, June). The ambiguities of intercultural dialogue: Critical perspectives on the European Union's new agenda for culture. *Journal of Intercultural Communication, 23*. Retrieved from http://www.immi.se/intercultural/

Oetzel, J., & Ting-Toomey, S. (2006). *The Sage handbook of conflict communication*. Thousand Oaks, CA: Sage.

Witteborn, S. (2011). Discursive grouping in a virtual forum: Dialogue, difference, and the "intercultural". *Journal of International and Intercultural Communication*, *4*(2), 109–126. doi:10.1080/17513057.2011.556827

Ethical communication and intercultural responsibility: a philosophical perspective

Giuliana Ferri

Department of Culture, Communication and Media, Institute of Education, University of London, London, UK

The ethical dimension of dialogue represents a major concern in the context of current research in intercultural responsibility. In this paper, I discuss the modalities in which the notion of competence is used to conceptualise responsibility and the relationship between self and other in intercultural research, in order to critique the Cartesian presuppositions of intercultural communication theory. I argue that models of competence and responsibility that are employed to design intercultural training operate within the paradigm of the autonomous rational agent that informs Kantian ethical thinking. I contrast the model of the competent intercultural speaker that emerges in intercultural research with the distinction proposed by Levinas between the saying and the said (le dire and le dit, meaning the event of speech and the content of speech), to suggest two scenarios of intercultural interaction that show two different approaches to responsibility, one operating in the dimension of the said and the other in the dimension of the saying. Thus, in this paper, I discuss the implications of Levinas's reflection on the nature of language for the development of an ethical framework that addresses the limitations of current conceptualisations in intercultural communication theory of competence and responsibility.

La dimensione etica del dialogo rappresenta una delle preoccupazioni maggiori nell'ambito della ricerca sulla responsabilità interculturale. In questo articolo analizzo in maniera critica le modalità in cui la nozione di competenza è usata per concettualizzare il concetto di responsabilità e la relazione con l'altro nel contesto della teoria della comunicazione interculturale, in modo da discuterne le presupposizioni Cartesiane. I modelli di competenza e responsabilità che sono utilizzati nel training interculturale operano all'interno del paradigma dell'agente autonomo razionale della tradizione etica kantiana. Ho intenzione di contrastare il modello del "competent intercultural speaker" che emerge dalla ricerca interculturale con la distinzione creata da Levinas tra il dire e il detto (le dire e le dit, l'evento della parola e il contenuto della lingua), per suggerire due scenari di interazione interculturale che mostrano due approcci alla responsabilitá, uno nella dimensione del dire e l'altro nella dimensione del detto. Quindi, in questo articolo discuto le implicazioni delle riflessioni di Levinas sulla natura del linguaggio per lo sviluppo di una comprensione etica che riconosce i limiti delle concettualizzazioni delle nozioni di competenza e responsabilità nella teoria della comunicazione interculturale.

INTERCULTURAL DIALOGUE

Introduction

This paper is theoretical and exploratory in nature. Its aim is twofold: to describe the models of competence developed in the field of intercultural communication, and to introduce the categories of the *said*, meaning the content of speech, and the *saying*, which indicates the event of speech, elaborated by Levinas (1998). Using this distinction, I discuss the modalities in which the notion of competence is used to conceptualise responsibility and the relationship between self and other in intercultural research, and I suggest two scenarios of intercultural interaction, one operating in the dimension of the *said* and the other in the dimension of the *saying*.

In doing this, I describe the ethical relation formulated by Levinas (1969, 1985, 1998, 2006) to define the encounter with the uniqueness of the other through the open-ended character of dialogue, in order to critique the Cartesian presuppositions of intercultural communication (henceforth IC) theory. My contention is that models of competence and responsibility that are employed to design intercultural training (e.g. Deardorff, 2006, 2009; Guilherme, Keating, & Hoppe, 2010; Hofstede & Hofstede, 2004; Spencer-Oatey & Stadler, 2009) reflect the Kantian notion of the rational autonomy of the moral agent who is held accountable for the effect of his/her moral decisions on others, who become the recipients of his/her actions. The locus of this agency is the Cartesian subject of the 'I think', a bounded individual capable of autonomy and rationality, a concept that developed during the Enlightenment, and particularly through Kantian moral philosophy, with the internalisation of reason and judgement in the thinking subject according to universal norms of freedom and equality. In other words, the subject of this form of rationality that initiated the modern conception of ethical thinking is able to choose the right course of action according to what reason dictates (Furrow, 2005; Popke, 2003).

My argument develops as follows: in the first section, I begin with a reflection on the origins of interculturalism as a field of inquiry in North American foreign policy and trade, which informs a functionalist understanding of communicative competence as effective transmission of meaning across cultures (Martin & Nakayama, 2010). After touching upon critical formulations of intercultural competence in the context of language learning, I outline current research on the acquisition of communicative competences relating to the development of intercultural responsibility. Finally, I trace the connection that is established in intercultural research between the acquisition of communicative competences and the development of responsibility to the idea of the autonomous rational agent that informs Kantian ethical thinking. In contrast to the model of the competent intercultural speaker that emerges in intercultural research, I intend to discuss the implications of Levinas's reflection on the nature of language for the development of an ethical framework that addresses the limitations of current conceptualisations in intercultural communication theory of competence and responsibility.

The field of intercultural research

The origins of IC as a field of inquiry in North American foreign policy and trade inform the idea of communication as effective transmission of meaning across cultures. The genealogical reconstruction of the field of IC conducted by Moon (2010) attributes the narrow understanding of culture in terms of national boundaries and the preference for microanalysis focused on communicative practices between interactants from different national cultures, to the agenda set by the US Foreign Institute in the 1950s in order to create intercultural training to use in trade with foreign countries. Moon concludes that:

INTERCULTURAL DIALOGUE

Intercultural communication developed in the midst of World War II as a tool of imperialism and that much of its foundations were infused with a colonial perspective. (2010, p. 35)

Moon attributes the formulation of the concepts of adaptation and competence to this dominant intercultural discourse that has narrowed the field of research to a set of categories that are based on the dichotomy self/cultural other. A significant consequence for intercultural studies is the development of competence training with its practical applications in a variety of contexts. In research conducted in this field (e.g. Berardo & Deardorff, 2012; Deardorff, 2006, 2009; Hammer, Bennett, & Wiseman, 2003; Hofstede, Pedersen, & Hofstede, 2002; Spitzberg & Changnon, 2009), the ideal of an intercultural performer who can apply the skills of intercultural training in a number of contexts, such as education, management, tourism and intercultural mediation, contributes to the creation of what can be defined as an intercultural industry. An illustration of this intercultural industry is represented by the research of Hofstede (2001) on cultural difference, which offers a model of training in intercultural contexts that reduces culture to a pattern of standardised models of behaviour. The principal claim is that knowledge of behavioural patterns pertinent to a culture, or a cluster of cultures, reduces stress, anxiety and miscommunication in intercultural encounters. A particular essentialist feature is the opposition between individualism and collectivism, the former considered a value characteristic of Western societies that nurtures initiative and critical thinking, whilst the latter promotes reliance on tradition and group cohesion typical of Eastern cultures.

From a similar perspective, Hall (1995) delineates two main dimensions of culture: high/low assertiveness and high/low responsiveness, so that each style is seen as conforming to a specific national culture. Behind the neutrality of academic research, these values are ideologically attributed to a fundamental, yet unproven difference between freedom in Western societies and the sacrifice of the individual to cultural values in all other societies. According to Jack (2009) this form of interculture is hegemonic, in the sense that this partial and simplified understanding of culture has become a dominant paradigm, assuming the posture of scientific truth. The idea of cultural differences in communication is thus used in guiding communicative exchanges in elite situations, such as business and management, in which recognition of the other is essentialised. Martin and Nakayama (2010) describe hegemonic interculturalism within a functionalist paradigm deriving from post-positivist social psychological research (e.g. Barnett & Lee, 2002; Gudykunst, 2003), that focuses on consciousness and on the competences of the intercultural speaker in terms of acquisition of skills, effectiveness and appropriateness in language use. In this context, Wiseman's definition of intercultural competence is illustrative of the functionalist paradigm:

ICC competence involves the knowledge, motivation and skills to interact effectively and appropriately with members of different cultures. (2003, p. 192)

This ability is further described as the process of identifying "meanings, rules and codes for interacting appropriately" (p. 200). According to Wiseman, this epistemological approach to competence is accompanied by another ontological dimension that foregrounds the dialectical process of negotiation of separate cultural identities in the course of interaction. In this sense, epistemological factors, including awareness of the other culture, self-awareness and knowledge of the language of interaction, contribute to the successful negotiation of cultural identities that results in competent and effective communication. For example, in Deardoff's model of competence (2006, 2009), the goal of intercultural communication is to communicate effectively and appropriately, showing adaptability and flexibility in selecting appropriate and effective styles that are culture-specific, reflecting the culture of the other relative to the context of interaction.

Blommaert (1991, 1998) highlights this preoccupation with the practical applications of IC to education, training and management, which leaves unproblematised the notion of culture and the power dimension at work in intercultural communicative exchanges. Similarly, Scollon and Scollon (1995), and Piller (2011) claim that the influence of culture is often inflated in determining behaviour and communication, hiding the socio-economic inequality that underlies the urban, multicultural and multilingual contexts in which much intercultural communication takes place. From this perspective, Roy and Starosta (2001) argue that a positivist and scientist approach is counter-productive when applied to human sciences, particularly intercultural communication, because it essentialises cultural identity, whilst ignoring the political, social and economic factors that determine the context of interaction. Furthermore, Curtin (2010) positions intercultural competences within the broader ideological and structural contexts in which they are "*enacted, judged and challenged*" (p. 279), thus problematising competence intended in terms of performance, effectiveness and appropriateness. From a similar critical perspective, Cheng (2010) and DeTurk (2010) problematise the focus on competence training in order to facilitate intergroup dialogue as the process of reinforcing dominant discourses.

An illustrative example of this form of essentialism is the intercultural project *Global People*, which provides guidance in developing intercultural awareness and competence in international educational contexts. In the competency framework delineated by Spencer-Oatey and Stadler (2009), the formulation of competence in terms of acquisition of effective and appropriate communicative skills recalls the neo-essentialism that Holliday (2011) ascribes to the use of language of scientific neutrality in relation to culture and communication. In this excerpt, the acquisition of effective and appropriate communicative skills is presented as an essential pre-requisite in building trust and mutual understanding in international exchanges:

> One of the key resources we bring to building trust and mutual understanding with our international partners is the quality of our communication skills. We may have come to some useful initial conclusions about what they want and how they operate, but unless we can build on this through effective and appropriate communication strategies and skills, the potential for building shared meaning will be lost. Often international partnerships can be beset by misunderstandings based on problems in overcoming the language barrier as well as a failure to draw on the right mix of listening, speaking and perceptiveness skills in order to construct, explore and negotiate meaning. Often people underestimate the amount of background information that is required to be shared up-front to create a platform for mutual understanding, as well as the different styles needed for communicating effectively with their international partners. (Spencer-Oatey & Stadler, 2009, p. 5)

This model of competence is built on previous knowledge of communicative styles and behavioural patterns in order to direct the ability to frame interlocutors within a national tradition. What transpires from these formulations of communicative competence is the possibility to achieve a form of transparent communication once the cultural other has been identified and categorised, marginalising the crucial task of intercultural studies to highlight the processual character of communication as an activity that is always situated and negotiated between speakers in both intercultural and intracultural situations (Dervin, 2011). Phipps (2007, 2010) critiques the idea of the acquisition of intercultural competence as a quick fix to resolving conflict and misunderstanding, and the practices of the intercultural industry, or "*consciousness raising industry*" (Phipps, 2013, p. 10), in directing intercultural communication research towards the production of training courses and manuals that offer practical applications and ready-made solutions to the complex endeavour of human understanding. Instead, Phipps emphasises the complexity of communication and *'the mess of human relatedness in languages'* (2007, p. 26).

In this context, the emergence of theoretical interventions that challenge the divide self/other along cultural lines signals the movement towards a redefinition of intercultural communication beyond current models of acquisition, assessment and reliable testing of communicative competences. The post-structuralist approach of Monceri (2003, 2009) rejects culture as the principal model to understand and explain behaviour, emphasising flux and becoming over cultural categorisation. Similarly, Dervin (2010, 2011) employs the concept of 'space-time' instead of the word culture, in reference to Bauman's (2000) liquid modernity, meaning that culture is always situated, and as such, it is a joint construction between self and other shaped by the context of interaction.

The competence model in critical intercultural language pedagogy

Byram (2008) addresses critically the priority accorded to the teaching of English over other languages, which drives formulations of communicative competence in terms of the hegemonic interculturalism outlined in the previous section. In his words, learning a foreign language is now almost synonymous with learning English:

> The role of English thus often dominates the development of language education policies and the teaching of English has been a major influence on the methods of teaching all foreign languages. (Byram, 2008, p. 9)

Furthermore, the prevalent version of English used in international exchanges is Business English, considered a *lingua franca* in intercultural business communication (Jack, 2009; Louhiala-Salminen, Charles, & Kankaanranta, 2005). From this perspective, Hüllen (2006) contrasts the utilitarian motivation for learning English as a foreign language to intercultural language learning, outlining a notion of competence that takes into account the socially constructed nature of culture and the context of interaction. This latter understanding of competence is illustrated by Byram's model of Savoirs (Byram & Zarate, 1997a, 1997b), which was influential in the development of the common European Framework of Reference for Languages (Council of Europe, 2001). In this model, the intercultural speaker acquires communicative competence not by casting off his or her social identity in the pursuit of a model of native speaker competence, but by developing the ability to assess the relationship between cultures and mediate between them. This is particularly evident in the case of non-native speakers communicating through a third language, or lingua franca, which increases complexity in communication (Byram & Risager, 1999). Similarly, Phipps and Gonzalez (2004) introduce the notion of languaging to highlight the complex nature of culture and the role of language in shaping social environments. According to the authors, the intercultural skill of languaging enables negotiation, understanding and transformation in the figure of the languagers-in-action, intercultural beings that cross borders and engage reflectively with self and other. Guilherme (2010) also draws on the notion of situatedness, recognising the necessity to develop a form of competence appropriated to context in order to facilitate communication and understanding in multicultural settings.

However, despite the transnational paradigm of Risager (2006), the redefinition of intercultural competence and language learning in terms of critical intercultural citizenship (Byram, 2008; Guilherme, 2002), and the notion of languaging (Phipps &

Gonzalez, 2004), I agree with Dervin (2010) that critical models of intercultural competence are far from becoming embedded in the practice of language teaching. Indeed, learning a foreign language still rests on the idealised notion of the nation state, built on the ideal of a common language and of a native speaker reflecting a homogeneous national culture opposed to other national identities (*see* the notion of imagined communities in Anderson, 1991; the unproblematic use of the word 'foreign' in language teaching and learning in Pavlenko, 2003; and the description of the national paradigm in language and culture pedagogy in Risager, 2008). The origins of this national paradigm in German Romanticism in the late Eighteenth and early Nineteenth centuries is a well-rehearsed argument (e.g. Hardcastle, 1999; Risager, 2006); therefore, I will only mention von Humboldt's (1988) and Herder's conceptualisation of language as connecting individual consciousness to the wider cultural and spiritual life of a nation, promoting the educational value of the ability to establish comparisons between different peoples and cultures, both past and present, through the study of other languages. This ability formed an important part in von Humboldt's educational ideal of *Bildung* as personal and cultural maturation, based on the Kantian presupposition of the value of moral qualities in the development of the individual, and it is powerful to this day in shaping national educational policies (Hardcastle, 1999).

Kramsch (2009) addresses critically both national cultural paradigms and the understanding of communication as information exchange with the idea of symbolic competence. In this model of competence, the reality of computer-mediated communication and the simultaneous coexistence of different languages and other signifying practices in everyday life displace traditional spatial/temporal positioning. These signifying practices are referred not only in terms of different linguistic codes, but include all the semiotic resources that contribute to the making of a hybrid identity and allow multilingual speakers to appropriate and manipulate multiple symbolic systems. This symbolic entity is formed in interaction with the environment through the discursive practices of others, which are then re-appropriated through the conscious activity of interpretation of signs and symbolic forms and the unconscious activity mediated by the conative sphere involving emotions, feelings, memories and desires. Kramsch attributes the construction of the self to this complex process of interaction:

> We only learn who we are through the mirror of others, and, in turn, we only understand others by understanding ourselves as Other. (2009, p. 18)

In other words, according to Kramsch, the process of acquiring symbolic competence entails a decentering of the self. I adopt this idea of decentering of the self to suggest that research on competence described in reference to Deardorff (2006, 2009), Hofstede (2001), Spencer-Oatey and Stadler (2009) and Wiseman (2003), as well as the model of responsibility delineated in Guilherme et al. (2010) which I describe in the next section draw on the philosophical tradition of the autonomy of the individual. Thus, the relationship self/other is posited in terms of tolerance, leaving open the question of critical engagement and dialogue with differing ethical frameworks in intercultural encounters.

Communicative competence and intercultural responsibility

Guilherme et al. (2010) describe intercultural responsibility in terms of "a dimension that aims to go beyond a straightforward notion of intercultural competence" (p. 79). Whereas intercultural competence provides the tools to communicate "appropriately and effectively across cultures" (Guilherme et al., 2010), responsibility adds an ethical layer to intercultural interaction. According to the authors, if communicative competence prevents conflict and misunderstanding due to a lack of cultural awareness, intercultural responsibility introduces respect of the other culture and of a different ethical framework. In their words, responsibility also contains an emancipatory aspect that develops from the exercise of intercultural ethics framed within the concept of global ethics, an approach that seeks to reconcile and balance universalistic and relativistic perspectives. This process happens through an ontological shift, a process of discovery and awareness that causes a change in being, transforming the individual into an "intercultural mobile being" (Guilherme, 2010) or an 'intercultural personhood' (Kim Yun, 2008). As a result of this critical cycle that causes the ontological transformation, difference is not only perceived in the cultural other, but it is also recognised within intra-cultural contexts and within the individual. The final outcome of this epistemological and subsequent ontological shift is the development of responsibility, the ability to interact effectively and to respect the other culture and a different ethical framework, leading to the acquisition of tolerance, which Guilherme describes as "a psychological readiness to be empathetic and to control one's emotions, that is, to be patient and tolerant towards the other" (2010, p. 8).

In this description of responsibility, the intercultural personhood is able to forsake both particularistic ethical perspectives and a superficial, or even opportunistic, acknowledgement of difference for instrumental purposes in the name of intercultural dialogue. This is accompanied by the claim that a flexible approach to ethical dilemmas achieved through intercultural responsibility will balance relativistic and universalistic perspectives, leading to emancipatory citizenship and the "corresponding re-framing of institutions and organisations" (Guilherme, 2010, p. 81). The form of responsibility, advocated by Guilherme, Keating and Hoppe with particular reference to multicultural workplaces, demands that:

> Every member is responsible not only for identifying and recognising the cultural idiosyncrasies of every other member-in-interaction, but also for developing full and reciprocally demanding professional relationships with them. (2010, p. 79)

In this context, the principal elements that allow the negotiation of conflicting and relativistic viewpoints, promoting intercultural responsibility, are represented by coherence, empathy and solidarity, described as the ability to work in a collaborative attitude to others and to adapt ethical principles to interactional contexts whilst maintaining 'underlying moral principles' (Guilherme et al., 2010, p. 79). From this standpoint, an intercultural being is able to interact using effective communicative strategies that display a degree of intercultural competence in handling difference, shifting perspective, adopting the viewpoint of the other and negotiating differing values. As a consequence, intercultural communication aims to reduce uncertainty in communicative exchanges when difficulties in establishing dialogue are attributed to culture, with the resulting differences in styles of communication. In this regard, responsibility in communication is translated as the acquisition of intercultural competences in communicating with other speakers from different cultural backgrounds, negotiating between differing ethical frameworks. However, the emphasis placed on transformation and dialogue over the simple acquisition of competences is problematic, because the other is still identified with a foreign language and culture, and responsibility emerges as tolerance of the other. In this sense, this account of responsibility reflects Holliday's (2011) description of neo-essentialist intercultural research, characterised by the use of the category of cultural difference to analyse the dynamics underlying intercultural communication, initiating a process of othering, or the creation of the dichotomy between the self and the cultural

INTERCULTURAL DIALOGUE

other. This dichotomy is further illustrated in relation to the ethical tradition of autonomy in moral philosophy, which I delineate in the next section in contrast to Levinasian ethics.

Kantian ethics and Levinasian ethics

Kant (1979) defines ethics as a theory of virtue, based on the strength of self-mastery with respect to the moral disposition, and distinguishes between pure and practical reason, the former concerning knowledge and the latter the conduct of beings possessed of free will. Kantian ethics formulates morality in terms of autonomy and redefines the relationship between individuals and society in terms of self-governance of the individual (Atwell, 1986; Schneewind, 1998). A crucial aspect of Kantian autonomy is that, as part of the noumenal realm (i.e. the realm of the thing-in-itself, unknowable to human experience), freedom is intended in transcendental terms, which means that moral action is not the result of natural causation. On the contrary, moral action follows instead the categorical imperative, a categorical obligation not influenced by the pull of desires and interferences from the sensible world.

Providing a comprehensive review of the subsequent developments of the role of autonomy and reason in moral philosophy falls outside the scope of this paper. To this end, I will describe two approaches to ethical thinking that are relevant in order to introduce Levinasian ethics: critical theory and the postmodern turn. The critique of the Enlightenment, started with Adorno and Horkheimer in the Frankfurt School, focused on the notion of the abstract transcendental subject, particularly the identification between instrumental reason and the ensuing understanding of human action as determined by utilitarian motives and the imperative of self-preservation:

> The self (which, according to the methodical extirpation of all natural residues because they are mythological, must no longer be either body or blood, or soul, or even the natural I), once sublimated into the transcendental or logical subject, would form the reference point of reason, of the determinative instance of action. (Adorno & Horkheimer, 1997, p. 29)

The second generation of critical theory, starting with Habermas, rediscovered the Enlightenment project with a critique of instrumental reason and of the self-founding Cartesian subject, through an appreciation of the role of reason understood in the relation to its historical, social and embodied incarnations (Habermas, 1987; Jacobs, 2001). This project of revaluation, based on the notion of communicative ethics that Habermas envisaged in situated reason, is realised in the communicative practices of ordinary interactions oriented to mutual understanding (Habermas, 1987). The other approach to ethical thinking, the postmodern turn, highlighted the principal argument of Dialectic of Enlightenment (Adorno & Horkheimer, 1997), the role of reason in excluding the 'other' of thinking in the name of uniformity and sameness (Honneth, 1995). This attention towards the heterogeneous, the non-identical and the excluded from the self-transparency of the Cartesian Self represented the starting point of postmodern ethical thinking (Derrida, 2001; Lyotard, 1984, 1988; Poster, 1989). In this context, Honneth (1995) indicates the notion of asymmetrical obligation between people, developed by Derrida on the basis of Levinas, as the only real challenge to modern theories of morality in the Kantian tradition. Whereas postmodern attention towards the particularity of each individual person and their rights to articulate interests and claims recalls Habermas' model of communicative action, asymmetrical obligation counters the Kantian perspective of equal treatment, initiating a unique model of postmodern ethics. The premise of this reversal of Kantian autonomy is that we become ethical beings only in accepting the obligation towards the other, which breaks the egocentrism of interest-oriented action of instrumental reason and the disembodied, abstract dictates of the Kantian categorical imperative.

In Derrida, this obligation translates in the ideas of unlimited care and hospitality, and the notion of deferred justice (for an account of hospitality and deferred justice, see Derrida, 1992, 2000, 2001). In the ethical relation described by Levinas (1969, 1985, 1998, 2006), the relation to the other lived as pure exteriority is devoid of any form of intentionality, for the self previously enclosed in the solitude of egoism and self-preservation is exposed to the other in an asymmetrical relation. Levinas writes that:

> The freedom of another could never begin in my freedom, that is, abide in the same present, be contemporary, be representable to me. The responsibility for the other cannot have begun in my commitment, in my decision. The unlimited responsibility in which I find myself comes from the hither side of my freedom, from a 'prior to every memory', 'an ulterior to every accomplishment', from the non-present par excellence, the non-original, the an-archical, prior to or beyond essence. (1998, p. 10)

The essence to which Levinas refers is ontological knowledge, or comprehension of beings in terms of generalisation, identity and universality of concepts. Ontological thinking, or thinking about beings, leaves all irreducibility and singularity outside of the relation established by the thinking subject towards the objects of knowledge: "The work of ontology consists in apprehending the individual not in its individuality but in its generality" (Levinas, 1969, p. 44). According to Levinas, ontology is a philosophy of power, based on the impersonal universality of concepts that turn difference and singularity into sameness. Ontological thinking is in other words a form of impersonal knowledge that predominates over the relation with the concrete other in its singularity, in order for the thinking subject to "comprehend or grasp it" (Levinas, 1969, p. 46). Although ontological thinking predominates in the tradition of Western philosophy, Levinas finds in the ethical relation with the other an originary form of thinking that 'overflows the capacity of thought' (1969, p. 49), adopting the idea of infinity that Descartes (1993) described in the Third Meditation. The argument of that meditation, aimed at establishing the existence of god by the fact that the idea of the infinite cannot have been generated by a finite being, is turned by Levinas to designate the encounter with the other in the form of irreducible alterity, "the relation with a being that maintains its total exteriority to him who thinks it" (1969, p. 50). Following this relation of exteriority in the ethical encounter, the other eludes the self and interrupts the dialectic process of representation, when the other is enveloped into a theme and identity is reaffirmed through the creation of a totality. This passage from the solitude of the thinking self to the sociality that is established with the other encountered in her/his singularity is constituted through language, from the dimension of the *said* to that of the *saying*.

The two modalities of the *saying* and *the said* are explored in Otherwise than Being (Levinas, 1998) in relation to language and temporality, when phenomena emerge in consciousness from the flow of perceptions. Levinas describes experience unfolding in two temporalities, the diachronic and the synchronic. In this latter form of temporality, consciousness organises experience in a coherent flow of past, present and future, and the impressions given to consciousness from the external world are categorised and identified with the use of language. This activity of categorisation, that Levinas defines as thematisation, proceeds from a proclamatory, or *kerygmatic*, expression: which is to say that to identify a being -to acknowledge a being- is to pronounce a proclamation, the fact that a phenomenon is "this as that" (Levinas, 1998, p. 35). With this activity, experience is shaped and organised into categories that belong to the *doxa* (i.e. the historical and cultural horizon in which the self is situated). This cultural horizon is the *said:*

> Giving to historical languages spoken by people a locus, enabling them to orient or polarise the diversity of the thematised as they choose. (1998, p. 36)

This means that kerygmatic proclamations organise immediate experience into intelligible phenomena that are consequently transmitted in the form of narration in the context of cultural traditions, what Levinas calls the "thematised" (Peperzak, 1989). The other dimension of language, the saying, operates beyond the language of identification and categorisation. In this dimension, diachrony is an event that interrupts the synchronicity of time, the orderly flow of past, present and future, through the encounter with the singularity- or uniqueness- of the other person.

This relation between temporality, being and language in the *saying* and the *said* is explicated by Levinas in the ambiguity of being thought at the same time as a verb, to be, and the noun indicating a simple being or the totality of beings. When being is expressed as noun, it means that the object of experience is isolated from the flow of time and is fixed in synchronic temporality by consciousness into a theme, concept, category, through the *said*. However, the presence of verbs in language reveals temporality in terms of process, becoming, event in the *saying*. Rather than placing the two modes of language into a dialectic opposing relation, requiring a synthesis and a totality in which the two elements would rest, Levinas describes the *saying* in terms of resonance, a diachronic temporality that allows a phenomenon to appear to consciousness before it is absorbed by the *said*. In other words, the two elements complement each other, as the saying needs a said in order to be processed by consciousness, but it dwells in the *said* as an irreducible remainder of difference between the content expressed in the *said* and what escapes categorisation:

> It is only in the said that, in the epos of saying, the diachrony of time is synchronised into a time that is recallable, and becomes a theme. (…) But the signification of saying goes beyond the said. (Levinas, 1998, p. 37)

Here, I understand that the presence of the *saying* underlying the *said* challenges the idea of the transparency of language, or the perfect correspondence between word and meaning. Levinas employs this understanding of language to illustrate two modalities of existence, the ontological relation to being expressed in the *said*, in which meaning is fixed, and the ethical relation to the other that emerges in the *saying*. The ethical relation is also referred in terms of non-relation, to emphasise the irreducibility of the other to the categories of the self, which brings about the loss of the "Cartesian privilege" of consciousness (Levinas, 1996, p. 60). In other words, when the other is encountered in this modality, the *saying* is expressed in the form of the uncertainty of open-ended dialogue.

In the next section, I will contextualise the two categories of the *saying* and the *said* in the field of intercultural research. I contrast the ethical relation described by Levinas to the notion of autonomy that guides the formulation of competence and intercultural responsibility, in other words the formulation of the self in terms of the Cartesian "I think" and characterised by autonomy and self-sufficiency. With this contrast, I bring forward on the one side the notion of responsibility in terms of open-ended dialogue and critical engagement (the *saying*), and on the other a conception of responsibility understood as tolerance of the other (the *said*).

The saying and the said: two scenarios of responsibility

To summarise, the *said* fixes and establishes meanings, it categorises, enveloping an object of knowledge into a theme, it is speaking about something and not to someone. Language as information, the *said*, expresses the symmetry of self and other in the form of communication of content. In this dimension of the *said*, after being reduced to the known categories of sameness by the active synthesis of the knowing subject, the other becomes the recipient of the moral action in the form of responsibility, tolerance, sensitivity to cultural difference. On the other hand, the *saying* is a 'speaking to' in the form of dialogue, when the self does not occupy a central position bestowing meaning on the other. The saying is proximity, commitment of the one for the other (Levinas, 1985). Levinas describes this proximity in terms of vulnerability of the subject destitute of sovereignty as an autonomous, self-sufficient being, and exposed to the other. This encounter with alterity is the unveiling of a physical vulnerability 'from which we cannot slip away' (Butler, 2005, p. 101), grounding our responsibility as ethical beings in presence to the other (Levinas in Robbins, 2001).

Levinas (1998) further qualifies this approaching as the uncovering of the one who speaks, a denuding of identity in front of the other, an entering of the diachronic temporalisation that is not actively synthesised by the knowing subject but lived in the experience of exposure as responsibility for the other. Thus, the *said* and the *saying* stand for two conceptions of speech: the former represents the transmission of content, or communicative competence; the latter is manifested in the presence of speakers to one another, the response to the singularity of the other when the self is addressed in speech (Blanchot, 1993). I suggest that the notion of language as information needing communicative competence to ensure effective transmission of content, which is prevalent in the notion of intercultural training, is a form of totalisation of meaning (Derrida, 1988), the fact that the intention of the speaking subject is in this way exhausted in the speech act, thus leaving no residue that escapes the transmission of intentional meaning. This totalisation is apparent in the idea of intercultural training, by which the competences required to interpret communicative behaviour as expression of a particular culture and to react with an appropriate response in order to communicate effectively are provided.

Such an instrumental understanding of communication is radically challenged by the *saying*, the relation established in speaking to one another, maintaining an asymmetry that defers the process of consensus and closure of meaning into the totality of being. In this way, using this distinction between the *saying* and the *said*, the ethical dimension of intercultural communication emerges as the open-ended character of dialogue, which is foregrounded over the idea of communicative competence as effective transmission of meaning. This main contrast between the two modes of communication of the *saying* and the *said* is further illustrated in the way in which they are defined by Levinas in the context of the relation between the self and the other. Whilst in the notion of intercultural competence the self and the other are beings enclosed within their own cultural horizon awaiting reciprocal recognition, in the *saying* self and other are inter-dependent because dialogue requires interaction between interlocutors, and the passage from the synchronicity of themes and categories to the diachrony of lived time. Thus, ethical responsibility resides in this relation between self and other established in the *saying*, which Levinas describes as a 'face-to-face' encounter: on the one hand, in the said, the other is reified into a cultural being, on the other hand in dialogue, the other is encountered in their own singularity, uniqueness. As such, the two categories of the *saying* and the *said* suggest two scenarios of intercultural interaction that show two different approaches to responsibility, one operating in the dimension of the said and the other in the dimension of the saying.

In the first instance, in the dimension of the *said*, communication develops on a set of assumptions regarding cultural belonging and identity. In this context, the notion of ethical responsibility is limited to the effort to understand the other as a cultural being and to avoid misunderstanding. In this case, the other is an object of knowledge, not an interlocutor, and responsibility is understood as tolerance of the other by the sovereign subject, the autonomous rational agent of Kantian tradition. In the second instance, in the dimension of the *saying*, dialogue unfolds in ways that are unpredictable and that can question our assumptions about culture, identity and belonging through reciprocal interaction between others. Thus, responsibility is revealed not as a conscious act from a fully bounded, all knowing subject, but as finding oneself in a situation that is not of our making. In this regard, Levinas describes the situation of the self being singled out in his/her uniqueness by the call of the other as the 'originary place of identification' (cited in Robbins, 2001, p. 110), in contrast to being identified according to a principle of individuation based on the fact of belonging to a particular national or cultural group. According to Levinas, the status of the *saying* and the *said* in relation to alterity – or otherness – surfaces in its simplest forms in everyday acts of politeness, for instance in the act of being addressed by an other, when the saying resonates briefly in the presence of two interlocutors:

> In discourse I have always distinguished, in fact, between the *saying* and the *said*. That the *saying* must bear a *said* is a necessity of the same order as that which imposes a society with laws, institutions and social relations. But the *saying* is the fact that before the face I do not simply remain there contemplating it, I respond to it. The *saying* is a way of greeting the Other, but to greet the Other is already to answer for him. It is difficult to be silent in someone's presence; this difficulty has its ultimate foundation in this signification proper to the saying, whatever is the said. It is necessary to speak of something, of the rain and fine weather, no matter what, but to speak, to respond to him and already to answer for him. (1985, p. 88)

Adopting a Levinasian perspective, the ethical aspect of language emerges when the discourse of effectiveness, reliability and performance is superseded by concern for the other qua other.

Conclusion

Intercultural Responsibility: Saying or Said? A problematic aspect in the formulation of competence in intercultural communication is represented by the emphasis placed on the consciousness of the intercultural speaker, which focuses on the cultural divide between self and other. Communication is examined in reference to awareness of cultural differences and with the use of neutral, scientific vocabulary, expressed in the language employed in intercultural training such as competence, skills, training and effectiveness (e.g. Deardorff, 2006, 2009; Hofstede & Hofstede, 2004; Spencer-Oatey & Stadler, 2009). This emphasis on consciousness and on a functional, instrumental understanding of communication influences the ways in which ethical responsibility is understood in intercultural research (e.g. Guilherme et al., 2010). To this end, a challenging prospect for future research is represented by the development of forms of theoretical approaches that bring forward and engage with the partial, contested and situated nature of language. Ultimately, the dynamics underpinning communication cannot be readily translated into a formula with practical applications measured by the reliable testing of competences. Despite current articulations of the critical intercultural speaker (Byram, Guilherme) and the languaging subject (Phipps, Gonzalez) which are increasingly attentive towards the hybrid and shifting nature of the self and the socially constructed nature of language, more theoretical engagement is needed to challenge the reliance on the functionalist paradigm of communication described in Martin and Nakayama (2010), that characterises models of communicative competence and responsibility. However, as Phipps argues (2013), the problematic divide between theoretical explorations of ethical issues on the one side, and empirical research driven by the collection of data according to established methodologies in social research on the other, raises questions that need addressing in the field of intercultural research, particularly in relation to the role of the researcher in eliciting, collecting and analysing data.

This ethical issue brings to light another under-theorised aspect of intercultural communication, namely the aporia of praxis between relativism and a politics of presence (MacDonald & O'Regan, 2012). In other words, critical intercultural theory embraces and celebrates cultural difference whilst also aiming at unearthing essentialised truths behind perceived ideological falsifications and hegemonic interpretations. Intercultural discourse thus finds itself posited amidst competing validity claims, each asserting their own truth, but incapable of deciding between them. Instead, in the name of universalised ethics of tolerance, it is obliged to support them all. As a result, the vision of ethics promoted in critical interculturalism relies on the idea that intercultural communication will create a fusion of cultural horizons through the idea of universal tolerance, although critical interculturalists have to face other competing claims, for instance those emanating from visions of cultural purity which reassert nationalistic values and divisive arguments across ethnic, linguistic, cultural and historical lines. As a tentative approach, this reading of Levinas suggests that although we are culturally situated, and our cultural horizon is the first instrument that we use in interpreting the world, the ethical encounter opens up a dialogic dimension of communication that is also critical engagement and concern for the concrete other, rather than simple tolerance towards an abstract 'cultural other'. According to this notion of ethical commitment, human individuals cannot be reduced to members or organs of any given community, in the sense that cultural categorisation and the notion of 'fixing' communication reduce the ethical force of the encounter with the other.

To conclude, I suggest that there are a number of factors that need to be accounted for in order to develop an ethical model of intercultural communication that challenges preconceived ideas of the other and of culture. First of all, an appreciation of the interdependence of self and other and an awareness of the complexity of real life in which interactions take place, including ideological constructions of culture and the discursive practices that surround the perception of the other (Dervin, 2011; Holliday, 2011; Kramsch, 2009). Furthermore, a consideration of the power dimensions at play in communication, particularly socio-economic inequality and sociolinguistic competence in the use of a dominant language in intercultural encounters (Blommaert, 1998; Piller, 2011; Scollon & Scollon, 1995). Finally, an acceptance of uncertainty in the form of responsible engagement with others in dialogue, through the awareness of the position of the self as potential all-knowing subject that silences the other and ignores the "needs, beliefs, feelings, desires, interests, demands, or injustices faced by interlocutors in any event" (Smith, 1997, p. 330).

In this last sense, responsible engagement in dialogue demands that the Cartesian presuppositions that underlie IC theory are acknowledged and critiqued by interculturalists. Perhaps, an ethical approach to IC entails taking the risk of meeting the other qua other, without the safety net of cultural categorisation, and at the same time being aware that the encounter with the other does not occur in a vacuum, because we are always positioned within networks of power.

INTERCULTURAL DIALOGUE

References

Adorno, T. W., & Horkheimer, M. (1997). *Dialectic of enlightenment*. London and New York, NY: Verso.

Anderson, B. (1991). *Imagined communities: Reflections on the origins and spread of nationalism*. London and New York, NY: Verso.

Atwell, J. E. (1986). *Ends and principles in Kant's moral thought*. Dordrecht, Boston, and Lancaster: Martinus Nijhoff.

Barnett, G. A., & Lee, M. (2002). Issues in intercultural communication. In W. B. Gudykunst & B. Mody (Eds.), *Handbook of international and intercultural communication* (pp. 275–290). Thousand Oaks, CA: Sage.

Bauman, Z. (2000). *Liquid modernity*. Cambridge: Polity.

Berardo, K., & Deardorff, D. K. (2012). *Building cultural competence: Innovative activities and models*. Sterling, VA: Stylus.

Blanchot, M. (1993). *The infinite conversation*. Minneapolis, MN: University of Minnesota Press.

Blommaert, J. (1991). How much culture is there in intercultural communication? In J. Blommaert & J. Verschueren (Eds.), *The pragmatics of intercultural communication* (pp. 13–33). Amsterdam: John Benjamins.

Blommaert, J. (1998). Different approaches to intercultural communication: A critical survey. Plenary Lecture, University of Bremen. 27-28 February. Retrieved December 13, 2013 from http://www.cie.ugent.be/CIE/blommaert1.htm.

Butler, J. (2005). *Giving an account of oneself*. New York, NY: Fordham University Press.

Byram, M. (2008). *From foreign language education to education for intercultural citizenship*. Clevedon: Multilingual Matters.

Byram, M., & Risager, K. (1999). *Language teachers, politics and cultures*. Clevedon: Multilingual Matters.

Byram, M., & Zarate, G. (1997a). *Sociocultural competence in language learning and teaching*. Strasbourg: Council of Europe.

Byram, M., & Zarate, G. (1997b). *The socio-cultural and intercultural dimension of language learning and teaching*. Strasbourg: Council of Europe.

Cheng, H. (2010). A critical reflection on an intercultural communication workshop: Mexicans and Taiwanese working on the US-Mexico border. In T. K. Nakayama & R. T. Halualani (Eds.), *The handbook of critical intercultural communication* (pp. 549–564). Chichester, West Sussex: Wiley-Blackwell.

Council of Europe. (2001). *Common European framework of reference for languages: Learning, teaching, assessment, council of Europe, modern languages division*. Strasbourg and Cambridge: Cambridge University Press.

Curtin, M. L. (2010). Coculturation: Toward a critical theoretical framework of cultural adjustment. In T. K. Nakayama & R. T. Halualani (Eds.), *The handbook of critical intercultural communication* (pp. 270–285). Chichester, West Sussex: Wiley-Blackwell.

Deardorff, D. K. (2006). Identification and assessment of intercultural competence as a student outcome of internationalization. *Journal of Studies in International Education, 10*, 241–266. doi:10.1177/1028315306287002

Deardorff, D. K. (Ed.). (2009). *The SAGE handbook of intercultural competence*. London: Sage.

Derrida, J. (1992). *The other heading: Reflections on today's Europe*. Bloomington and Indianapolis: Indiana University Press.

Derrida, J. (1988). *Limited Inc*. Evanston: Northwestern University Press.

Derrida, J. (2000). *Of hospitality*. Stanford: Stanford University Press.

Derrida, J. (2001). *On cosmopolitanism and forgiveness*. Abingdon, Oxon and New York: Routledge.

Dervin, F. (2010). Assessing intercultural competence in language learning and teaching: A critical review of current efforts in higher education. In F. Dervin & E. Suomela-Salmi (Eds.), *New*

INTERCULTURAL DIALOGUE

approaches to assessing language and (inter-)cultural competences in higher education (pp. 157–174). Frankfurt: Peter Lang.

Dervin, F. (2011). A plea for change in research on intercultural discourses: A 'liquid' approach to the study of the acculturation of Chinese students. *Journal of multicultural discourses, 6*, 37–52. doi:10.1080/17447143.2010.532218

Descartes, R. (1993). *Meditations on first philosophy*. Indianapolis: Hackett.

DeTurk, S. (2010). "Quit whining and tell me about your experiences!": (In)tolerance, pragmatism, and muting in intergroup dialogue. In T. K. Nakayama & R. T. Halualani (Eds.), *The handbook of critical intercultural communication* (pp. 565–584). Chichester: Wiley-Blackwell.

Furrow, D. (2005). *Ethics: Key concepts in philosophy*. London and New York, NY: Continuum.

Gudykunst, W. B. (Ed.). (2003). *Cross-cultural and intercultural communication*. Thousand Oaks, CA: Sage.

Guilherme, M. (2002). *Critical citizens for an intercultural world*. Clevedon: Multilingual Matters.

Guilherme, M. (2010). Mobility, diversity and intercultural dialogue in the cosmopolitan age. In M. Guilherme, E. Glaser, & M. del Carmen Méndez Garcia (Eds.), *The intercultural dynamics of multicultural working* (pp. 1–17). Bristol: Multilingual Matters.

Guilherme, M., Keating, C., & Hoppe, D. (2010). Intercultural responsibility: Power and ethics in intercultural dialogue and interaction. In M. Guilherme, E. Glaser, & M. del Carmen Méndez Garcia (Eds.), *The intercultural dynamics of multicultural working* (pp. 77–94). Bristol: Multilingual Matters.

Habermas, J. (1987). *The philosophical discourse of modernity*. Cambridge: Polity Press.

Hall, W. (1995). *Managing cultures: Making strategic relationships work*. Chichester, West Sussex: Wiley & Sons.

Hammer, M. R., Bennett, M. J., & Wiseman, R. (2003). Measuring intercultural sensitivity: The intercultural development inventory. *International Journal of Intercultural relations, 27*, 421–443. doi:10.1016/S0147-1767(03)00032-4

Hardcastle, J. (1999). Von Humboldt's children: English and the formation of a European educational ideal. *Changing English, 6*(1), 31–45. doi:10.1080/1358684990060104

Hofstede, G. (2001). *Culture's consequences, comparing values, behaviours, institutions and organisations across nations*. Thousand Oaks, CA: Sage.

Hofstede, G., & Hofstede, G. J. (2004). *Cultures and organisations: Software of the mind*. New York, NY: McGraw-Hill.

Hofstede, G. J., Pedersen, P. B., & Hofstede, G. (2002). *Exploring culture*. Yarmouth, ME: Intercultural Press.

Holliday, A. (2011). *Intercultural communication and ideology*. London: Sage.

Honneth, A. (1995). The other of justice: Habermas and the ethical challenge of post-modernism. In S. K. White (Ed.), *The Cambridge companion to Habermas* (pp. 289–323). Cambridge: Cambridge University Press.

Hüllen, W. (2006). Foreign language teaching – A modern building on historical foundations. *International Journal of Applied Linguistics, 16*(1), 2–15. doi:10.1111/j.1473-4192.2006.00103.x

Jack, G. (2009). A critical perspective on teaching intercultural competence in a management department. In A. Feng, M. Byram, & M. Fleming (Eds.), *Becoming interculturally competent through education and training* (pp. 95–114). Bristol: Multilingual Matters.

Jacobs, B. (2001). Dialogical rationality and the critique of absolute autonomy. In P. U. Hohendahl & J. Fisher (Eds.), *Critical theory, current state and future prospects* (pp. 139–153). New York, NY and Oxford: Berghahn Books.

Kant, I. (1979). *Lectures on ethics*. Whitstable, Kent: Methuen.

Kim Yun, Y. (2008). Intercultural personhood: Globalisation and a way of being. *International Journal of Intercultural Relations, 32*, 337–348. doi:10.1016/j.ijintrel.2008.04.003

Kramsch, C. (2009). *The multilingual subject*. Oxford: Oxford University Press.

Levinas, E. (1969). *Totality and infinity*. Pittsburgh: Duquesne University Press.

Levinas, E. (1985). *Ethics and infinity*. Pittsburgh: Duquesne University Press.

Levinas, E. (1996). *Proper names*. London: Athlone Press.

Levinas, E. (1998). *Otherwise than being*. Pittsburgh: Duquesne University Press.

Levinas, E. (2006). *Entre Nous*. London and New York, NY: Continuum.

Louhiala-Salminen, L., Charles, M., & Kankaanranta, A. (2005). English as a lingua franca in nordic corporate mergers: Two case companies. *English for specific purposes, 24*, 401–421. doi:10.1016/j.esp.2005.02.003

INTERCULTURAL DIALOGUE

Lyotard, J. F. (1984). *The postmodern condition: A report on knowledge*. Manchester: Manchester University Press.

Lyotard, J. F. (1988). *The different*. Minneapolis: University of Minnesota Press.

MacDonald, M. N., & O'Regan, J. (2012). The ethics of intercultural communication. *Educational Philosophy and Theory, 45*, 1005–1017. doi:10.1111/j.1469-5812.2011.00833.x

Martin, J. N., & Nakayama, T. K. (2010). Intercultural communication and dialectics revisited. In T. K. Nakayama & R. T. Halualani (Eds.), *The handbook of critical intercultural communication* (pp. 59–83). Chichester, West Sussex: Wiley-Blackwell.

Monceri, F. (2003). The transculturing self: A philosophical approach. *Language and Intercultural Communication, 3*, 108–114. doi:10.1080/14708470308668094

Monceri, F. (2009). The transculturing self II: Constructing identity through identification. *Language and Intercultural Communication, 9*(1), 43–53. doi:10.1080/14708470802444282

Moon, D. G. (2010). Critical reflections on culture and critical intercultural communication. In T. K. Nakayama & R. T. Halualani (Eds.), *The handbook of critical intercultural communication* (pp. 34–52). Chichester, West Sussex: Wiley-Blackwell.

Pavlenko, A. (2003). 'Language of the enemy': Foreign language education and national identity. *International Journal of Bilingual Education and Bilingualism, 6*, 313–331. doi:10.1080/13670050308667789

Peperzak, A. (1989). From intentionality to responsibility: On Levinas's philosophy of language. In A. B. Dallery & C. E. Scott (Eds.), *The question of the other* (pp. 3–23). Albany: State University of New York Press.

Phipps, A. (2007). *Learning the arts of linguistic survival. Languaging, tourism, life*. Clevedon: Multilingual Matters.

Phipps, A. (2010). Training and intercultural education: The danger in good citizenship. In M. Guilherme, E. Glaser & M. del Carmen Méndez Garcia (Eds.), *The intercultural dynamics of multicultural working* (pp. 59–77). Bristol: Multilingual Matters.

Phipps, A. (2013). Intercultural ethics: Questions of methods in language and intercultural communication. *Language and Intercultural Communication, 13*(1), 10–26. doi:10.1080/14708477.2012.748787

Phipps, A., & Gonzalez, M. (2004). *Modern languages: Learning and teaching in an intercultural field*. London: Sage.

Piller, I. (2011). *Intercultural communication: A critical introduction*. Edinburgh: Edinburgh University Press.

Popke, E. J. (2003). Poststructuralist ethics: Subjectivity, responsibility and the space of community. *In Progress in human geography, 27*, 298–316. doi:10.1191/0309132503ph429oa

Poster, M. (1989). *Critical theory and Post-structuralism in search of a context*. Ithaca and London: Cornell University Press.

Risager, K. (2006). *Language and culture: Global flows and local complexity*. Clevedon: Multilingual Matters.

Risager, K. (2008). *Towards a transnational paradigm in language and culture pedagogy*. AAAL 2008 Annual Conference, Washington, DC, USA. Retrieved January 3, 2013, from http://www.academia.edu/200448/Towards_a_transnational_paradigm_in_language_and_culture_pedagogy

Robbins, J. (Ed.). (2001). *Is it righteous to be? Interviews with Emmanuel Levinas*. Stanford: Stanford University Press.

Roy, A., & Starosta, W. J. (2001). Hans-Georg Gadamer, language, and intercultural communication. *Language and Intercultural Communication, 1*(1), 6–20. doi:10.1080/14708470100866 8060

Schneewind, J. B. (1998). *The invention of autonomy: A history of modern moral philosophy*. Cambridge: Cambridge University Press.

Scollon, S., & Scollon, S. W. (1995). *Intercultural communication: A discourse approach*. Oxford: Blackwell.

Smith, A. R. (1997). The limits of communication: Lyotard and Levinas on otherness. In M. Huspek & G. P. Radford (Eds.), *Communication and the voice of the other* (pp. 329–351). New York, NY: Suny Press.

Spencer-Oatey, H., & Stadler, S. (2009). *The global people competency framework: Competencies for effective intercultural interaction*. Warwick occasional papers in applied linguistics, 3. Retrieved November 8, 2012, from http://www.globalpeople.org.uk/, http://warwick.ac.uk/al/

Spitzberg, B. H., & Changnon, G. (2009). Conceptualizing intercultural competence. In D. K. Deardorff (Ed.), *The SAGE handbook of intercultural competence* (pp. 2–53). London: Sage.

von Humboldt, W. F. (1988). *On language: The diversity of human language-structure and its influence on the mental development of mankind*. Cambridge: Cambridge University Press.

Wiseman, R. L. (2003). Intercultural communication competence. In W. B. Gudykunst (Ed.), *Cross-cultural and intercultural communication* (pp. 191–208). Thousand Oaks, CA: Sage.

Zones of interculturality and linguistic identity: tales of Ladino by Sephardic Jews in Bulgaria

Richard Fay[a] and Leah Davcheva[b]

[a]*The Manchester Institute of Education, The University of Manchester, Manchester, UK;*
[b]*AHA Moments, Centre of Intercultural Learning, Education and Research, Sofia, Bulgaria*

Ladino, the heritage language of cultural affiliation for many Sephardic Jews in Bulgaria and beyond, is often discussed in terms of language endangerment and of cultural loss for this community and humanity more widely. However, for intercultural communication specialists, especially those with a linguistic focus, the Ladino experiences of Sephardic Jews in Bulgaria, as set against the backdrop of their changing political and social realities, provide rich insights regarding the linguistic complexities of identity. Through the Ladino-framed narratives of (often elderly) members of this community, we have learned how they drew, and continue to draw, upon their diverse linguistic and cultural resources to define themselves, to articulate their various identities, and to communicate within and beyond Bulgarian society. In order to connect these insights to current discussions of interculturality, and as informed by intercultural thinking, we developed the following five-zone framework: (1) *the (intra-)personal*, that is a zone of internal dialogue; (2) *the domestic*, that is a zone for the family; (3) *the local*, that is a zone for the Sephardic community in Bulgaria; (4) *the diasporic*, that is a zone for the wider Sephardic Jewish community; and (5) *the international*, that is the international community of Spanish-speakers. Further, the project presented here is methodologically innovative involving: several languages (i.e. it was researched multilingually as well as focused on multilingual communities) and therefore issues of translation and representation; and the use of researcher narratives as an additional means for managing the inherent reflexivities in our work.

Ладино, езикът на наследствената и културна обвързаност на сефарадските евреи в България, както и другаде, често бива дискутиран като застрашен език и като предстояща културна загуба не само за тази общност, но и за цялото човечество. За изследователите на междукултурното общуване, и най-вече за тези с лингвистични интереси, житейският опит на сефарадските евреи, свързан с използването на ладино и случващ се в непрекъснато променящи се политически и социални реалности, е неизчерпаем източник на знания за езиковите измерения на идентичностите. Посредством разказите на предимно възрастни членове на сефарадската общност - те описват как са използвали и продължават да използват езиковите и културните си възможности, за да се самоопределят, да изразяват множеството свои идентичности, и да общуват в и извън пределите на българското общество - научаваме за жизнения им път, рамкиран от общуването на ладино. За да свържем изникналите идеи и нови разбирания с текущото дебатиране на явлението междукултурност и в духа на междукултурното мислене, развихме следната рамка, състояща се от пет зони на междукултурност: (1) личностна, т.е. зоната на вътрешен диалог; (2) домашна, т.е. зоната на дома и семейството; (3) локална, т.е. зоната на сефарадската общност в България; (4) диаспорична, т.е. зоната на глобалната сефарадска

INTERCULTURAL DIALOGUE

общност; и (5) международна, т.е. зоната на международната общност на испаноговорящите. Методологията ни е новаторска: включва работа с няколко езика (и следователно въпроси свързани с превод и пресъздаване), както и рефлексивните разкази на двамата автори.

Kon estos tres chikos
So de Rotshild mas riko.
Este es mi oro
Ke tanto anyoro. (Francés, 2006, p. 71)
[Having these three kids
Makes me richer than Rothschild.
They are the gold
I treasure and wish for.]. (transl., Leah Davcheva, 2012)

Ladino – endangered language or intercultural opportunity?

The above poem – by one of the storytellers in our study – is written in the heritage language of the Sephardic Jews in Bulgaria and beyond (i.e. wherever the Sephardim settled after they were expelled from the Iberian Peninsula in the late fifteenth century). The language has various names; from habit rather than ideology, we use *Ladino* whereas others prefer *Judesmo, Judæo-Spanish*, or *Spanyol* amongst others (Alfassa, 1999; Annavi, 2007; Gelber, 1946, p. 105; Harris, 1994; Moscona, 2004; UNESCO, 2002). Ladino is based on mediaeval Spanish as enriched with elements from Arabic, Bulgarian, French, Greek, Hebrew, and Turkish. Its fortunes have changed over the centuries as have those of its users. For Elias Canetti (a Bulgarian-born Sephardic Jew and Nobel Prize Winner for Literature), Ladino – or Spanish as he termed it – was very much present in multilingual Bulgaria in the early twentieth century:

> … through the centuries since their expulsion from Spain, the Spanish they spoke with one another had changed little. The first children's songs I heard were Spanish, I heard old Spanish romances; but the thing that was most powerful and irresistible for a child, was a Spanish attitude. […] To each other, my parents spoke German, which I was not allowed to understand. To us children and to all relatives and friends, they spoke Ladino. That was the true vernacular, albeit an ancient Spanish, I often heard it later on and I've never forgotten it…. All events of those first few years were in Ladino or Bulgarian. It wasn't until much later that most of them were rendered into German within me. (1979, p. 10)

Kushner (2011) estimates that only 160,000–300,000 Sephardim worldwide (i.e. approximately less than half the global Sephardic population) have some knowledge of Ladino today. It is therefore a 'definitely endangered language' (Moseley, 2010). In Bulgaria, the Sephardim are now just 3000 strong and, although there are no reliable statistics (e.g. census data), we estimate that only a small subset (e.g. 500) of these know some Ladino.

At this point, we pause, recognising that we have slipped into a narrative of Ladino based on an 'endangered languages' storyline, invoking a tale of Ladino as a once thriving but now endangered language, and – using Canetti as a literary hook for our argument – alluding also to the loss of this cultural resource of value to the Sephardim and humanity more generally. We could continue in this vein, pointing out how the community of fluent Ladino users is rapidly dwindling thereby leaving the language in

INTERCULTURAL DIALOGUE

the hands of 'terminal speakers', 'semi-speakers', and 'near-passive bilinguals' (Dorian, 1977, 1982; Horak, 2005; Lipski, 1990). Further, we might note Ladino's 'tenuous position' and share Harris' difficulty in being 'optimistic about the state of the Ladino language' (2011, p. 54, 51). Mourning the loss of this cultural pearl, we would then write passionately for posterity about the insights gained through our narrative study into the largely lost world of Ladino-using Sephardic Jews.

A related storyline would note the ways in which Sephardic and Ladino-based cultures are currently being re-vitalised through song (e.g. Mor Karbasi and Yasmin Levy), literature (e.g. Annavi, 2007; Cohen, 1998; Kaufman, 2010), and online discussion groups with global spread (e.g. Ladinokomunita).[1] This (relatively minor) renaissance could be used to challenge, but not reject, the storyline of language decline.

Both lines of discussion see Ladino as something precious but at risk. As such, they represent the kind of discourses of language endangerment that have been problematised in recent years. For example, Duchêne and Heller (2007, p. 11) consider the benefits and losses of understanding languages in this way and ask 'what is at stake for whom, and how and why language serves as a terrain for competition'.

Bearing the above points in mind, we neither wish to follow the language-at-risk storyline nor question how and why Ladino is discoursally constructed as endangered. Rather, we report on a narrative study (see below) which: (1) initially sought, as influenced by the traditions of oral history, to preserve – in several languages – the Ladino-focused life stories of a largely elderly group of Sephardic Jews in Bulgaria; and (2) was subsequently expanded to explore these stories for intercultural insights and to develop a conceptual framework for them.

Through our analysis of Ladino-focused narratives, we explore an earlier, essentially twentieth century, age of interculturality, of transnational migrations and affiliations, and this exploration surfaced some of the linguistic and cultural affordances that these Sephardim were able to call upon as they performed their diverse identities against a rapidly changing sociocultural, politico-historical backdrop. These narratives reveal some of the intercultural complexities of these earlier times and remind us that intercultural communication is not simply a current phenomenon.

Some design considerations

In this section, before reporting how the study was undertaken, we briefly consider the collaborative, narrative, and reflexive aspects of the design.

Researching collaboratively

The study had a collaborative impulse developed through previous jointly undertaken projects and narrative research studies and the Ladino focus flows from our shared intercultural and linguistic professional backgrounds as coupled to our Balkan and Jewish preoccupations. One consequence was that our developing research practice had to accommodate but also become enriched by, these differing linguistic, cultural, contextual, methodological, and other resources.

Researching narratively

Although narrative-based research is not particularly new – for example the 1946 Holocaust survivor testimony research by David Broder (Rosen, 2010) is stimulating regarding the complexities of multilingual narrative research with Jewish participants – during the second half of the twentieth century, and particularly in the last 30 years, there has been something of a 'narrative turn' in which researchers have embraced *'biographical methods in social science'* (Chamberlayne, Bornat, & Wengraf, 2000, p. 1) to such an extent, perhaps, as to mark *'the demise of the positivistic paradigm in social science ...'*. (Lieblich, Tuval-Mashiach, & Zilber, 1998, p. 1). The basis for much of the wealth of this recent narrative work lies in Bruner's appreciation of the undervalued narrativised understandings of human experience, and his view on meaning-making as *'the narrative construction of reality'* (e.g. Bruner, 1991, 1996).

Associated with this foundation, a range of narrative research traditions have developed including: autobiography, autoethnography, case history, case study, ethnography, interpretive biography, life narrative or life history, narrative accounts, narrative, oral narratives or oral history, personal experience story, personal history, and story (Cole & Knowles, 2001, pp. 14–16). We were influenced by an oral history approach to narrative research, seeking to capture – for the first time – the stories of a particular community (of Ladino-speakers) before they passed away. We were also influenced by Clandinin and Connelly's narrative inquiry (2000) which Creswell (2003, p. 15) delineates as:

> ... a form of inquiry in which the researcher studies the lives of individuals and asks one or more individuals to provide stories about their lives. This information is then retold or restoried by the researcher into a narrative chronology. In the end, the narrative combines views from the participant's life with those of the researcher's life in a collaborative narrative ....

Further, the distinction between *life story* and *life history* – Goodson distinguished the *'story we tell about our life'* and the locating of this story within its historical context (1992, p. 6) – is helpful. We were interested in the Ladino-framed life-stories of some of the remaining Sephardic community in Bulgaria, stories which cannot be divorced from the often traumatic events of the last century as experienced by Sephardim. Nonetheless, as the study progressed, we sought less to locate them in larger sociopolitical and geo-historical contexts and more to explore them in terms of the storytellers' performance of interculturality.

Researching multilingually

Whilst researchers in linguistic ethnography and multilingualism provide insights into multilingual research practice,[2] the exploration of the complexities and opportunities of working multilingually for a wider spectrum of researchers has only recently begun to gather pace (Andrews, Holmes, & Fay, 2013; Holmes, Fay, Andrews, & Attia, 2013).[3] Leah has Bulgarian as a mother tongue, English as a professional language, and fragments of Ladino as a heritage language, and Richard has English as a first and professional language, reasonable Spanish, but very limited Bulgarian. Further, our previous collaborations have been conducted through shared English-medium professional spaces. However, for this study, we felt that it was ethically important to respect, value, and utilise the linguistic-cultural resources not only of the storytellers but also of the researchers, all of whom made the study what it was. Therefore, we embraced the multilingual possibilities of our study, focusing on insights about life experience framed by one language (Ladino), with data generated in another (Bulgarian) and processed, restoried, and analysed bilingually (Bulgarian and English), and leading to obvious dissemination possibilities in three languages (English, Bulgarian, and Spanish). We hope that we contribute to the growing debates about researching multilingually, especially through the use of reflexivity as a means of not only foregrounding the assumptions and beliefs that each of us brought to the study but also of taking account of the multilingual richness of the research process.

Developing reciprocal researcher reflexivity

To some extent, we both bring complementary insider and outsider perspectives to the study – we say 'to some extent' mindful of the limitations of insider–outsider terminology but appreciative of the differing perspectives we were both able to bring to the research. Leah is from the Sephardic community in Bulgaria but is, to some extent, an outsider to UK-based English-medium research communities; and Richard is part of the UK-based English-medium academic world but has no direct heritage connection with the Sephardic community or with Bulgaria. Thus, we brought varied insights, interests, and preoccupations to the analytical processes, including our differing: cultural and linguistic backgrounds; exposure to literatures relevant to the topic; experiences of narrative research; levels of involvement in the data generation and restorying processes; and relationships with the storytellers.

In order to manage these subjectivities and to strengthen the multilingual dimension of the study, we developed the technique of researcher narratives in which, as coherent with our narrative methodology, we told each other our own Ladino-framed and researcher stories. In this way, we individually surfaced and then shared what each of us might be bringing to the processes of data generation and analysis.

Data generation and analysis

Generating the stories

Leah's Bulgarian and Sephardic-heritage identities enabled access – initially through personal contacts, and then snowballing to friends of friends – to our 14 storytellers (aged between 43 and 93), all drawn from the Sephardic community in Bulgaria. The selection criteria were that they had (some) knowledge of Ladino and were willing to tell us, with Ladino-foregrounded, their life experiences. Many of them were members of the Ladino Club at the Shalom Jewish Centre in Sofia, where Leah was then a largely unfamiliar face. Initially, the club members seemed reluctant to trust such an outsider with their narrativised life-experiences. However, the theme of the research, a genuine desire to spread the word about the importance of Ladino, and their curiosity about Richard's co-researcher role, led to them sharing their experiences and agreeing to their stories being recorded, then transcribed, restoried and translated into English, and finally becoming public. The narrative-generating encounters were managed through, and in, Bulgarian. Leah was the story-prompter and immediate audience. Her prompts were based on a desire to learn more about what they did with Ladino in their lifetime, how they did it, with whom, where, and when.

Restorying the narratives for presentation and analysis

Leah transcribed each story into Bulgarian which she shared with the storytellers (to ensure that it captured what they had said and wanted to say). Then, following the narrative inquiry tradition, she used these transcripts to create Bulgarian-medium, restoried prose versions of the narratives. For various reasons – for Richard's benefit, to enable our English-medium researcher collaborative discussion, and for dissemination/representation purposes – Leah translated these restoryings into English (see Appendix 1).

INTERCULTURAL DIALOGUE

The study therefore led to a corpus of Bulgarian and English prose restoryings of stories originally told in Bulgarian. The restoryings were shared with the storytellers prior to them being made public (e.g. via the project website).[4]

In a thematic analysis process – which we liken to double-distillation – Leah worked with restoried texts in both languages and Richard with the English version. His response to the stories was therefore at one remove from the restoried data and two steps removed from the original storytellings. We then shared, in English, our responses to the versions of the restoried texts, and, from this exchange, developed a conceptual framework for capturing the insights we took from the stories.

Developing a conceptual framework

Our overarching approach to the restoried texts was informed by a post-structural, interpretative, transnational stance in which we recognised the non-unitary fluidity of identity and viewed the individual as culturally complex and culturally unique (e.g. Singer, 1998). More particularly, the analysis was informed by our earlier work on 'zones of interculturality' in international doctoral student supervision (Davcheva, Byram, & Fay, 2011). There, we located interculturality in zones of dynamic interaction and negotiation between individuals, a position on interculturality informed in many ways by Bhabha's (1990) *third space*, Kramsch's (1998) *intercultural space*, and Holliday's (1999) *small culture* approach. We hoped to extend this conceptual frame to the narrativised understandings of our storytellers as articulated through the restoried texts.

Further, following Street's (1993) formulation 'culture is a verb', and mindful of Johnson's (1997, p. 23) extension, 'gender is a verb', we were interested in what the narratives revealed about the storytellers' processes of becoming as well as of being. Underpinning these formulations is the notion of *identity work*, or the performance of gender, culture, and other identities through social interaction (Brittan, 1989, p. 36). This notion is itself underpinned by the concept of *performativity* drawn from speech act theory (e.g. Austin, 1961; Butler, 1990; Cameron, 1997).

From these starting points, and by way of the double-distilled thematic analysis outlined above, we developed the five-zoned framework which we used to make sense of the Ladino-foregrounded interculturality of our storytellers. This framework has wider applicability we hope.

Five zones of interculturality

As set against the Bulgarian context (in all of its historical, national, social, political, cultural, and linguistic complexity as this has developed over their lifetimes), the storytellers can be understood to be performing their identity in terms of five, to some extent overlapping, zones, namely:

(1) *the (intra-)personal*, that is a zone of internal dialogue;
(2) *the domestic*, that is a zone for the family;
(3) *the local*, that is a zone for the Sephardic community in Bulgaria;
(4) *the diasporic*, that is a zone for the wider Sephardic Jewish community; and
(5) *the international*, that is the international community of Spanish-speakers.

In each of these zones, in keeping with our earlier conceptual work on zones of interculturality, our analysis of the stories identifies dynamic interactions and negotiation between individuals. Further, the first zone below extends the original framework from the interpersonal only to the intra-personal as well.

The (intra-)personal zone

The storytellers reflect on how their knowledge, and/or use of, Ladino provide a special marker of identity for them in a society often uncomfortable with linguistic and cultural diversity:

> I remember the way I felt exceptional when I realised that I knew a language which was not typically spoken in Bulgaria. (Aron)[5]

> My sense of being an heir to this language is special. It enthuses and empowers me with a kind of primary and fundamental force. I think that the significance of being different changes, i.e., from originally being a disadvantage it has now become a huge advantage. We seek our sense of uniqueness and find it in this language. It is a symbol, a token of our otherness. (Andrey)

For Gredi, it provides '*a sense of belonging to something larger...* [giving me] *the freedom of choice – I can choose the culture I want to belong to'*. Even though it '*is not the language that I use now ...it just pops up in certain situations and this makes me realise that there's this language inside me, lurking there, deep inside'*. However, faced by the societal pressures for linguistic-cultural conformity, this Ladino potential is not shared by all – '*I sometimes wonder about my* [Ladino] *accent or my intonation – perhaps they bear some Jewish traces and give me away'* (Andrey) – and some stories report unhappy experiences of self-control and anxiety about their Ladino voice being unmasked.

Most prominent here, in this zone of intra-personal dialogue, is the power of choice the narratives evoke. Supported by critical self-awareness of the opportunities that their different identities afford, the storytellers make decisions about when to use particular linguistic resources. As discussed below, this element of choice is evident also in the other zones.

The domestic zone

It is at home that all the storytellers began shaping a sense of themselves as Ladino speakers. In an essentially Bulgarian- but also Turkish-speaking environment their stories tell how they were exposed to Ladino and how they acquired it in the home setting. For the more elderly ones, it was a first language – '*Judesmo is my mother tongue ... at home we spoke Judesmo ... with my aunts, grannies, everybody ...*' (Yvette, aged 92); but others did not become fluent in Ladino because it was less 'present' in their upbringing – '*We lived with my maternal grandparents, Grandad Gershon and Grandma Rachel .... they spoke to me in Spanyol* [Ladino] *but I didn't understand much at first'* (Gredi). Some storytellers acquired Ladino 'in passing', whereas for others, a conscious effort had to be made to learn the language. Take Reina, for example: at home, until she was five, they spoke Bulgarian, and then ...

> ... my Grandma moved in with us. [...] She could not speak Bulgarian and she took it upon herself to teach me Ladino. She must have been a good 'teacher' because in less than three months, I was able to communicate with her in Ladino. I don't think I could fully understand everything she was saying but we somehow managed to talk with each other.

For most of the storytellers, life at home involved a complex navigation between different languages and ambiguities. Similar to Canetti's account of his multilingual household, in

Yvette's childhood home, family life ran in Ladino but *'our domestic help were Bulgarian girls and we spoke Bulgarian with them'*. The choice of whether to use Ladino or other languages at home was also influenced by the political climate of the time in question. Yvette began raising her own family in the post-war 'socialist' era, a time when advertising one's Jewishness was politically ill-advised. As a result, *'in the years when the first socialist government came into power ... gradually Judesmo* [Ladino] *stopped being the language of my family – during socialism, we did not speak Judesmo'*. Yvette and her husband chose Bulgarian to perform not only their roles as good citizens of the newly established socialist society but also their family and parenting roles. Notable in this zone of interculturality is the purposefulness of identity work. When Ladino became a political liability, they dropped it.

Ladino in the home setting was both a means of inclusion and exclusion, a dynamic interplay between a sense of belonging and of being on the outside. For example, Reina's participation in family life, as framed by Ladino, changes over time. Before she was 'taught' Ladino, she experienced moments of exclusion (finding herself in the same boat with her Russian nanny) when her parents and other members of older generations used *Spanyol* [Ladino] whenever they *'wanted to remain discreet or say something private'*. Many stories reveal a sense of annoyance at being left out, leading to a sense of 'home-grown' outsider-ness. However, this is balanced by the equally powerful experiences of insider-ness and being included:

> My memories go back to my childhood – I grew up in a Jewish environment ... I remember that the first thing I learned was the word *pashariko* and only later, many years later, I realised that my grandmother had been actually calling me 'my little chicken'. And this is very pleasant of course. Later on, I learned *ijo de azno* (son of a donkey) or *cavesa di tuch* (wooden head). And I knew I was somewhere between the small chicken and the donkey's son, and it felt the most natural thing in the world. (Solomon)

The home also provides opportunities to become an insider to family wisdom through proverbs and story-telling, wisdom to be safeguarded and passed on. Ladino enables family members to move across time and space, connecting them with the larger world through the family zone.

> My Dad knew a lot of funny stories from his grandfather and he was in the habit of saying the introductory sentences in Spanish [Ladino], thus giving them an especially vivid flavour. The Spanish part of the story would also become its leading and central idea, its leitmotif. For example, he would start like *'Unos campos longar ... distant roads, I could hear neither a dog barking nor a cock singing/ crowing'*. I have always connected this saying with what I think is a very Jewish sense of being lost in the physical space of this world. There is a particular family meaning for me in all this. (Andrey)[6]

In the family context, people move between languages depending on what their resources are and how they are needed. In this linguistically rich environment, Ladino had the power to inculcate belongingness but also to exclude especially the children from fully participating in family life.

The local zone of the Sephardim in Bulgaria

This is where the endangered storyline is most evident as the storytellers reflect on the dwindling Sephardic community in Bulgaria. They perform their various identities in an environment strongly influenced by significant geopolitical changes and social

INTERCULTURAL DIALOGUE

transitions. Revisiting their childhoods, they talk with nostalgia about the use of Ladino by their relatives, friends and Jewish neighbours:

> In Plovdiv, my father used to go to the Jewish club on a daily basis. He played cards with his friends. All their jokes, curses and playful bantering was done in Judesmo. [Eli].

However, even in the 1930s and 1940s, *'the version of Ladino they used was interspersed with Bulgarian words'* (Sami). This usage signalled affiliation to both the (Jewish) community and the Bulgarian society. Some of the younger members of the community went further and questioned the taken-for-granted richness of their inherited language. Instead, they asserted their new, 'modern' (non-Ladino) identities in the community of Sephardic Jews:

> When she was young, my paternal Grandma Blanca regarded herself a modern young woman and tended to speak Bulgarian only. In those times, they apparently believed that speaking Ladino was something that only the lower classes did, or just old women anyway. Competence in correctly spoken literary Bulgarian was very highly valued. [Andrey].

Those storytellers who can remember the immediate post-war period experienced the loss of Ladino as their language of communication. They grew up in their own Jewish neighbourhoods but spoke Bulgarian among themselves, trying to lose the tell-tale 'nasal drawl' which betrayed their origins. They played around with their identities, deliberately stepping beyond the linguistic line which, for centuries, used to define them as Sephardic Jews. They experimented, consciously and consistently, in order to 'pass' as Bulgarians, and do so even inside their own community:

> … we had a similarly large number of people – 45,000 Jews. And then, all of a sudden, the numbers drastically dropped. A terrible pressure for integration was exerted, both from the inside and from the outside. I grew up in the Jewish neighbourhood where we spoke Bulgarian with a peculiar distinctive accent. …. We did not like sticking out like this and did our best to get rid of the accent – so that nobody could tell. (Aron)

However, *'if you go to the Jewish cemetery in Sofia you can see some of the older graves written out in Ladino with Hebrew letters'* [Sami]. Thus, no matter how fast Ladino disappears from the world of the living, posterity will be left with a reminder of their centuries-old inherited identity.

The stories reveal the deeply felt loss of Ladino as the most significant marker of Sephardic identity. However, the storytellers also report their efforts to rescue the language and thus preserve its distinctiveness and beauty. For Aron, *'Ladino is a like a live coal hidden among the ashes'*, and he and his son's family all sing in the Dulce Canto choir. His son notes how, *'when I started singing in the Dulce Canto choir we sang Ladino songs there and I felt I was able "to hear" this language and identify with it'* (Solomon). Similarly, when she was in her late 1980s, Yvette began, missionary like, to run a course in Ladino in order to preserve and revive the language for members of the Jewish community in her city of Plovdiv:

> The secretary of the Plovdiv Jewish community … asked me whether I could organise and teach a Judesmo course for several people, who were not very keen to participate in the meetings of the 'Ladino' club. Mostly old people attended the club and they [the younger ones] did not find the pace of learning fast enough. I was willing to get the course started. The arrangement was that they get themselves organised and I take care of the learning materials. … There was a core of 12–15 people who remained faithful to their desire to learn

the language of their grandmothers and about the traditions, life and values of the Jewish neighbourhood in the past.

It is noticeable how the functions and status of Ladino in the Bulgarian Sephardic zone have changed over the years. Members of this community have gone from using the language naturally as part of their daily lives, to willingly, but also reluctantly, dropping it from their linguistic agenda, to becoming its revival advocates. Negotiating this new identity for themselves only became possible following the political changes in 1989. To complete our earlier discussion of the endangerment storyline, their sense of loss is challenged, but not overthrown, by the missionary revival ardour.

The diaspora zone of the wider Sephardim community

Beyond the local community, the storytellers narratively construct themselves as competent users of Ladino with Sephardim from countries such as Turkey, Greece, France, and Israel. They use Ladino as a lingua franca and their stories do not dwell on broken or unsuccessful communication but rather speak of easy moves between languages and cultures: *'from time to time, I go to Istanbul, in Turkey … half of my communication is in Turkish, the other half – in Spanyol'* (Aron); and *'I have been using Ladino as an international language and I have a whole range of experiences to share'* (Sami).

Through Ladino, Solomon finds an explanation for how the Sephardic Jews in Bulgaria find it 'natural' to identify with the wider Jewish community in the Balkans:

> If you think of it, we became 'Bulgarian Jews' only 70–80 years ago. Before that we used to be Balkan Jews. Should we find ourselves among Jews from other Balkan countries, there would hardly be anything to make us inherently different from each other – except for the language our passports have been written out in. We behave in very much similar ways. Everywhere on the Balkans I feel at home. My great Grandad was born in what is now Turkey. What was he? What kind of Jew was he exactly? My Grandma used to tell me about her family and relatives who are no longer among us. They came from what today is Serbia and Macedonia.

A sense of common Sephardic origin emerges in the reports of these Ladino-based diasporic encounters with complete strangers, long-time friends, business partners, and fellow professionals, a commonality transcending the bounds and bonds of national, class, profession, economic, social, political, and other affiliations:

> At this event, I had the chance to speak Ladino with the ex-president of Israel, Yitzhak Navon. Navon was born in Israel but, in his family, Ladino had been spoken for centuries. He was chairperson of the Sephardic Institute in Israel. We communicated in Ladino and could understand each other perfectly well. There were differences in the way we spoke it but this didn't surprise me. Over the centuries, Spanyol has absorbed features from many other languages. [Sami]

With Ladino providing entrée into an inclusive international community, other differences turn out to be less salient. Our storytellers no longer need to balance their Ladino and Bulgarian affiliations, and as they move into the wider Sephardic community their sense of self-esteem is enhanced. Even a small degree of fluency in Ladino grants the right of entry and provides a confidence boost:

> If I could speak Ladino [properly], I could easily communicate with people in Greece and Turkey, and elsewhere, especially with the elderly. I would have been very well positioned, exactly because of that. But even as it is, I am being well-positioned and accepted now. (Solomon)

The storytellers seem no longer to be the nostalgic losers of their linguistic and cultural heritage as they were in the previous zone. Instead, they have become active members of the wider Sephardic community. Thus, Sami writes for the Ladino-written *El Amanecer* (At Dawn) page of the Shalom newspaper issued in Istanbul and Yvette writes prolifically in Ladino and she subscribes to every possible newspaper and journal containing some Ladino.

The international community of Spanish-speakers

In this zone, the storytellers move beyond the boundaries of the Sephardic community and connect in differing ways with members of transnational Spanish-speaking communities from countries such as Cuba, Spain, Argentina, Mexico, and Chile. These connections, although also international in character, differ from the more in-group, community bonding of the previous zone. Here, the process of engagement, with individuals or groups, is based on shared ownership of closely related and mutually intelligible languages (Ladino and modern Spanish varieties).

Until his first encounter with living speakers of Spanish, Aron did not think that he could travel any of the distance between Ladino and modern Spanish:

> Have you ever heard Cubans speak Spanish? They tend to swallow their consonants and it's hard to understand them. For a whole week I kept my mouth shut and did not dare speak. By and by, I gathered courage and would put in a word here and a word there.

However, he closely observed the impact of his Ladino on the Cubans:

> … the response of the Cubans was twofold. First, they thought they heard somebody who had risen from their grave. So obsolete was the language I produced. They were enormously delighted and would make me repeat what I said, time and time again.

Like Aron, Eli stays with Ladino and the discovery that he can make himself understood in this way takes him a step closer towards Spanish and generates a feeling of being at home in the Spanish-speaking environment:

> I remember my first visit to Spain. It was quite an emotional experience. I felt completely comfortable in the Spanish-speaking context and was pleasantly excited by listening to the people around me and actually being able to understand. Although I was not at home and in my own country, I still had this amazing sense of being in a linguistically familiar context. It must have all sounded ridiculous and primitive because I had never specially studied Judesmo, but it was very well received. People applauded me. I did a presentation at the Chamber of Commerce in Barcelona and I said my last couple of sentences in Judesmo–Espanyol. The same thing happened to me when I was in Brazil. They speak Portuguese there of course, but again, I felt at home and an insider.

In tune with his artistic self, Gredi creates his own version of Ladino-Spanish but is happy that he can '*get around*':

> I expressed myself by capturing the root of a word and then attached different things to it. The result was a mongrel-like language, a mixture of everything. But I managed to get around through this approximation of the Spanish language. […] Interestingly, I didn't feel any constraints when I was in Mexico.

INTERCULTURAL DIALOGUE

Friendships with Spanish-speaking people are more easily developed in Spanish than in Ladino and it is the desire to travel and connect with people that drives Itsko to take up learning Spanish. He revels in every little detail of his learner role:

> I bought myself a Spanish textbook. In Sofia, I became friends with a man from Cuba. He was a musician and I visited him in Cuba. I learned a lot of Spanish words from him. When I write email messages or letters to my relatives and friends, I try to write them in Spanish. My vocabulary of contemporary Spanish has increased and I make efforts to use the correct Spanish words.

Movement along the Ladino-Spanish axis does not always seem to be a unilateral shift performed by our Ladino speakers and gravitating towards Spanish only. Reina's story constructs an emerging mutuality of relationships framed by communication in both Ladino and modern Spanish where Spanish speakers from Spain, Chile and Cuba venture into Reina's Ladino world. For many long years Reina's Ladino speaker identity had remained dormant. She was close to losing it for good but an opportunity to speak it authentically and for communication arose when she, by chance, met a political immigrant from Spain:

> When we first met, I spoke to her in Ladino. I was amazed that Reyes could understand what I was saying and importantly, I could understand her too.

Becoming instrumental in starting a new relationship and in sustaining its growth into a close friendship, Reina's Ladino self was brought back into play. Although it may appear so on the surface, this was not just a return of an old and somewhat forgotten identity. Reina expanded her zone of expression to transcend the borders of family and Sephardic community and entered, through her friendship with Reyes, the international Spanish speaking world. What made this process even more interesting was the location where it unfolded. Reina and Reyes became friends in Bulgaria where the political regime in the 60s welcomed some of the political refugees from Franco's regime. Thus, paradoxically, the same political and ideological status quo which was responsible for marginalising Reina's inherited Ladino self nonetheless created the circumstances for this Ladino self to re-enter and assert itself on home soil. Initial contact between Reina and Reyes started on the overlapping ground between Ladino and Spanish. They were both language teachers and shared a professional curiosity about Ladino's relationship with modern Spanish: '*We both loved engaging with that – tracing the roots of various words – and for me, a Russian philology graduate, this was a pleasurable thing to do'*. Mindful of the perceptions and experience of her Spanish-speaking friends, Reina became aware of the respect and recognition speakers of Spanish had for Ladino. Guitarist Valentin Biesa from Madrid, for example …

> […] was keen to hear the language which he had never heard anybody speak before. The time we spent together made me aware of the special attitude the Spanish have for us, Sephardic Jews: they find it truly amazing that not only have we preserved Ladino for five centuries but we also cherish the warmest sentiments for Spain itself.

Reina's awakened Ladino identity stimulated her to learn Spanish:

> My developing relationship with Reyes and the exaltation that resulted from mutually understanding each other (mind you, my Ladino was far from perfect), inspired me to register on a course to learn Spanish. […] Soon after I completed the course, I was able to speak contemporary Spanish. Ladino helped a lot but surprisingly it also got in the way to some extent.

INTERCULTURAL DIALOGUE

Ladino thus became a springboard for Reina to start a journey into friendships and worlds she had not explored before. In some ways, she seemed to have made a leap across time to transition from the Spanish spoken at the end of the fifteenth century to the contemporary version.

Some intercultural implications

We feel greatly privileged to have been welcomed into the storied Ladino-framed worlds of these often elderly Sephardim in Bulgaria, and it is with sadness that we note that some of our storytellers are already no longer with us. However, in keeping with our initial oral history impulse, and as demonstrated through our reporting above, their stories and the insights they offer remain available to us and for others now and in the future. The worlds their stories create set their Ladino-informed identities against the complicated linguistic, cultural, political, and historical Bulgarian context as well as more broadly. As we immersed ourselves in these worlds, we gained a sense of the highly situated complexities of (language-based) identity performances. We are suggesting that the five-zoned framework enables us to appreciate and explore these complexities.

The stories in our study remind us that wherever we recognise and value the interculturality of individuals and their contexts, then before us a vast arena of identity-performance opens up in which languages, cultures, affiliations, and identities constantly interact. Such identity-performances are individualised, contextualised, and often expansive – whilst our storytellers' Ladino-informed identity-performances are now, unlike earlier eras, quite muted in Bulgaria (because of the markedly reduced Sephardic population), there are unexpected and self-affirming international possibilities also.

The stories remind us also that intercultural communication – despite the discussions of virtual worlds, global villages, transnational flows, and local complexities – is not a new phenomenon, and that whenever and wherever individuals are seen to be culturally- and linguistically complex, living in and between dynamic societies and in changing (political, etc) times, intercultural communication is an omnipresent possibility.

These stories provide case study material of great depth for exploring interculturality and thereby challenge the (still all too dominant) essentialising discourses evident in much discussion of intercultural communication. These discourses can so easily, and do so often, reduce the multiple and fluid identities of the individuals who, in ever-changing population configurations, generate the dynamic societies in which they live, work, and play. In place of such diversity, these reductivist discourses articulate a culturally homogenised view of people and societies, a view often based upon a single marker of identity, be it societal, linguistic, or cultural affiliation. The Ladino stories challenge such discourses and the vision they enshrine. In them, we witness individuals making their way in a changeable world. As they do so, they call upon the various linguistic and cultural resources at their disposal to smooth their passage through life, despite fickle political parameters and other obstacles.

It might seem that, by exploring Ladino identity performance (in the shadow of an endangered language storyline), we have focused on a linguistic and cultural backwater and concerned ourselves with a somewhat fraught (given particularities of twentieth-century history) cultural identity. Other researchers might focus instead on intercultural aspects of identity performance at the centre of current transnational flows and emergent twenty-first century identities. However, although these stories seem bound in time and place, we believe they reveal a great deal about the zones in which complex individuals perform their multiple identities as set in ever-changing contexts. As such, they are as relevant today and for the future as they are rooted in the past.

Notes

1. http://www.sephardicstudies.org/komunita.html.
2. For example, http://www.birmingham.ac.uk/research/activity/education/projects/researching-mul tilingualism.aspx.
3. E.g. http://researchingmultilingually.com/.
4. http://talesofladino.wordpress.com.
5. All data quotes are from Leah's English translation of the Bulgarian restoried texts co-constructed by her and the storytellers as based on the transcripts of the narrative encounters.
6. In this restoried text which is an English translation of Leah's Bulgarian re-storying, we have retained Andrey's original embedded use of a Ladino phrase in order to give some indication of how he uses his Ladino resources in his storytelling.

References

Alfassa, S. (1999). *A quick explanation* of *Ladino (Judeo-Spanish)*. New York, NY: Foundation for the Advancement of Sephardic Studies and Culture (FASSAC). Retrieved 24 February, 2011, from http://www.sephardicstudies.org/quickladino.html

Andrews, J., Holmes, P., & Fay, R. (Eds.). (2013). Researching multilingually' special issue. *International Journal of Applied Linguistics, 23*(3), 285–299.

Annavi, I. (2007). Explanatory notes about the name of the spoken language of the Sephardims. In M. Varol (Ed.), *Manuel de Judaeo-Espagnol* (p. 9). Sofia: Shalom [accessed via the Bulgarian text: Анави, И. (2007). "Обяснителни бележки за названието на говоримия език на сефарадите". Във Варол, М. *Ръководство по еврейско-испански* (стр. 9). София: Шалом].

Austin, J. L. (1961). *How to do things with words*. Oxford: Clarendon Press.

Bhabha, H. K. (1990). The third space. In J. Rutherford (Ed.), *Identity: Community, culture, difference* (pp. 207–221). London: Lawrence and Wishart.

Brittan, A. (1989). *Masculinity and power*. Oxford: Blackwell.

Bruner, J. S. (1991). The narrative construction of reality. *Critical Inquiry, 18*, 1–21. doi:10.1086/448619

Bruner, J. S. (1996). *The narrative construal of reality*. Boston, MA: Harvard University Press.

Butler, J. (1991). *Gender trouble: Feminism and the subversion of identity*. New York: Routledge.

Cameron, D. (1997). Performing gender identity. In S. Johnson & H. M. Meinhof (Eds.), *Language and masculinity* (pp. 47–64). Oxford: Blackwell.

Canetti, E. (1979). *The tongue set free*. New York: Farrar, Straus and Giroux.

Chamberlayne, P., Bornat, J., & Wengraf, T. (Eds.). (2000). *The turn to biographical methods in social science: Comparative issues and examples*. London: Routledge.

Clandinin, D. J., & Connelly, F. M. (2000). *Narrative inquiry: Experience and story in qualitative research*. San Francisco, CA: Jossey-Bass (Wiley).

Cohen, D. (Ed.). (1998). *The river flows away, the sand remains*. Sofia: Shalom [accessed via the Bulgarian text: Коен, Д. (ред) (1998). Реката изтича, пясъкът остава. София: Шалом].

Cole, A. L., & Knowles, J. G. (Eds.). (2001). *Lives in context: The art of life history research*. Oxford: Alta Mira Press (Rowman & Littlefield).

Creswell, J. W. (2003). *Research design: Qualitative, quantitative, and mixed methods approaches.* 2nd ed. London: Sage.

Davcheva, L., Byram, M., & Fay, R. (2011). Zones of interculturality in postgraduate doctorate supervision. In F. Derwin, A. Gajardo, & F. Lavanchy (Eds.), *Politics of interculturality* (pp. 127–149). Newcastle-upon-Tyne: Cambridge Scholars Press.

Dorian, N. C. (1977). The problem of the semi-speaker in language death. *International Journal of the Sociology of Language, 12,* 23–29. doi:10.3109/13682827709011305

Dorian, N. C. (1982). Defining the speech community to include its working margins. In S. Romaine (Ed.), *Sociolingustic variation in speech communities* (pp. 25–33). London: Edward Arnold.

Duchêne, A., & Heller, M. (Eds.). (2007). *Discourses of endangerment.* London: Continuum.

Francés, S. (2006). El ombre mas Riko [The richest man]. In V. Atanassova (Ed.), *Para ke no se olvide* (p. 79). Sofia: Shalom.

Gelber, N. H. (1946). Jewish life in Bulgaria. *Jewish Social Studies, 8*(2), 103–126.

Goodson, I. F. (1992). Studying teachers' lives: An emergent field of inquiry. In I. Goodson (Ed.), *Studying teachers' lives* (pp. 1–17). London: Routledge. doi:10.4324/9780203415177

Harris, T. K. (1994). *Death of a language: The history of Judeo-Spanish.* Newark, NJ: University of Delaware Press; London: Associated University Presses.

Harris, T. K. (2011). The state of Ladino today. *European Judaism, 44*(1), 51–61. doi:10.3167/ej.2011.44.01.07

Holliday, A. (1999). Small cultures. *Applied Linguistics, 20,* 237–264. doi:10.1093/applin/20.2.237

Holmes, P., Fay, R., Andrews, J., & Attia, M. (2013). Researching multilingually: New theoretical and methodological directions, in the 'Researching Multilingually'. *Special Issue of the International Journal of Applied Linguistics, 23,* 285–299. doi:10.1111/ijal.12038

Horak, A. (2005). Language death: A theoretical approach. *AnMal Electronic, 18.* Retrieved 5 April, 2011, from http://cats.informa.com/PTS/proof/external/prepareCorrectionsFrames.do?nopopup=true&manuscriptId=866122&t=MANUSCRIPT

Johnson, S. (1997). Theorizing language and identity: A feminist perspective. In S. Johnson & H. M. Meinhof (Eds.), *Language and masculinity* (pp. 1–26). Oxford: Blackwell.

Kaufman, N. (2010). My mother's songs. *La Estreya, 4,* 48–54 [accessed via the Bulgarian text: Кауфман, Н. (2010). Песните на майка ми. *La Estreya,* 4:48–54].

Kramsch, C. (1998). The privilege of the intercultural speaker. In M. Byram & M. Fleming (Eds.), *Language learning in intercultural perspective* (pp. 16–31). Cambridge: Cambridge University Press.

Kushner, A. (2011). *Ladino today.* Retrieved 1 April, 2012, from http://www.myjewishlearning.com/culture/2/Languages/Other_Jewish_Languages/Ladino/Today.shtml

Lieblich, A., Tuval-Mashiach, R., & Zilber, T. (1998). *Narrative research: Reading, analysis and interpretation* (Applied Social Research Methods Series, vol. 47). London: Sage.

Lipski, J. M. (1993). Creoloid phenomena in the Spanish of transitional bilinguals. In A. Roca & J. M. Lipski (Eds.), *Spanish in the United States: Linguistic contact and diversity* (pp. 155–182). Berlin: Walter de Gruyter.

Moscona, I. (2004). *Language, everyday life and spirituality of the Balkan Jews.* Sofia: Shalom [accessed via the Bulgaria original: Москона, И. (2004). *Език, бит и душевност на балканските евреи.* София: Шалом].

Moseley, C. (Ed.). (2010). *Atlas of the world's languages in danger.* 3rd ed. Paris: UNESCO. Retrieved 27 March, 2013, from http://www.unesco.org/culture/en/endangeredlanguages/atlas

Rosen, A. (2010). *The wonder of their voices: The 1946 Holocaust interviews of David Broder.* Oxford: Oxford University Press.

Singer, M. H. (1998). *Perception and identity in intercultural communication.* Yarmouth: Intercultural Press.

Street, B. (1993). Culture is a verb: Anthropological aspects of language and cultural process. In D. Graddol, L. Thompson, & M. Byram (Eds.), *Language and culture* (pp. 23–43). Clevedon: Multilingual Matters (in association with BAAL).

UNESCO. (2002). *Saving the Judæo-Spanish language and culture.* UNESCO Press 2002–15. Retrieved 26 February, 2011, from http://portal.unesco.org/en/ev.php-URL_ID=4311&URL_DO=DO_TOPIC&URL_SECTION=201.html

INTERCULTURAL DIALOGUE

Appendix 1. A sample restoried narrative

Reina Lidgi is in her early eighties. Leah met her for the first time in December 2010, at one of the regular gatherings of the Ladino club, where (mostly) elderly Jews speak Ladino with each other and revisit old proverbs, jokes and popular tales. Reina readily responded to Leah's request for an interview where she would tell her about some of her experience in and with the Ladino language.

Reina was five when her grandmother moved in with her son's family. Until then, Bulgarian was the main language of communication in the family and Reina's parents would only speak Ladino when they wanted to share something private – something Reina was not meant to hear and know about. The situation changed because:

> My grandmother could not speak Bulgarian and took it upon herself to teach me Ladino. She must have been a good 'teacher' because in less than three months I was able to talk with her in Ladino.

Ladino was a language only for home, though. Reina was enrolled at a Bulgarian school and Ladino had absolutely no place there and became a site of repression:

> I would not utter a single word in Ladino. It was non-existent as far as the school was concerned. This was one kind of border which I came across when I was growing up.

After her grandmother died, Reina and her mother still used Ladino with each other but this happened less and less regularly. As no literature in Ladino was available and nobody they knew was reading or writing in that language, Reina did not regard it very highly. With time, it slowly disappeared from her world, until:

> In the summer of 1961 I met, quite by chance, one Reyes Bertral, a political emigrant from Spain. When we first met, I spoke to her in Ladino. I was amazed that she could understand what I was saying, and importantly, I could understand her too. I had studied French and Italian and the knowledge of these two languages might have also helped. By and by, we became very close friends and would meet on a daily basis. She communicated with my mother in Ladino too and they understood each other perfectly well.

> Before the Civil War, Reyes was a teacher of Spanish and language matters intrigued her. Sometimes she would catch a word in our conversation which did not look as if it were of Spanish origin. On hearing such a word she would start looking for its root. For example, in Ladino, we use the word *medlar* for read. All her efforts to find out where this word came from were in vain because this is a Hebrew word and she couldn't have known it from before. We both loved engaging with that – tracing the origins of various words – and for me, a Russian philology graduate, this was an intellectually stimulating thing to do.

Reina's developing relationship with Reyes and her 'exaltation' at their mutually understanding each other prompted her to take a course in Spanish. She was soon able to speak modern Spanish and many numerous opportunities arose for her to practice it and establish contact with Spanish-speaking people from Latin America and Spain itself. Her memory is still vivid with the verbal detail:

> When I opened my mouth to speak to them in Spanish, their first question was, "Where does you Spanish come from?" or "How come you know this language?"I always responded by first saying, "Lo aprendi de mi abuela, que avlava el Ladino", meaning that I could speak Spanish thanks to the Ladino which I had learned from my grandma. A long conversation about Ladino would then follow. When they heard me speak Ladino, they would say one of two things – either that my Ladino sounded like the language of Cervantes, or that I spoke the Castilian dialect which is regarded as the foundations of modern Spanish. We, the Sephardic Jews, have actually preserved that ancient language after we were expelled from Spain in 1492.

In all of Reina's encounters and friendships with Spanish speakers Ladino played a part, used either as a channel of communication or emerging as a theme of conversation:

INTERCULTURAL DIALOGUE

> Jorge spoke Ladino with my mother and from time to time comic situations arose. We laughed a lot together. One day Jorge came to visit, bringing along a friend of his from Cuba. In one part of our sitting room my mother was chatting with a friend, and in the other part of the room I was talking with the two Cuban men. All of a sudden, we heard my mother say to her friend, *"Mi 'sta comiendo las tripas!"*. The two Cubans burst out laughing – this wasn't a phrase they would ever use in Spanish. Its literal meaning is "Let him eat my guts", and its figurative meaning is "He is getting on my nerves."

This and similar experiences were making Reina aware of the curiosity and special appreciation the Spanish had for the Sephardic Jews. They found it truly amazing that not only they had preserved Ladino for five centuries but also cherished the warmest sentiments for that country.

In her old age, Reina has few opportunities to use Ladino for spontaneous communication. Her story finishes with an episode whereby she tells of her ongoing work on collecting and publishing Sephardic proverbs and sayings:

> Time passed and my mother died. In 1993, researcher David Cohen published a small book of Ladino proverbs entitled *The River Flows Away and the Sand Remains*. During the first stage of writing, I helped David gather, arrange and translate the proverbs. When the book came out, I continued working on my own.

Cultural identities in international, interorganisational meetings: a corpus-informed discourse analysis of indexical *we*

Michael Handford

The Institute for Innovation in International Engineering, The University of Tokyo, Tokyo, Japan

To date, there have been very few studies employing corpus techniques in the analysis of intercultural interactions. This study analyses the indexing of cultural identities in international, interorganisational meetings. The approach used draws on methods and insights from corpus linguistics and discourse analysis, professional communication, intercultural studies and identity studies. It explores how a statistically significant single item, *we*, in specialised corpora of authentic professional meetings, signals different identities at different moments in the unfolding discourse. Specifically, two research questions are answered:

1. What cultural identities are explicitly indexed in business meetings through *we*?
2. What can corpus linguistics contribute to IC studies?

While the first question comprises the bulk of the paper, the second question is discussed in the final section, along with limitations of the approach applied here.

現在まで、コーパス分析法に基づく異文化間相互行為 (Spinizi, 2011) の先行研究はごくわずかしか行われていない。本研究では異文化間および組織間のミーティングにおける、参加者の文化的アイデンティティ示唆について分析する。本研究はコーパス をベースとしたディスコース分析法を行い、プロフェッショナルコミュニケーション研究、国際文化およびアイデンティティ研究に基づき分析結果を解明する。 これらの分析では実際の国際ビジネスミーティングにおける対話を編纂したコーパス使用し、ミーティング中に展開される対話中の単語"we"の使用について統計分析を行う。さらに単語"we"の使用によるアイデンティティ示唆およびそのタイミングについて言及している。

本研究の研究テーマは下記の通りである：

1.ビジネスミーティングにおける、単語"we"の使用によって示唆される文化的アイデンティティ

2.コーパス言語の異文化研究への貢献

本研究の主要研究テーマは上記1となる。文字制限を考慮し、研究テーマ2については論文最終章にて議論を行った。

Background

The signalling, or indexing, of cultural identities in professional meetings is analysed in this study. The paper draws on methods and insights from corpus linguistics and discourse analysis (Baker, 2006; Gee, 2005; Handford, 2010; Sinclair, 1991; Stubbs, 1996), professional communication (Alvesson, 2002; Handford, 2013; Tijhuis & Fellows,

2012), intercultural studies and identity studies (Benwell & Stokoe, 2006; Bucholtz & Hall, 2005; Collier & Thomas, 1988; Dervin, 2011) to explore how a statistically significant single item, *we*, in corpora of authentic professional meetings signals different identities at different moments in the unfolding discourse. In this section, the thorny issue of cultural identities will be discussed, followed by a discussion of previous work applying corpus methods to intercultural studies, and this study's approach and research questions.

Cultural identities

The term 'cultural identity' is 'immensely challenging' (Dervin, 2011, p. 182), as there has been much debate about its nature and meaning as well as that of other related terms such as social identity, collectivist identity or sociocultural identity (Bucholtz & Hall, 2005; Collier & Thomas, 1988; Dervin, 2011; Simon, 2004; Spencer-Oatey, 2007). The prevailing view of identity, in both public and in many academic arenas over an extended timeframe, is essentialist (Benwell & Stokoe, 2006): people have a 'core' identity that is stable and absolute, and which governs their action (Benwell & Stokoe, 2006, p. 3). Essentialism has found a fertile application in the cross-cultural work of Hofstede (1980, 1991, 1998), who argues for a high degree of causal determinacy in terms of national culture and behaviour (e.g. 1991, p. 107). It has also influenced some business research to explicitly equate culture with nationality (for example Lewis, 1999; Sussman, 2000). The work of Hofstede has been strongly critiqued in terms of its methodology, rigour and epistemology (e.g. Jameson, 2007; McSweeney, 2002), but remains highly influential in management and business schools and consultancy organisations (Holliday, 2011; Jameson, 2007).

An alternative view of identity proposes that identity is not an a priori singular entity (Collier & Thomas, 1988). Rather than *identity*, we have *identities* which can be personal, relational or collectivist (Simon, 2004; Spencer-Oatey, 2007). Collectivist identities can be categorised as social, cultural, or sociocultural (see Spencer-Oatey, 2007 for a discussion). Such identities emerge and are dynamically constructed in and through unfolding discourse (Benwell & Stokoe, 2006; Bucholtz & Hall, 2005; Collier & Thomas, 1988; Dervin, 2011; Gee, 2005; Hall, 2000). In other words, they are indexed and occasioned (Antaki & Widdicombe, 1998). As Hall states, identities are 'points of temporary attachment to the subject positions which discursive practices construct for us' (2000, p. 19). Thus, identities become *relevant* at different moments of the interaction: 'each participants has a portfolio of possible identities that can be invoked at any moment in the interaction, by orienting to a particular identity, participants are making that identity relevant' (Clifton & Van De Mieroop, 2010, p. 2450). However, this is not to suggest interlocutors are able to invoke any identity they wish. As is implied in Hall's mention of discursive practices, constraint is a feature of identity: there are context-dependent limitations on the range of identities that can be appropriately invoked and made relevant. While it is arguably the case in other contexts, in professional contexts, these constraints and possibilities are often linked to power and its negotiation (Gee, Hull, & Lankshear, 1996).

'Intercultural communication' can be categorised as such when there are differing avowed and ascribed cultural identities apparent in the discourse (Collier & Thomas, 1988). Conceptions of cultural identity often include a range of potential avowed and ascribed categorisations and roles, such as nationality, ethnicity, religion, gender (see Benwell & Stokoe, 2006; Dervin, 2011). Within the context of professional discourse, it is argued here that organisational identity (Alvesson, 2002) is also part of a person's store of cultural identities. For instance, Alvesson argues that (2002, p. 165): 'different work cultures and identities become salient' at different moments at work, depending on whom the person is interacting with and the purpose of the communication (also Jameson, 2007). In discussing the role of culture within the construction industry, for instance, Tijhuis and Fellows (2012) give the example of contrasting cultural practices and identities of engineers and architects.

This paper therefore examines the indexing of 'cultural identities', which include national, organisational and more local instantiations in authentic meetings. By local instantiations I mean those identity categories that may have developed among a small group working together, and equate, within the professional context, to Holliday's 'small cultures' (1999). Furthermore, a dynamic, reflexive understanding of context and discourse is proposed: shifts in identities can reflexively index shifts in the context, and vice versa, through language choices (Gee, 2005). As such, the present study adds to the recent body of work in 'interculturality' (Dervin, 2011; Higgins, 2007; Young & Sercombe, 2010; Zhu Hua, 2013).

Corpora and intercultural studies

This study has two main themes: exploring what cultural identities are indexed in professional meetings and what corpus linguistics can contribute to intercultural studies. While addressing the first theme comprises the bulk of this paper, and involves the description and application of a corpus-informed methodology, the second theme is inherently more general and will be discussed in the final part. The second theme is important, given the potential corpora provide for empirical testing of assumptions and assertions within intercultural studies, and relates to Collier & Thomas's (1988) call to analyse interactional discourse in intercultural settings. Despite this potential, even compared to discourse-based studies of identity (Benwell & Stokoe, 2006; Clifton & Van De Mieroop, 2010), there are notably few studies combining corpus methods, discourse analysis and intercultural communication (Spinzi, 2011).

One area that has seen research combining these approaches is within the field of corpus-informed descriptive translation studies. The research has focused on the search for language universals across multilingual corpora (meaning those features that tend to reoccur across translated texts), culture-specific phenomena (including the distance between source culture and target culture), and the investigation of Anglicisms in a variety of languages (relating to discussions of cultural diversity and unity, transnational identities and multilingualism) (Laviosa, 2012). Methodologically, such studies often use traditional corpus tools such as word frequency lists, statistically significant keyword lists and keyword in context (KWIC) concordance lines (Laviosa, 2012; Spinzi, 2011).

KWIC are lines of text from the corpus that contain a 'node' word. They allow the word's surrounding language to be examined both vertically and horizontally, in other words syntagmatically and paradigmatically (Sinclair, 1991). Below are three concordance lines from an international, inter-organisational business meeting, which contain the node keyword *we*. They were all uttered by the Chair, and will be discussed in the methodology section.

(1) Sounds good. So we've got a way ahead (1 sec) on that.
(2) So should we put we put them all through to Hezer?
(3) So I g= I guess for me if we look at the logistics action we* took cos I

Concordance lines usually contain around 10–14 words each, meaning interpretation of deictic, vague or polysemous items, like *we* in such constrained co-text can be problematic. For this reason, in this study a speaker's whole turn, and if needed surrounding turns, are analysed.

One of the tenets of corpus linguistics is that frequent items are important items (Sinclair, 1991). Frequency lists show the most used words in a corpus, but tend to be a blunt tool, as the most frequent words across different corpora tend to be relatively uninteresting: there are many 'functional' words, such as articles and prepositions. Therefore, like concordance lines, they have not been employed in this study; however the keyword tool was used. Statistically significant 'keywords' (Scott, 2011), like frequency lists, are produced using corpus software such as AntConc or Wordsmith Tools; the target corpus is compared to a larger reference corpus, to see which words typically occur in the target corpus in comparison to some norm. However unlike frequency lists, keyword lists tend to feature a far higher proportion of content words (Scott, 2011).

The professional corpora and research questions

The data examined here are from two corpora of spoken interactions: the CANBEC[1] corpus of spoken business meetings (see Handford, 2010), and an in-progress corpus of construction industry interactions[2] (hereafter CCC; see Handford & Matous, 2011; Handford, 2013). Both sets of data have been collected and compiled by me; as well as the recordings, I collected a considerable amount of background data on the participants, the companies they work for and so on, in the form of pre- and post-recording interviews, and observation notes, and interviews with expert informants. CANBEC is a one-million word corpus of authentic business discourse, with over 50 fully transcribed meetings from a range of organisations. Approximately a quarter of the data is from inter-organisational interactions, and approximately 15% of the speakers and recordings are from outside the UK. CCC at present contains approximately 250,000 words, and is mainly comprised of ELF interactions in Asian contexts. The reference corpus used was SOCINT,[3] a 2.7 million word corpus of everyday spoken English.

In the keyword comparison of CANBEC and SOCINT (Handford, 2010, p. 106), showing which words are far more typical (with an error probability of less than 0.000001%) in business meetings than in everyday talk, the top three keywords are *we, okay* and *hmm* (the keyword list the construction corpus produced virtually identical results). This is somewhat counterintuitive because more business-specific words, such as *merger* or *invoice*, might be expected to occur at the top of the list. It is also possible to create negative keyword lists, which show words that are statistically far *less* likely to occur, in the CANBEC/SOCINT comparison we find the pronouns she, *I, he, and you* in the top ten (Handford, 2010, p. 103). This contrast emphasises the importance and relative ubiquity of *we* in business meetings. One considerable benefit of using corpora is their ability to produce counterintuitive, but empirically verifiable, results. Nevertheless, the interesting item then needs to be interpreted, hence many traditionally qualitative approaches use corpora as a first step into the data (Baker, 2006). Spinzi (2011, p. 14), discussing the potential synergy of corpus linguistics and intercultural studies, states:

> If corpora tell us what the important words are they do not tell us why. Intercultural studies might help explain the reason for that statistically high density.

As the above description and discussion below show, one important word in business interactions is *we*. Although this study draws on around a million and a quarter words of fully transcribed meetings for the keyword analysis, it explores the top keyword *we* to see which identities it indexes in context in three international, inter-organisational meetings. Why these particular meetings were chosen is discussed below.

Two research questions will be addressed with reference to the corpus data:

(1) What cultural identities are explicitly indexed in business meetings through *we*?
(2) What can corpus linguistics contribute to IC studies?

In the next section, the methodology developed and employed is discussed, looking specifically at indexicality, relevant research on *we*, further data description, and how quantification and categorisation were achieved. After that, the results and analysis section investigates instances of *we* in several longer extracts from each of the meetings. Finally, the second research question along with the limitations of the methodology, are discussed.

Methodology
Indexicality

This paper draws directly on the part of the methodology proposed by Bucholtz and Hall (2005) for analysing sociocultural identity in interactions, as well as Gee's discourse analysis methodology (2005), and combines aspects of these two methodologies with corpus linguistics to analyse potentially intercultural interactions. As with other discourse-based approaches, Bucholtz and Hall argue that identity should be seen as the emergent product of discursive practices rather than its pre-existing source. Their second argument is that there are different categories of identity: (1) 'macro-level demographic categories; (2) local, ethnographically specific cultural positions, and (3) temporary and interactionally specific stances and participant roles' (2005, p. 592; see also Holliday, 1999 and Young & Sercombe, 2010). While these two aspects of identity (its emergent nature and range of categories) reflect the ontology of identity, the third principle of their approach, indexicality, demonstrates the mechanism through which identity is constituted, and is therefore of particular relevance to the methodology employed here. There are several indexical processes through which identity can emerge in discourse (Bucholtz and Hall, 2005, p. 594), specifically:

(1) Overt mention of categories and labels
(2) Evaluative/epistemic orientations and interactional footings
(3) Implicatures regarding own/other identity
(4) Use of ideologically associated linguistic structures and systems

While all of these processes could be explored using a suitably contextually-informed corpus, this paper analyses the indexing of particular footings through the use of the statistically significant deictic *we*. The process of indexicality applied here corresponds with Gee's notion of 'situated meanings': words do not have general meanings once we start analysing discourse, but instead have 'different specific meanings in different contexts of use...the meanings of words are also integrally linked to and vary across different social and cultural groups' (Gee, 2005, p. 53).

We

As consistently reoccurring words can be expected to have an underlying functional cause (Biber, 1988, p. 13), statistically significant keywords are one method for choosing which items to explore as instances of situated meanings. As discussed above, the top keyword in business meetings is the pronoun *we*, as it is uttered far more frequently in business meetings than it is in talk between friends, family and so on. Figure 1 shows the comparative frequencies.

We is of interest here for various other reasons:

- it is one of the key deictics which indexes identity in workplace settings, for example, Drew and Heritage (1992), Bargiela-Chiappini and Harris (1997), Poncini (2004), Handford (2010).
- it is one of the key deictics through which identity can be marked in various other institutional settings (e.g. Zupnik (1994), De Fina (1995), Fairclough (2000), Mulderrig (2012) in political discourse; Oliveira (2010) in classroom discourse; Fairclough (1993) in higher education discourse; O'Keeffe (2006) in media discourse.
- it can index national identity for example, Wodak, de Cillia, Reisigl, and Liebhart (1999, p. 45).
- it is inherently versatile, and can index different identities (Mulderrig, 2012; Poncini, 2004).
- it can mark shifts in footings and frames, and as such is in a reflexive relationship with the context (Gee, 2005; Levinson, 1983; Poncini, 2004; Wortham, 1996).

Furthermore, on a practical note, compared to other markers of identity in multiparty settings like business meetings, pronouns are 'easier to quantify for the purpose of analysis' (Poncini, 2004, p. 87). Poncini's (2004) work on multinational meetings is discussed in more detail below. It is, to date, one of the most rigorous studies of *we* in business meetings, and the categorisation applied here draws on her work. Each occurrence of *we* in the data is counted and categorised, and both the linguistic co-text and the wider context are considered when allocating a particular category. Background data on the speakers and their organisations allows for plausible interpretation; for

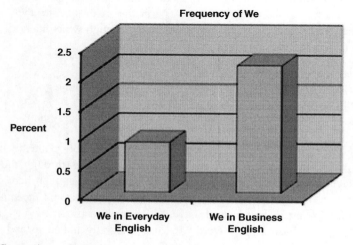

Figure 1. 'Comparison of We'.

instance, in the concordance lines from the introduction, distinguishing between the different *we*s requires such knowledge (the first concordance line indexes both companies, the second only the speaker's company, and the third indexes the participants present at the meeting).

(1)   Sounds good. So we've got a way ahead (1 sec) on that.
(2)   So should we put we put them all through to Hezer?
(3)   So I g= I guess for me if we look at the logistics action we took cos I

Data description

As stated above, the initial keyword analysis compares meetings and other professional spoken interactions totalling around a million and a quarter words with 2.7 million words of everyday English. As it would be impractical to manually interpret every instance of *we* in the professional corpora (there are well over 20,000), three meetings, with just over 10,000 words and lasting around one hour each, are analysed. These three meetings were chosen because they all involve different participants from different nationalities, locations, organisations and work groups, and therefore, should provide opportunity for the participants to index a range of identities (or indeed just one). Furthermore, a considerable amount of background data had been collected on each meeting.

'Meeting 1' occurs in Germany, and is between three British and three German representatives of two very large (UK and USA) pharmaceutical companies. The meeting occurs at a relatively early stage of the project on which the two project teams (each made up of logistics, supply chain and finance staff) are collaborating: the US company will be taking over the supply chain management of a range of the UK company's products. The main focus of meeting 1 is to ensure that this process is run as effectively as possible. The next meeting (hereafter 'meeting 2') is held in a country in South Asia (which will not be named for confidentiality purposes), and is part of a series of meetings on the design process of a large bridge project. There are 15 participants from seven different nationalities, including several from the host nation and three from Japan, as well as several from Western Europe; there are representatives of the national bridge authority, the design consultancy company, a panel of experts (PoE), as well as government officials. 'Meeting 3' takes place in England in a vehicle manufacturing company. The meeting is between three members of the company's IT department and two consultants from a Belgian consultancy company, and the consultancy company is offering advice on how the manufacturer's IT systems can be changed in preparation for relocation and downsizing. Participants are British and Belgian.

Therefore, while all meetings differ in terms of geographical location, industry, and nationality of the speakers, they are all inter-organisational, international and inter-professional. This allows us to see which identities are indexed across very different contexts, and whether any interesting comparisons arise that might be suggestive of wider patterns. All three meetings are conducted in English.

Categorisation of 'we'

The fully transcribed corpus data used here allow for a turn-by-turn analysis of the statistically significant keyword *we* and the identities it indexes. An interpretation of each indexed identity was made, through reference to the speaker (hence turn-level analysis, rather than concordance lines), the co-text, and when necessary the contextual background information. Following Bucholtz and Hall (2005), macro and micro identities were expected to be indexed, such as national identity, organisational identity and more local *we*. These were quantitatively categorised (see results section), using the categories discussed below, and then explored in longer extracts.

The categories employed here partly draw on Poncini's coding system of the manufacturer-distributor meeting she analysed (2004). It is made up of three main categories, related to the presence of the distributors (2004, p. 108): '*we*-exclusive', which excludes the distributors; '*we*-inclusive', which includes the distributors, and '*we*-ambiguous'. One of Poncini's key findings is the degree of ambiguity in uses of *we*, a finding apparent in the data analysed here. Furthermore, the distinction between inclusive and exclusive *we* was apparent in all meetings, and helps explain the frequency of the item in business. However, the present categorisation differs from Poncini's in several ways.

Poncini's (2004) categorisation is unidirectional: it only takes account of the manufacturer's use of *we* in the meeting in terms of how it identifies themselves and their identity-relationship with the distributors/others. The present study analyses all uses of *we*, irrespective of the speaker's identity. Furthermore, while Poncini (2004) prioritises the inclusive/exclusive distinction, the different indexed cultural identities are emphasised here. Also, extra categories have been added to account for instances that do not fit under Poncini's labels. Following an analysis of the meetings, the following main categories have been developed:

Local *we*

- Inclusive local (all people present at the meeting)
- Exclusive local (the speaker plus at least one other person present, but not all)

Organisational *we*

- Inclusive organisational (both, or all, organisations)
- Exclusive organisational (the speaker's organisation, but not other organisation(s))

National *we*

- Inclusive national (both or all nationalities present)
- Exclusive national (only the speaker's nationality)

Vague *we*

- Uses of *we* which could not be confidently categorised, but which indexed a group identity. These include several incomplete clauses.
- Empty *we*
- Usually uses of *we* which formed part of an idiomatic expression, but which did not index an identity (for example the phrase *here we go* upon finding something in a document)

Extract 1 below is from meeting 1 (the pharmaceutical meeting), and shows some of the different identities that can be indexed through *we*. The Chair is discussing the need for each organisation to collaborate effectively on the proposed supply chain process. Each *we* is numbered (e.g. #1).

Extract 1

<$1> I guess I can photocopy this but I think w= what's more important is (swallows) we (#1) actually discuss this information in terms of what we (#2) need to do with it. Because you mean f= for instance we're (#3) assuming everything's five days so if we (#4) built a ninety-eight day lead time into our system for the standard five-day markets (inhales) we (#5) therefore, know that your aim is to have everything ready and passed eight days before dispatch.

The first *we* is an inclusive personal *we*, referring to all the people in the room, and like many of the instances of the local *we* it collocates with a verb meaning talk (here *discuss*). The second *we* is also inclusive, but refers to both organisations. The third *we* is also inclusive organisational, as both organisations are assuming that five days is the norm. Uses four and five, in contrast, index the speaker's organisation and not the other company (because he is referring to his own organisation's system – stated in a follow-up interview), and are therefore exclusive. This extract shows that some uses can be categorised wholly from the co-text, whereas others require reference to outside sources of data.

Bargiela-Chiappini (1997) and Poncini (2004) argue that different meetings will feature different groups depending on the specific context of the communication. Analysis of meetings 2 and 3, following discussions with expert informants and some of the participants, showed that a large majority of the organisational *we* in fact indexed the project team representing the organisation and carrying out the work (for example uses two and five in extract 1). Meeting 1, in contrast, did not feature project teams as such. Therefore, the proportion of organisational *we*s that referred to project teams is outlined below.

Results and analysis

The following three graphs (Figures 2–4) show the results of the quantitative analysis per meeting according to the categories outlined above.

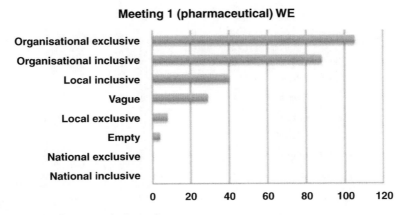

Figure 2. We in pharmaceutical meeting.

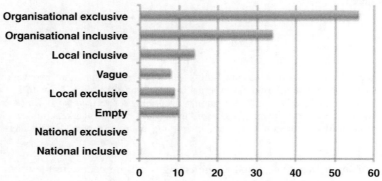

Figure 3. We in pharmaceutical meeting.

One point to note is the variation in the frequency of *we* across the three meetings, despite all three data-sets each totalling around 10,400 words.[4] In meeting 1, there are 271 uses of *we*, in meeting 2 there are 131, and in meeting 3 there are 274. Nevertheless, a keyword search (Scott, 2011) of the meeting 2 data shows that *we* is still one of the top ten keywords when compared to everyday English.[5] This difference can partly be explained by the context of the meetings: whereas meetings 1 and 3 are primarily concerned with exploring how two project teams from two different companies can work together, meeting 2 is less collaborative in nature, with a lot of the meeting being concerned with the Panel of Experts and the National Bridge Association evaluating the proposals of the bridge design company (Scott, 2011).

When comparing all three meetings, one clear pattern is that the most frequent identity in all three meetings is the external organisational. In meetings 1 and 3, the majority of these invoke project team exclusive identities: 104 out of 109 and 146 out of 172, respectively. When considering the use of such exclusive *we*, Poncini raises the important point that they do not 'reflect an antagonistic situation. Rather, these uses can indicate cooperative or reciprocal aspects of the business relationship' (Poncini, 2004, p. 86). For instance in extract 2, taken from the later stages of meeting 3 where the manager from the vehicle company has just finished outlining where his project team

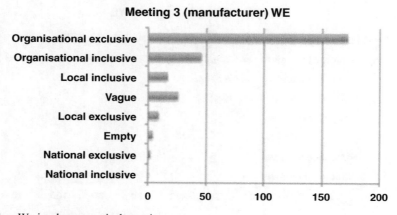

Figure 4. We in pharmaceutical meeting.

INTERCULTURAL DIALOGUE

needs help from the consultants, we find two instances of exclusive project team organisational *we* that are highly convergent.

Extract 2

<$1> Okay. So I mean that's er basically where we (#1) are really and er and where we (#2) need the assistance. So er I mean I think from our point of view it's er it's really you know as much help as you can give us+
<$2> Mhm.
<$1> +in whatever form.

The majority of cases of exclusive organisational *we*, especially those indexing project team identities, while avowing (Collier & Thomas, 1988), and by implication ascribing, distinct cultural identities, do not signal divergence – as is the case in extract 2. Indeed in extract 3 from meeting 1, the positioning of the speaker's organisation as exclusive allows for banter, with the Chair ironically suggesting to his colleague that his company is not responsible for the action, because there is no mention of time in the minutes of the previous meeting.

Extract 3

<$1> You know what= You know the only thing we're (#1) saved by Helen is the fact that on these minutes it doesn't actually say when the f= action was first taken.
<$6> Blackmail.
<$1> (laughs)

However, there are instances where organisational *we* can signal problems, and problems that can be of a cultural nature. For instance, in extract 4, taken from meeting 1, the Chair ($1) is discussing the other pharmaceutical company's perceived lack of willingness to be guided in this project by his company despite his company (here given the pseudonym Novartis, with their Head Office in Staines) having considerably more experience in the area. In follow-up interviews the Chair talked about his continuing frustration over this, combined with the need to 'tread carefully'. The phrase *Staines way of working* refers to the cultural practices of his company, and just preceding this extract he had raised concerns over the other company's different practices.

Extract 4

<$1> I'm not sure. But+
<$3> Yeah.
<$1> +certainly there's a lot of experience within the Novartis* camp and that's that's a good thing and it's a bad thing cos we (#1) can be perceived as interfering. (laughs) You know we (#2) can be seen very much in that light and I'm s= I'm sure we (#3) are. But at the same time there there'd be some good advice.
<$3> Yeah.
<$1> And I think the o= the only thing I would stress is that we (#4) want it to work and what we (#5) don't wanna do er is impose lots of Staines ways of working. But at the same time you might say "Well actually like that don't like that like that don't like that". And (1 second) I'm just concerned that (1 second) as I haven't seen anything yet. And we've (#6) got such a big commitment to take three weeks out of a schedule having just started up a new facility.

51

All of the *wes* in this extract are exclusive, and while all are organisational, the first three are most directly aligned with the organisational identity of the company in its (somewhat negatively) perceived corporate sense; thus *we* occupies the subject position in passive clauses. The remaining uses index *we* the company as an understanding yet concerned partner-as-agent, while highlighting the different cultural practices between the companies. Hence, exclusive *we* can be a very flexible deictic term, signalling cooperation or divergence even within the same speaker turn.

It is interesting that the speaker in extract 4 also uses terms other than *we* to avow organisational identity, specifically the company name and the metonymic use of the place where the Head Office is located (Staines). On this point, Mulderrig (2012) quotes Wilson (1990, p. 62), who states 'indicating self-reference by means other than *I* or *we* is said to represent a distancing strategy on the part of the speaker, because the choice of pronoun indicates how close-distant the speaker is to the topic under discussion, or the participants involved in the discussion'. This seems to be the case here, as the indexing of the company identity through the name and place are used when the speaker is framing the company's behaviour in potentially negative terms. This provides distance between his team and the potentially negative perception of the company, which in turn potentially creates convergence between the two teams. It also obfuscates and downplays the speaker's responsibility for the potential interference through objectification of the institution (van Leeuwen, 1996).

This extract is thus also interesting from a power (Gee et al., 1996) perspective, as the Chair is the most senior person present and hence the most senior representative of his company, but he is seemingly trying to hedge the force of his comments through such distancing. However, given that more powerful people have access to a wider range of identities (Zupnik, 1994), his ability to signal such distance arguably highlights his power.

The second most frequent category in all meetings is inclusive organisational *we*. Extract 5 shows a typical example, where the group has just heard a presentation from the environmental consultant on the Panel of Experts.

The independent checking engineer ($11) is suggesting that following the consultant's proposal is a good idea, and his use of *we* in the first line signals that this requires the agreement of all organisations.

Extract 5

<$11> I'm I'm I I have a feeling that i= if we (#1) do this it's er nice to do an environmental assessment.

Inclusive *we* can also be used strategically. For instance, in extract 6 from meeting 1 (the pharmaceutical meeting) both occurrences of *we* are inclusive organisational *we*. While the second *we* thus implies both organisations will combine the orders, in fact it is the other pharmaceutical company that will need to carry out the combining. The use of an inclusive *we* here therefore serves to soften the face-threat of the implied directive (the use of *you*, for instance, would be more direct).

Extract 6

<$1> So we've (#1) got three different orders. So I guess the question is assuming it's the same delivery address can we (#2) combine any of those orders.

INTERCULTURAL DIALOGUE

Another finding from the quantitative analysis, with clear implications for the topic of this paper, is the use of inclusive or exclusive national *we*: there are only two instances across all three meetings. Extract 7 shows these two uses of the national *we*, which occur towards the beginning of meeting 3. The manager of the vehicle manufacturer is trying to arrange dates for their next meeting.

Extract 7

<$1> Erm that would take us then up to the week commencing the twenty-sixth of August, which is a short week really, because it's the Bank Holiday week.
<$4> Right.
<$1> We (#1) have a day off. It's a national holiday.
<$2> Mhm.
<$1> What we (#2) call August Bank Holiday.
<$2> Mhm.
<$3> Mm.
<$1> Yeah. You perhaps have similar things in Belgium. We (#3) had a <$G1>.
<$2> Mhm.
<$1> It started off as a Bank Holiday+
<$2> Mhm.
<$1> +because you know the financial institutions they all used to close down+
<$2> Yeah.
<$1> +and had sort of quarter days and things.
<$2> Mhm.
<$1> Erm traditionally everybody used to have holidays then. That was before we (#4) used to have things like you know 'Oh you're entitled to four weeks holiday a year' that type of thing.
<$2> Yeah.
<$1> Yeah. I mean you've probably got similar things run in Belgium anyway.
<$2> Oh yes. <$G?>

The first *we* is organisational, and the third is an example of an incomplete (vague) *we*. Uses two and four however index (exclusive) nationality, the only instances in all the data; interestingly, the issue of differing nationality and the cultural practice of Bank Holidays is not directly relevant to the task at hand, but is an instance of what Koester (2004) terms a 'relational sequence': it seems 'to have more to do with the way in which speakers relate to each other, rather than with getting the job done' (Koester, 2004, p. 1407). As such, we see the overt indexing of nationality employed as a convergent, off-topic resource, in the search for similarity as in this somewhat clumsily-handled example. Also, unlike extract 3 where the speakers are negotiating cultural (i.e. organisational) differences, this extract involves no negotiation of cultural practices, but is merely communication *about* culture. Aston (1993) noted similar use of nationality by 'non-native' speakers' of English, but here it is used by an English L1 speaker in an international setting.

An analysis of national *we*, or rather the lack of it, across three meetings cannot support strong conclusions about identity and the role of national identity in professional contexts, partly because national identity could be marked in other ways, and partly because such analysis would benefit from more data. Nevertheless, how and when nationality is indexed in international meetings would warrant further study.

Conclusions

Although categorical conclusions about identity cannot be drawn based on the analysis of a single item, *we*, this study arguably adds support to the view that the discursive construction of identity is more complex and less fixed than an essentialist position assumes. For instance, in extract 1, there are three different identities indexed by the speaker through *we* alone in the space of around 30 seconds, and in extract 4, the Chair strategically avows contrasting degrees of distance towards his own organisation again within a single turn. Moreover, this fine-grained analysis demonstrating the dynamism of *we* arguably helps explain its ubiquity in this context: it is a cultural as well as statistical keyword as it incrementally constitutes the collaborative tenor of much professional discourse.

When evaluating the findings of this study, there are several limitations in the present study that need to be considered. Firstly, the analysis has focused on a single item, *we*, and its indexing of cultural identities. There are evidently many other overt and implicit ways that identity can be indexed, as listed in Bucholtz and Hall (2005) above, that have not been analysed here. There are also other items that can index the organisational identity specifically, such as the metonymic forms noted in extract 4. Furthermore, while the quantitative analysis drew on 1.25 million words, only three meetings were analysed in depth, meaning that other possible identities could be indexed in other contexts. Also, while the meetings were chosen because they combined a variety of nationalities, professional contexts and purposes, they do not represent the full range of meetings in CANBEC and CCC, or indeed in business at large. Moreover, while the meetings are all international, interorganisational and involve different professions, thus allowing for potential comparison across this range of features, as discussed above the specific contexts of the meetings themselves strongly affect the language used. For instance, in the construction meeting, there were comparatively fewer uses of *we*, which can partly be accounted for by the highly transactional, evaluative and informational focus of the meeting.

When we consider the first research question, 'What cultural identities are explicitly indexed in business meetings with *we*?', clearly organisational identity is the most frequently indexed, although this may mean the local team representing the organisation. In contrast, the national identity is not indexed at all in the on-topic, transactional meeting interactions through *we*, and only occurs in an off-topic relational sequence (Koester, 2004). Its relevance to the task at hand can therefore be queried. The extent to which such a finding problematises the Hofstedian essentialist prioritisation of nationality is open to debate; nevertheless, the results here do at least suggest the need for further discourse-based research into the indexing of national identities, for instance through explicit labels.

In order to ascertain the participants' perspective on the issue of which identities they think are relevant in meetings, I emailed several of them, explaining that I was exploring the issue of national, organisational and local identities in meetings. I asked them what was 'most relevant to the way people communicate and the differences in the meeting in terms of communication'. Consistently, the respondents said that organisational identity was the most relevant. For instance, one member of the Panel of Experts (PoE) from meeting 2 answered:

> As for your question about the identity, I can almost confidently say that we were assuming our identities according to the *roles* assigned. For example, I am a POE member with specialization in social safeguard. My counterpart, Dr Zxxxx, for example, speaks as the safeguard group leader of the consultant team. Indeed we communicate with each other like

friends (as we are) in private, but in the meeting we kind of play the roles (not necessarily saying he was the one to grill).

The response shows the participant had a clear sense that different identities become relevant in different contexts, and that he saw his membership of the PoE as the key identity during the meeting. While such triangulation of findings does not mean nationality is not relevant in this context, it does suggest further research exploring how nationality may or may not be indexed through other discursive means in professional meetings is worthwhile.

In terms of whether the use of *we* signals instances of intercultural communication, for example through the use of exclusive *we*, the picture is complex. For instance, it is problematic to state categorically that 'exclusive organisational we a priori signals inter-cultural communication': as discussed above, exclusive organisational *we* may signal cooperation and alignment rather than difference (also Poncini, 2004), and stance towards the avowal of one's organisational identity can vary considerably within one speaker turn, as in extract 4. Nevertheless, distinct cultural identities can be indexed through excusive *we*, but in order to interpret whether this is the case a careful consideration of each situated meaning, combined with reference to background information, is needed. Furthermore, it goes without saying there are many other ways intercultural commun-ication may be occurring interactionally beyond the use of *we*.

In answer to the second research question, concerning the contribution that corpus linguistics can make to intercultural studies, as noted above there are few such studies (Spinzi, 2011). It is argued here that the potential contribution of corpus linguistics, as an empirical approach, has parallels with other areas of research. Baker (2006) and Mautner (2009) for instance, argue that corpus linguistics has contributed to the rigour and range of discourse analysis approaches in terms of allowing researchers to work with much larger data-sets, helping reduce researcher bias by broadening the empirical base, and enabling the combination of quantitative and qualitative analyses, thus allowing the potential for generalisability of findings. While corpus linguistics cannot replace the need for interpretation, the methodology produces 'results and language patterns that have been discovered in a relatively neutral manner' (Baker, 2006, p. 18); furthermore, these patterns of use may not be obvious prior to analysis. Arguably, the same benefits for intercultural studies can be gained from the application of appropriate corpus tools and insights, and the present study is intended to illustrate such an application, notwithstand-ing the limitations listed above. As with this study, the combination of a larger, quantita-tively analysed corpus with a smaller, mainly qualitatively analysed, carefully chosen sub-section of the data allows for a greater degree of context-specific interpretation than a purely quantitative approach would allow. It also helps answer Collier and Thomas's (1988) call for intercultural communication to be analysed in discourse. Overall, a corpus approach may not allow us to see the whole elephant, but it can unearth hitherto unidentified and even surprising linguistic patterns which occur in and incrementally construct specific contexts of use.

Transcription conventions

= sound abruptly cut-off, for example, false start
+ speaker's turn breaks and continues after back channels or overlaps
/$G/ inaudible utterances (number or question mark refers to number of syllables)
<$5?> probable speaker

INTERCULTURAL DIALOGUE

() words in these brackets indicate non-linguistic information, for example, pauses of 1 second or longer (the number of seconds is indicated), speakers' gestures or actions, or the presence of *we* e.g. (#1)

Acknowledgements

I would like to genuinely thank the two anonymous reviewers who offered perceptive, critical yet encouraging comments and suggestions on an earlier draft of this paper, and to the editors for further feedback and support. I would also like to thank Tony Young and Alex Gilmore for comments on the paper.

Notes

1. Cambridge and Nottingham Business English Corpus, copyright Cambridge University Press. Directors Profs Ronald Carter and Michael McCarthy. Extracts 1, 2, 3, 4, 6 and 7 are taken from the CANBEC corpus.
2. The CCC corpus is funded by a grant from the Japanese Society for the Promotion of Science, No. 25370423. Copyright M. Handford. Extract 5 is taken from the CCC corpus.
3. SOCINT is part of the CANCODE corpus, copyright Cambridge University Press. Directors Profs Ronald Carter and Michael McCarthy.
4. The shortest meeting, meeting 3, contains 10,412 words in total. Meetings 1 and 2 are longer, therefore, only the first 10,400 words of these meetings were analysed.
5. It is the top keyword in the other two meetings.

References

Alvesson, M. (2002). *Understanding organizational culture*. Newbury Park, CA: Sage.

Antaki, C., & Widdicombe, S. (1998). Identity as an achievement and as a tool. In C. Antaki & S. Widdicombe (Eds.), *Identities in talk* (pp. 1–15). London: Sage.

Aston, G. (1993). Notes on the interlanguage of comity. In G. Kasper & S. Blum-Kulka (Eds.), *Interlanguage pragmatics* (pp. 224–250). Oxford: Oxford University Press.

Baker, P. (2006). *Using corpora in discourse analysis*. London: Continuum.

Bargiela-Chiappini, F., & Harris, S. (1997). *Managing language: The discourse of corporate meetings*. Amsterdam: John Benjamins.

Benwell, B., & Stokoe, E. (2006). *Discourse and identity*. Edinburgh: Edinburgh University Press.

Biber, D. (1988). *Variation across speech and writing*. Cambridge: Cambridge University Press.

Bucholtz, M., & Hall, K. (2005). Identity and interaction: A sociocultural linguistic approach. *Discourse Studies, 7*, 585–614. doi:10.1177/1461445605054407

Clifton, J., & Van De Mieroop, D. (2010). 'Doing' ethos—A discursive approach to the strategic deployment and negotiation of identities in meetings. *Journal of Pragmatics, 42*, 2449–2461. doi:10.1016/j.pragma.2010.03.008

Collier, M. J., & Thomas, M. (1988). Cultural identity: An interpretive perspective. In Y. Y. Kim & W. B. Gudykunst (Eds.), *Theories in intercultural communication* (pp. 99–120). Newbury Park, CA: Sage.

De Fina, A. (1995). Promotional choice, identity and solidarity in political discourse. *Text, 15*(3), 379–410.

Dervin, F. (2011). Cultural identity, representation and othering. In J. Jackson (Ed.), *Routledge handbook of intercultural communication* (pp. 181–194). Abingdon: Routledge.

Drew, P., & Heritage, J. (1992). Analysing talk at work: An introduction. In P. Drew & J. Heritage (Eds.), *Talk at work* (pp. 3–65). Cambridge: Cambridge University Press.

INTERCULTURAL DIALOGUE

Fairclough, N. (1993) Critical discourse analysis and the marketization of public discourse: The universities. *Discourse and Society, 4,* 133–168. doi:10.1177/0957926593004002002

Fairclough, N. (2000). *New labour, new language?* London: Routledge.

Gee, J. P. (2005). *An introduction to discourse analysis.* Abingdon: Routledge.

Gee, J. P., Hull, G., & Lankshear, C. (1996). *The new work order.* London: Allen and Unwin.

Hall, S. (2000). Who needs identity? In P. du Gay, J. Evans, & P. Redman (Eds.), *Identity: A reader* (pp. 15–30). London: Sage.

Handford, M. (2010). *The language of business meetings.* Cambridge: Cambridge University Press.

Handford, M. (2013). Context in spoken professional discourse: Language and practice in an international business meeting. In J. Flowerdew (Ed.), *Discourse in context* (pp. 113–132). London: Continuum.

Handford, M., & Matous, P. (2011). Lexicogrammar in the international construction industry: A corpus-based case study of Japanese – Hong-Kongese on-site interactions in English. *English for Specific Purposes, 30*(2), 87–100. doi:10.1016/j.esp.2010.12.002

Higgins, C. (2007). Introduction: A closer look at cultural difference: 'Interculturality' in talk-in-interaction. *Pragmatics, 17*(1), 18.

Hofstede, G. (1980). *Culture's consequences: International differences in work related values.* Beverly Hill, CA: Sage.

Hofstede, G. (1991). *Culture and organisations.* New York, NY: McGraw-Hill.

Hofstede, G. (1998). Attitudes, values and organizational culture: Disentangling the concepts. *Organization Studies, 19,* 477–493. doi:10.1177/017084069801900305

Holliday, A. (1999). Small cultures. *Applied Linguistics, 20,* 237–264. doi:10.1093/applin/20.2.237

Holliday, A. (2011). *Intercultural communication and ideology.* London: Sage.

Jameson, D. (2007). Reconceptualising cultural identity and its role in intercultural business communication. *Journal of Business Communication, 44,* 199–235. doi:10.1177/00219436 07301346

Koester, A. J. (2004). Relational sequences in workplace genres. *Journal of Pragmatics, 36,* 1405–1428. doi:10.1016/j.pragma.2004.01.003

Laviosa, S. (2012). Corpora and translation studies. In K. Hyland, M. H. Chau, & M. Handford (Eds.), *Corpus applications in applied linguistics: Current approaches and future directions* (pp. 65–81). London: Continuum.

Levinson, S. (1983). *Pragmatics.* Cambridge: Cambridge University Press.

Lewis, R. (1999). *Cross cultural communication: A visual approach.* Warnford: Transcreen.

Mautner, G. (2009). Checks and balances: How corpus linguistics can contribute to CDA. In R. Wodak & M. Meyer (Eds.), *Methods of critical discourse analysis* (pp. 122–143). London: Sage.

McSweeney, B. (2002). Hofstede's model of national cultural differences and their consequences: A triumph of faith – A failure of analysis. *Human Relations, 55*(1), 89–118.

Mulderrig, J. (2012). The hegemony of inclusion: A corpus-based critical discourse analysis of deixis in education policy. *Discourse and Society, 23,* 701–728. doi:10.1177/09579265 12455377

O'Keeffe, A. (2006). *Investigating media discourse.* Abingdon: Routledge.

Oliveira, A. W. (2010). Developing elementary teachers' understandings of hedges and personal pronouns in inquiry-based science classroom discourse. *Journal of Science Teacher Education, 21*(1), 103–126. doi:10.1007/s10972-009-9157-4

Poncini, G. (2004). *Discursive strategies in multicultural business meetings.* Bern: Peter Lang, Linguistic Insights Series.

Scott, M. (2011). *Wordsmith tools version 5.* Oxford: Oxford University Press.

Simon, B. (2004). *Identity in modern society: A social psychological perspective.* Blackwell: Oxford University Press.

Sinclair, J. (1991). *Corpus, concordance, collocation.* Oxford: Oxford University Press.

Spencer-Oatey, H. (2007). Theories of identity and the analysis of face. *Journal of Pragmatics, 39,* 639–656. doi:10.1016/j.pragma.2006.12.004

Spinzi, C. (2011). Corpus linguistics and intercultural communicative approach: A synergy. *Cultus, 4,* 9–20.

Stubbs, M. (1996). *Text and corpus analysis.* Oxford: Blackwell.

Sussman, N. M. (2000). The dynamic nature of cultural identity throughout cultural transitions: Why home is not so sweet. *Personality and Social Psychology Review, 4,* 355–373. doi:10.1207/S15327957PSPR0404_5

INTERCULTURAL DIALOGUE

Tijhuis, W., & Fellows, R. (2012) *Culture in international construction*. London: Spon Press.

van Leeuwen, T. (1996). The representation of social actors. In C. Caldas Coulthard & M. Coulthard (Eds.), *Texts and practices* (32–70). London: Routledge.

Wilson, J. (1990). *Politically speaking: The pragmatic analysis of political language*. Oxford: Basil Blackwell.

Wodak, R., de Cillia, R., Reisigl, M., & Liebhart, K. (1999). *The discursive construction of national identity*. Edinburgh: Edinburgh University Press.

Wortham, S. E. F. (1996). Mapping participant deictics: A technique for discovering participants' footing. *Journal of Pragmatics*, *25*, 331–348. doi:10.1016/0378-2166(94)00100-6

Young, T., & Sercombe, P. (2010). Communication, discourses and interculturality. *Language and Intercultural Communication*, *10*, 181–188. doi:10.1080/14708470903348523

Zhu Hua (2013). *Exploring intercultural communication: Language in action*. London: Routledge.

Zupnik, Y.-J. (1994). A pragmatic analysis of the use of person deixis in political discourse. *Journal of Pragmatics*, *21*, 339–383. doi:10.1016/0378-2166(94)90010-8

Faithful imitator, legitimate speaker, playful creator and dialogical communicator: shift in English learners' identity prototypes

Yihong Gao

Institute of Linguistics and Applied Linguistics, School of Foreign Languages, Peking University, Beijing, China

> This paper attempts to conceptualize identity prototypes regarding model L2 learners/ users of English over the past 50 years, as embedded in research discourses. For a long time, the ideal learner was a *faithful imitator* whose L2 use and cultural conduct were strictly modeled on the native speaker (NS). With postcolonial changes around the world, a *legitimate speaker* was born, claiming equal language standards and rights with NSs. Growing under the increased influence of globalization and postmodernism is a *playful creator*, who constructs unconventional hybrid language use for distinct self-expression. A Bakhtinian *dialogical communicator* is also emerging, who converses on the basis of respect and reflection. These prototypes are discussed with their respective characteristics, L2 research discourse, contexts, and constraints.

> 本文尝试概括过去半个世纪中英语二语认同的典型模式及其变化。理想的英语学习者很久以来都是"忠实的模仿者", 其语言使用和文化行为都严格以本族语者为模版。逐渐取代这一模式的, 是后殖民的环境下诞生的"正规的发言者", 以维护自己群体的语言标准和权利、争取与本族语者的平等地位为目标。在全球化和后现代主义影响加剧的背景下, 出现了"嬉戏的编创者", 以其标新立异的语言混杂方式表达自我。在此过程中还出现了"对话的交流者", 在巴赫金所言"对话"的意义上, 以尊重和反思为基础进行交流。文章讨论了这些演变中的模式的特征、二语研究话语、相关情境, 以及困境。

Introduction

This paper attempts to conceptualize identity prototypes regarding model L2 learners/ users of English over the past 50 years, as embedded in academic discourses. This conceptualization is admittedly subjective; thus, the paper is essentially an opinion piece, but I will ground my claim in selected research literature that has struck me as representative. I will reveal a shift in the model L2 learner/user of English from *faithful imitator* to that of *legitimate speaker*, and then to *playful creator* and *dialogical communicator*. While substantial research reviews of language and identity in general (e.g. Joseph, 2004) and L2 identities in particular (e.g. Block, 2007) have been conducted, I believe conceptualizing L2 identities embedded in abundant abstract theories into a few embodied *persons* will provide a clear and useful picture of the space for alternative targets. Also, compared with existing reviews that focus primarily on L2 theories developed in the West, I will include and put some emphasis on L2 identity models developed in Chinese contexts. Such an expanded and embodied picture may help English learners, educators, as well as researchers make better informed choices. For each of the identity prototypes, I will discuss its general characteristics, related L2 research discourse, social and intellectual contexts, and constraints.

The faithful imitator

Characteristics

The faithful imitator models his or her L2 on the norm of native speakers (NSs) of English, particularly that of the UK or USA, and makes the utmost effort to produce L2 identical to such norms. He or she is also fully acculturated into the target cultures (C2) of NSs. Ideally such a learner uses English in a native(-like) manner, well accepts target cultural values, and lives competently and comfortably in the C2. The ideal of faithful imitation is based on the assumptions that (1) the English language is bound to the culture of the NS, however 'culture' is defined; and (2) cultures have clear-cut boundaries that will not easily dissolve. Thus, L2 learning and use is associated with integration, acculturation or socialization into the C2 community of NSs, the most ideal being the adoption of its membership. For the faithful imitator, acquiring the accuracy and appropriateness of the L2 and C2 norms is of utter importance. He or she humbly heads toward the 'nativeness' target. 'You speak like a British/American!' and 'I thought English was your mother tongue!' would be the praise one loves to hear. Individuals may vary, however, in the dimensions of linguistic skill (e.g. accents, writing styles) and cultural norms (e.g. rituals on social occasions) they care most about. Psychologically, the faithful imitator resembles a child without a distinct self, eager to identify with parents and copy their conducts.

L2 research discourse

Most theoretical models of bilingualism developed in the 1970s and 1980s entailed the faithful imitator as the ideal learner. For example, Schumann's (1978) 'acculturation theory' focused on the social and psychological proximity between L2 learners and the target language community. The more learners acculturate themselves to the target language and culture group – the more faithful they are – the better the L2 learning results. Alberto, the empirical case on which Schumann's theory was based, was a failure for not changing *faith* from his native Hispanic culture to that of the target American culture. Likewise, Lambert's (1974) 'subtractive bilingualism' and 'additive bilingualism' entailed the acquisition of a C2 identity, the difference between the two lying in the loss or maintenance of the learner's mother tongue (L1) and original culture (C1) identity. By stressing the importance of 'integrativeness', i.e. the motivational orientation to integrate into the target language community, Gardner and Lambert's (1972) motivation theory had some implication of the faithful imitator. Integrativeness is associated with successful L2 learning, and much preferred over 'instrumental motivation'.

Apart from bilingual theories of the above, general English as Second Language (ESL) and English as a Foreign Language (EFL) research discourse of the latter half of the twentieth century also embraced the faithful imitator. Audiolingual (USA) and audiovisual (France/Britain) methods, which reached their peak in the 1960s, had a basis in behaviorist psychology of stimulus and response. The learners were expected to practice drills in NS linguistic patterns until the norm became internalized and automatic. The imitator here had even less agency than in the above theories of 'acculturation' and 'motivation'; they were treated more or less as mindless parrots doing mechanical repetition. In a broad range of research, the division between 'native speaker' and 'non-native speaker' (NNS) was essential; it generated abundant empirical studies which measured the learning success of the latter by comparing their linguistic production with that of the former. While heading toward the NS model, learners' language was considered 'interlanguage', at a half-way point in terms of faithful imitation. Learners should target not only linguistic 'accuracy', but also communicative 'appropriateness', and watch out for 'pragmatic errors'. Good language teaching should use 'authentic' materials that provide 'genuine' NS models for imitation. Such research discourse dominated the second half of the twentieth century, and still prevails now in many contexts.

Contexts

Without doubt, the faithful imitator model has its constant and justified practical basis, such as reducing the risk of misunderstanding by keeping to a common standard, and the economy of learning effort investment. However, the model is also related to particular social and academic contexts. Sociohistorically, the faithful imitator was particularly suited to a modern, industrialized context, with a legacy of colonialism. 'Culture' was primarily associated with the nation state, which was secluded within closed boundaries. International traveling was limited, not a common lifestyle. Large power distances existed among different nations, particularly between the UK and USA as NS countries on the one hand, and 'ESL' and 'EFL' countries on the other. The linguistic hegemony of the UK and USA was taken for granted.

In the social sciences, hierarchical social structures were perceived to be essentially given and stable; so were group boundaries. The room for individual choice of social identity, though present, was highly constrained. For example, Tajfel's (1982) theory of social identity posited the basic *social categorization* between 'ingroup' and 'outgroup'. Intergroup *social comparison* in terms of status and power is an important mechanism for *positive distinctiveness*, which motivates individual behavior. This theory exerted great influence on L2 identity theories, for example, Giles and associates' 'Intergroup Model' and 'Ethnolinguistic Identity Theory' (Giles & Johnson, 1987).

On the whole, the faithful imitator fits well in contexts where hierarchical sociocultural structures and intergroup boundaries are (perceived as) largely stable and fixed, where the individual is believed able to choose how 'good' a learner he or she wants to be according to given standards. This prototype dominated the 1960s, 1970s, and 1980s, and remains popular at present in some English-teaching communities. The NS as target of imitation, after being scrutinized from an applied linguistic perspective, is claimed to be 'both myth and reality' (Davies, 2004, p. 431).

Constraints

The faithful imitator, if eventually successful in becoming a full member of the NS group, should be free from dilemmas and live a happy life hereafter. However, most learners never reach that goal, and even if linguistically successful, may suffer great pain when their faith in the C2 is in conflict with that in their home culture (C1). 'The issue of loss of identity' (Davies, 2004) is central to the NS belief.

Schumann's unsuccessful learning example 'Alberto', for instance, chose to be socially and psychologically distant from NSs so as to maintain his bond with Spanish-speaking C1 community members:

> He made very little effort to get to know English speaking people. In Cambridge he stuck quite close to a small group of Spanish speaking friends. He did not own a television and expressed disinterest in it because he could not understand English. On the other hand, he purchased an expressive stereo set and tape deck on which he played mostly Spanish music. (Schumann, 1978, p. 36).

The perceived split of faith or betrayal of his C1 identity lay at the root of Alberto's self-imposed distance from the L2 and the C2.

A 'successful' learning example that impressed me personally comes from Richard Rodriguez, as written in his autobiography *Hunger of Memory* (1982). The story was of a Spanish-speaking Mexican boy who immigrated to the USA with his family at an early age. He 'begins his schooling in Sacramento, California, knowing just 50 words of English and concludes his university studies in the stately quiet of the reading room of the British Museum'(back cover of book). The success was won at the price of painful separation from his family, past, and C1. Rodriguez calls himself 'a comic victim of two cultures' (Wikipedia), and takes a strong stance against bilingual education:

> Behind this screen there gleams an astonishing promise: One can become a public person while still remaining a private person. At the very same time one can be both! There need be no tension between the self in the crowd and the self apart from the crowd! Who would not want to believe such an idea? Who can be surprised that the scheme has won the support of many middle-class Americans? If the barrio or ghetto child can retain his separateness even while being publicly educated, then it is almost possible to believe that there is no private cost to be paid for public success. (Rodriguez, 1982, pp. 34–35)

In a 'foreign language' environment, learners may not suffer such poignant pain of identity loss, but nor will they necessarily enjoy a vision of success either, and so may find themselves stranded in hopelessness. A senior Chinese professor of English whom I greatly respected spent several years before retirement proof reading transcriptions of talks given by an English NS. He lamented upon retirement: 'We English teachers in China spend the whole life trying to speak and write like a native speaker, but are bound to fail in the end'.

The legitimate speaker
Characteristics

From the 1980s, the faithful imitator model in L2 learning and use became increasingly challenged by that of a legitimate speaker of the English language. The legitimate speaker criticizes the traditional dichotomy of NS vs. NNS and the preferential status ranking of the former over the latter, and claims equal rights of using the language as well as setting variety standards. In the view of the legitimate speaker, language is not exclusively owned by the 'native culture'. English has multiple varieties with respective standards and equal status. L2 users in different parts of the world have developed their own varieties with respective local standards modeled on educated users of the language; these varieties are equally standard and 'good' as native varieties such as British or American English. The legitimate speaker targets not at perfect imitation of NSs, but at effective communication and identity expression. Thus, accents of English, for example, were no longer seen as deficiencies, but neutral or positive markers of group identity, and of equal and distinct participants in communication.

L2 research discourse

Several new concepts regarding the position of English contributed to the rise of the legitimate speaker. A prominent one is Kachru's (1982/1992) 'world Englishes' (WE) paradigm, referring to indigenized varieties of English, especially those varieties that were developed in nations colonized by the UK or influenced by the USA. Kachru further divided WE varieties into three concentric circles. With the emergence of WE organizations and academic journals (e.g. *World Englishes*), and publication of extensive research (e.g. on China/Chinese English: Bolton, 2003; Li, 1993; Li, 2006), the existence and legitimacy of WE varieties have been widely accepted, at least within the WE field.

Concepts related to WE have emerged in the past decades, such as 'English as an International Language (EIL)', 'international English', 'global English', and 'English as Lingua Franca (ELF)'. More recently, Jenkins (2007) proposed 'ELF' to replace EIL, further stressing the role of English among NNSs, though NSs were not excluded. Jenkins (2007, p. 13) explicitly claimed that ELF as a functional variety is 'legitimate English'. While WE related indigenized English varieties with local cultures, ELF largely eliminated cultural elements and stressed the Lingua Franca function in communication. Yet in breaking the NS vs. NNS dichotomy, these theories shared a common stance.

From the 1990s, L2 identity research from a social constructivist perspective enriched the image of the legitimate speaker. Drawing on Bourdieu's (1977) 'cultural capital', Norton (1995, 2000) proposed 'L2 investment' to replace 'L2 learning motivation'. Later she (Norton, 2001) further borrowed from Wenger (1998) and proposed that the investment target was the L2 learner's chosen 'imagined community' (cf. Anderson, 1983/1991; Wenger, 1998) and 'imagined identity'. Norton showed how immigrant learners of English in Canada negotiated with people in their social contexts for their imagined identity as legitimate speakers, and how those people in the contexts responded. In some cases, learners chose 'non-participation' (Norton, 2001) as a protest to the contexts' failure in recognizing and legitimizing their imagined identities. In an ESL class, for instance, the teacher invited students to share information about their home country. Yet in the teacher's summary, Felicia's points about Peru were left out. When Felicia questioned this, the teacher explained that Peru was not a major country under consideration. Felicia never returned to class. It was found that Felicia identified herself as a 'wealthy Peruvian' rather than a recent immigrant. Her Peruvian identity was validated at work, but denied in the ESL class. While the same kind of nonparticipation might be explained by faithful imitator models as a learner's individual failure in C2 acculturation, Norton legitimized it and called for critical reflection on the social contexts.

More recently in the description of L2 competence, 'symbolic competence' proposed by Kramsch and Whiteside (2008) also has an empowering function for the legitimate speaker. In their definition, symbolic competence is 'the ability to shape the multilingual game in which one invests – the ability to manipulate the conventional categories and societal norms of truthfulness, legitimacy, seriousness, originality – and to reframe human thought and action' (Kramsch & Whiteside, 2008, p. 667). If conventional 'communicative competence' stressed the faithful observation of NS norms, then 'symbolic competence' has emphasized the ability to manipulate and reframe existing norms.

Blommaert's (2010) 'sociolinguistics of globalization' is very much about legitimacy in the reordered social structure of globalization. With concepts such as 'sociolinguistic scales', 'orders of indexicality', and 'policentricity', his theory leaves room for people to move up social scales by making use of symbolic resources such as English, but much more emphasis is put on inequality, rigidity of structural hierarchy, and obstacles for grassroots people with 'truncated repertoires' to become legitimate speakers.

In China, 'Chinese cultural aphasia' in EFL education – the inability to describe and explain Chinese culture in English – has aroused much critical attention and corrective attempts in the past decade (e.g. Song & Xiao, 2009). Some empirical research and teaching projects have been carried out from the perspective of critical pedagogy, to empower learners as legitimate and creative English writers (Ye, 2012). Calls have also been made concerning the legitimacy of English publication of previously published research in authors' L1, with reframing for international readers (Wen & Gao, 2007).

Shi-xu's (2009) stance of 'reconstructing Eastern paradigms of discourse studies' is that of vehement fighting for the legitimate speaker identity, at national and transnational levels. Publishing widely in English in the field of discourse studies but often at a grand 'East vs. West' level without fine-grained discourse analysis of specific textual data, he makes repeated calls to 'undermine the global universalization of Western ideas and ideologies, and reclaim cultural identity and diversity of the underdeveloped and developing cultures' (2009, p. 32).

Contexts

The legitimate speaker of English was born in a postcolonial era, in which the colonial power of the UK was broken in various parts of the world. Linguistic hegemony, along with other types of hegemony, was seriously challenged. Increasingly, the use of English was separated from the 'native culture' of the previous colonizers. A strong sense of autonomy was growing, including identification with local English varieties, and critical awareness of language rights. The civil rights movement which emerged in the USA in the 1960s also had a dimension of language rights, which engaged efforts from dis-privileged racial, ethnic, and gender groups.

Critical strands of intellectual thinking contributed greatly to the growth of the legitimate speaker. Neo-Marxist theory, feminist theories, and critical theory all helped to shape critical awareness of power in language. For example, following French-thinker Michel Foucault, power is perceived to be omnipresent in human activity. It has a positive side when enhancing people's capacity to act, and a negative side when constraining such capacity. French sociologist Pierre Bourdieu expanded Marx's theory of capital to include not only economic, but also social, cultural, and symbolic dimensions. In his view, language competence, or linguistic capital, is an embodied form of cultural capital, able to be transformed into other capital forms. Following his conceptualization of cultural capital and 'the economics of linguistic exchange' (Bourdieu, 1977), NNSs were competing with NSs for the position of 'legitimate speaker' in the linguistic market. Positioned by himself as 'constructivist structuralism' and 'structuralist constructivism' (Bourdieu, 1990, p. 123), Bourdieu's theory drew attention to both social structural constraints on language use, and possibilities of symbolic negotiation from below.

Schools of critical thinking created room for reconceptualizing L2 learner/user identities. While the 'faithful imitator' does not have an independent voice, the legitimate speaker is determined to articulate him- or herself.

Constraints

The concept 'legitimate speaker' contains a paradox, i.e. the need to fight for legitimacy marks and possibly strengthens disadvantaged power positions. Also, a disparity exists between legitimacy and equality as an ideal, and discrimination and inequality as reality. Though room exists for power negotiation, all too often L2 users are subject to social structural constraints. For example, while researchers enthusiastically propose 'China English' as a legitimate variety of world English, teachers show far less interest, and students are mostly uninterested. With increased competence in differentiating English varieties, Chinese netizens recently laughed at and put shame on a China Central Television (CCTV) journalist who communicated effectively when interviewing a Zambian official, yet with a heavy Chinese accent: 'The Chinese accent of English shocked (雷翻) netizens'; 'English teachers will be made mad!'[1] The reasoning behind the strong emotion was that CCTV, the official national media, represented China's national 'face' and was thus expected to use 'standard' English pronunciation – British or American. Language users are driven by realistic principles of social comparison, and will target the most powerful varieties. There is a long way to go toward the legitimacy goal. Perhaps only when 'legitimacy' is no longer an issue, can one say it is realized.

Another potential problem of legitimate speakers is that, in their passionate fight against inequality, there is a danger of slipping into a dichotomized, essentialist view of culture. Simplistic categorization may conceal linguistic and cultural complexities, and excessive focusing on one particular social dimension of inequality (ethnic, national, religious, socioeconomic, gender, etc.) may serve to conceal inequalities in other dimensions.

The playful creator

Characteristics

The idea of L2 legitimacy was further extended by postmodernists in the new millennium, to formulate an identity that can be labeled 'the playful creator'. The playful creator lives not within a language but across languages; he or she constantly reinvents and reconstructs language or discourse by mixing different linguistic codes. Unconventional hybridization, fragmentation and juxtaposition of linguistic and cultural elements at surface level are conventionally employed, to form distinct ways of self-expression. These creators are critically playful; they can be regarded as a type of legitimate speaker in their challenge of existing standards. However, instead of claiming to be 'equal' users of the same language, they actually 'disinvent' the L2 and create their own L2 related 'creole' (Makoni & Pennycook, 2007). Their typical way of interacting with the social environment is not serious negotiation or bitter fight, but rather indirect forms of playful or cynical self-expression. The playful creator is typically young, and his language (dis) invention is intertwined with a form of pop culture.

L2 research discourse

Alastair Pennycook has made a leading contribution to the portrayal of the playful creator. His empirical work has captured features of the transnational phenomena of hip-hop and English (Pennycook, 2007). Hip-hoppers' use of English is not imitative, but a mix with local languages in the form of 'creoles'. As an example, hip-hopper Joe Flizzow sang at a night club in Kuala Lumpur, Malaysia (Pennycook, 2007, p. 1):

INTERCULTURAL DIALOGUE

> Hip hop be connectin' Kuala Lumpur with LB
> Hip hop be rockin' up towns laced wit' LV
> Ain't necessary to roll in ice rimmed M3's and be blingin'
> Hip hop be bringin' together emcees.

In this English rap, Kuala Lumpur of Malaysia is tied with Long Beach of the USA, which might imply the global spread of the American culture and its domination over the local cultural forms. Yet the African-American flavor in pronunciation and syntax ('Hip hop be connectin') implies resistance to the US cultural mainstream. Its juxtaposition of Louis Vuitton clothes and BMW 3 series wheel rims demonstrates identification with the contemporary global popular culture of fashion and consumption, yet at the same time it claims distance from and rejection of such cultural elements ('Ain't necessary').

With the language of hip-hop and English woven together, Pennycook argues that such language use becomes part of a localized subculture in many parts of the world: hip-hop operates as a global code, while simultaneously creating a sense of locality. Pennycook uses 'transcultural flows' to capture the movements, changes and reuses of cultural forms in disparate contexts. For him, 'there are many flows in many directions' (2007, p. 117), instead of a one-directional flow. Also, he uses 'global Englishes' to replace Kachru's 'world Englishes'. In Pennycook's critical view, WE with its concentric circles are still centered on NS varieties; the various varieties are far from 'equal'. Under global Englishes, however, language conventions are being 'disinvented' and 'recon-structed' (Makoni & Pennycook, 2007) by their creative (L2) users around the world.

With a stance more toward the social structuralist side, Blommaert also notes the mixed uses as norms, including those of pop songs. In his view, such hybrid language use 'becomes creative because it is measurable against normative hegemonic standards' (Blommaert, 2005, p. 106). They serve to 'disorder' and 'reorder' the conventional hierarchy of speech norms set by the society. Yet, the hegemonic forces will not easily surrender. Although with competence to manipulate symbolic sources for self expression and communication, the creators may or may not succeed in making their discourses accepted in a higher or broader social 'scale'. Thus, L2 creators in the view of Blommaert are only occasionally 'playful' compared to those of Pennycook; they are more often fighting the hard battle of legitimate speakers.

Along with 'creativity' tied with 'hybridity', concepts such as 'performativity' (Butler, 1997), 'transculturation' or 'transculturality' (Pennycook, 2007), and various '-ity' and 'trans-' affixed terminologies have become popular, replacing the more structuralist '-ism' concepts such as 'bilingualism'. The multiplication of new termino-logy creation shows the postmodernist attempts and eagerness to disform and reform ideologies in the entire field, which interestingly parallel the hip-hoppers' language or discourse (dis)invention.

In Chinese contexts, a number of collections included images of the playful creator. Doreen Wu's (2008) collection examined various discourses in 'Cultural China' (mainland China, Hong Kong, Macao, Taiwan, Singapore, and Chinese diasporas in other parts of the world), with a 'glocalization' perspective. Her own serial studies on advertisements in Hong Kong and mainland China have maintained a focus on hybridity and creativity. Yet, the discourses she researched on were mostly quite formal and carefully designed, and often with a dimension of historical change, which were different from playful improvisations of the hip-hoppers. Tian and Cao's (2012) collection, on the other hand, had quite a broad concern over discourse and 'reinvention of identities' in mainland China. The discourses examined ranged from hybridized shop signs, the

INTERCULTURAL DIALOGUE

localized English teaching genre of 'Crazy English', and Chinese political discourse in English translation. In the same discourse book series, Ding and Shen's (2013) collection focused on 'marginal discourses' such as rock and roll, Internet talk, and movies with homosexual themes.

Contexts

The playful creator grows up in an era of increased globalization. The rapid development of new media technology facilitates world-wide linguistic and cultural flows, though disparity exists among socioeconomic classes. The Internet has become indispensable for an increasingly large number of people. According to *New Weekly* (2013), China had 538,000,000 netizens by 2012. International traveling is becoming common, even a lifestyle for some. In 2011, the number of international visitors entering China was 54,120,000; the number of Chinese tourists traveling abroad was 70,250,000. The World Tourism Organization predicts that by 2020, the annual number of Chinese tourists going abroad will reach 100 million. Consumerism and cosmopolitanism are cherished, accompanied with policentricity of power. Geographic boundaries are no longer important. Languages and cultures are being deterritorialized, acquiring global mobility. 'Never say what you want to say in a (conventionally) "good" manner' (有话就不好好说) has become a spirit of the era for the young. When word games saturate genres such as advertisements, Twitter, TV series, and titles of articles and posts in an L1 other than English, code mixing from English has become a common source for playful creation.

Intellectually, poststructuralist, postmodernist, and social constructivist/constructionist theories have gained great influence. Unified stable structures are no longer in favor in social theories. Anderson (1983/1991) views nations as 'imagined communities', subjectively constructed. Giddens's (1984) structuration theory breaks the dichotomy of 'society' and 'individual', perceiving them as mutually structuring each other in interaction. Self-identity is an ongoing reflective narrative in search of 'ontological security' (Giddens, 1991, p. 47). Bauman (2005, p. 1) conceives 'liquid lives' of the postmodern era, where people 'act change faster than it takes the ways of acting to consolidate into habits and routines'. Regarding the constant tension between social structure and individual agency, there seems to be a general tendency in social science theories that more weight has been put on the latter (cf. Block, 2013).

Taken together, the late modern/postmodern era of globalization is (perceived as) essentially different from the previous ages. Hybridity, ambivalences, and fluidity have become norms of life. Individuals enjoy increased agency in identity construction, and at the same time suffer a decrease in their sense of stability and security. Such perceived and actual changes in social environments have exerted a great influence on the formation of the playful creator.

Constraints

The playful creator, while leading the direction of language change, is constrained in several ways. First, their creation is largely confined to particular 'marginal' domains of language use (e.g. recreation, informal talk), separated from major domains such as politics, economy, and education. Its influence on the mainstream of social life is restricted. Second, playful creators are mostly young people whose social power is limited, at least in 'vertical cultures' such as China. Third, while playful creations are often praised as heroic resistance against hegemony of linguistic standards, it remains to be further investigated how 'free' they are. Much like the legitimate speaker in general and perhaps to a greater extent, the playful creator appears to be powerful in L2 research, but may remain quite powerless in social reality.

The dialogical communicator

Characteristics

The dialogical communicator is an ideal L2 learner/user identity that I have proposed, based on Bakhtin's theory of dialogue and empirical data of intercultural communication (Gao, 2010). Following Bakhtin, human beings are by nature dialoging agents. The dialogicality for L2 learners/users can be characterized at two levels. In inter-subject communication, dialogical communicators converse – speak and listen – on the basis of mutual respect. Communication gains its end value; creative discourses and effective outcomes may turn out to be byproducts. In intra-subject communication, i.e. the dialogue between different consciousness or 'voices', the dialogical communicator has a reflective sensitivity, ready to discern, expand, deepen and reorganize various kinds of consciousness within him- or herself. These two levels of dialogicality are dialectical and mutually facilitating. Good quality self-consciousness is necessary for interpersonal communication.

The dialogical communicator has transcended various dichotomies such as listening vs. speaking, native culture vs. C2, and instrumental vs. integrative motivation. They are free from the superiority–inferiority complex. Different from the playful creator who mixes and combines selected elements from various cultures, the dialogical communicator respects the integrity and entirety of each and every culture. He or she enjoys mutual enhancement of L1/C1 on the one hand, and competence in the chosen L2 target discourse and identification with the chosen imagined community on the other.

L2 research discourse

Though the term 'dialogical communicator' was proposed recently, its characteristics such as transcendence of dichotomy appeared in my earlier studies on 'productive bilingualism' (Gao, 2001, 2002), based on Fromm's (1948) 'productive orientation' and empirical data of recognized 'best foreign language learners' in China. Contrasted with Lambert's (1974) 'subtractive' and 'additive' bilinguals, productive bilinguals enjoy mutually enhanced L2 and L2 competence, and mutually deepened C1 and C2 understanding. They are distinguished for openness and criticalness toward and incorporation of both cultures, in their own individual manner.

As a poetry translator, for example, one participant translated many ancient Chinese poems into English and French. The following is his rendering of Du Fu's 'Deng Gao' (On the Height):

Original couplet in Chinese and Pinyin:

无边落木萧萧下，Wubian luomu xiaoxiao xia,
不尽长江滚滚来。Bujin changjiang gungun lai.

Translation by Participant:

The boundless forest sheds its leaves shower by shower;
The endless river rolls its waves hour after hour.

INTERCULTURAL DIALOGUE

Compared with other translations which focused mainly on meaning[2] and rhyme, the translator's above rendering made an additional effort to capture the sound parallelism in Chinese:

> It is said that in English strict parallelism without the repetition of a word is nearly impossible, while parallelism involving repetition will quickly seem rigid and monotonous. But in the above version we may find only unimportant particles repeated without entailing rigidity or monotony. It is true that in the second line of Du Fu's original couplet the word 'roll' is repeated (gungun), while in this version it is not. Isn't it a loss? So it is, but the loss is compensated for by the repetition of 'hour', which cannot be found in the original. Then this may be called a loss at sunrise with a gain at sunset. (cited from Gao, 2002, p. 154)

Along with his translation practice, the translator proposes his principle of poetry translation: 'beauty in meaning, sound, and written form'. 'The West values truth; the East treasures goodness; as a poetry translator I pursue beauty. Truth, goodness and beauty are congruent with one another' (Gao, 2002). In his own field and in his own manner, he incorporated the beauty of L1 and L2, and actualized his own potential as a poetry translator.

In a later ethnography on student volunteers for the Beijing Olympic Games (BOG; Gao, 2010), it is found that the student volunteers underwent an identity change from the legitimate speaker to the dialogical communicator. The study captured a change of volunteer proposed slogans for their office wall in a competition venue:

When proposing 'We speak and the world will listen' prior to BOG (Figure 1), the volunteers wanted to convey 'our ambition, and our competence of exerting influence'. As Chinese volunteers, they felt 'ambitious, confident and courageous; the whole world is listening to us'. This ambitious slogan, setting 'we' and 'the world' apart as the speaker and the listener, was later replaced by an assembly of names of nations and languages represented by the competing teams in the venue (Figure 2). During BOG, volunteers developed empathy with international guests they served. In a post-BOG discussion, a volunteer reflected:

> I was very happy when I was being able to help, and received thanks for that. In my view, 'we speak' is an internal talk among (Chinese) foreign language learners. As volunteers, our focus should be serving the needs of the external. We should not impose on others. So when addressing the external, 'we speak' needs to be changed. After we've invited others, and they've got *their own* positive feelings, they'll naturally have a good impression of us. And we'll in turn feel proud of ourselves. Serving the needs of others – this is what a volunteer should do. (Gao, 2010).

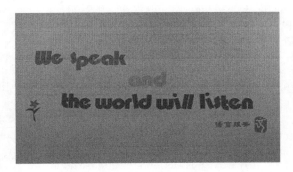

Figure 1. Initial slogan on the wall: Legitimate speaker identity.

Figure 2. Later change: Dialogical communicator identity.

Apart from the office wall slogan, the volunteers also reflected on their experience inside the Paralympics venue (Liu & Gao, 2013). In a table tennis competition, when the overwhelming majority of audience was cheering for Chinese athletes, a minority of volunteers started to cheer for the guest team. One volunteer reflected afterwards:

> If I were a foreign journalist sitting in the venue, my vision would be filled with Chinese faces and redness; foreign athletes seemed so negligible. Apart from respect, would this nation arouse my fear of some kind? I guess yes. Would this fear be a kind of awe, or disdain? Would this nation arouse my respect because of its strength/power, or would it impress me with nothing other than strength/power? :… I sometimes think – quite seriously – what kind of Chinese I want to be, what kind of nation China should be. Being powerful, becoming Number One and winning gold medals – these are important, but what is more important is how we treat others. BOG is a good opportunity to demonstrate what kind of nation China is. For friends who have never been to China, we hope you'll see we are not economically poor and culturally blank; we are not only economically promising, but also good in other respects. Every Chinese has such a responsibility of showing to the world what kind of nation China is'. (Liu & Gao, 2013, p. 77)

Taken together, student volunteers started with a rather narrow patriotic or nationalistic stance, claiming and celebrating the acquisition of a legitimate speaker identity. During and after BOG, they developed a growing capacity of critical self-reflection, and started to step beyond the 'we'–'they' opposition. Patriotism was deepened, through dialoging with an international perspective. The new position developed later was that of a dialogical communicator.

The spirit of dialogicality, particularly between the local and global, is widely found in research discourse, though terminologies vary. In portrayal of the cross-cultural awareness development, for example, Kramsch proposes the finding of 'the third place', which 'would enable learners to take both an insider's and outsider's view on C1 and C2' (Kramsch, 1993, p. 210). Explicitly drawing on Bakhtin's concept of dialogue, Kramsch conceives contexts of interaction as 'sphere of intersubjectivity', 'sphere of intertextuality', and 'sphere of interculturality' (Kramsch, 1993, p. 13). In this view, cultures are understood only in dialogical relation with other cultures. Bucholtz and Hall's (2005) 'sociocultural linguistic approach' to identity sees identity as intersubjectively produced and interactionally emergent. Dörnyei, Csizér, and Nemeth (2006) state that bicultural identity is partly rooted in local culture and partly rooted in global culture. Byram (2008) proposes a move from foreign language teaching to 'education for intercultural citizenship'. Holliday (2013) extends his nonessentialist notion of 'small cultures' to a grander 'grammar of culture', exemplifying how the self may dialogue with the 'other',

INTERCULTURAL DIALOGUE

and with social and political 'structures'. Wu Zongjie (2009) proposes English education in China should promote learners' dialogue with C1 history and local culture, with expanded competence of meaning interpretation of texts. His 'China study from an intercultural perspective' has already generated interesting ethnographic work and pedagogical practice.

Contexts

In the post-cold war world, relations among cultures have become a center of attention. Huntington (1996) proposed that instead of ideological differences, people's cultural and religious identities will be the major source of conflict, hence 'the Clash of Civilizations'. This theory generated heated discussion and debates. As a response to Huntington's perception, the former Iranian president Mohammad Khatami proposed the theory of 'Dialogue Among Civilizations', which caught international attention and became the basis for United Nations' resolution to name the year 2001 as the Year of Dialogue among Civilizations. After al-Qaeda's brutal 9/11 attacks on US targets in 2001, more international efforts have been made to promote such dialogues. In 2005, 'The United Nations Alliance of Civilizations' (UNAOC) was proposed by the Prime Minister of Spain, and co-sponsored by the Prime Minister of Turkey. The initiative seeks to galvanize international action against extremism through the forging of international, intercultural, and interreligious dialogue, with a particular emphasis on defusing tensions between the Western and Islamic worlds (Wikipedia). In 2010, a UNAOC forum was held at the Shanghai World Expo, paying special attention to dialogues in the Asian–Pacific region. Within nations, there has also been an increasing call for attention to isolation and segregation of ethnic minorities, for example, in the criticism of 'multiculturalism' in European countries and Australia in the past 10–20 years (Wikipedia). As a lasting theme in history, dialogue among cultures has acquired its particular importance in the present era when the world is becoming increasingly smaller, but violence and segregation are becoming common and easy solutions.

The dialogical communicator has both traditional and contemporary intellectual origins. Its direct theoretical resource is Bakhtin's theory of dialogism/dialogicality. According to Bakhtin, dialogical communication is the very essence of existence. 'In dialogues, people not only present themselves to the external world, but also become who they are for the first time' (Bakhtin, 1988, p. 344). 'Only in communication, in the interaction between human beings and about human beings, can one's 'inner human being' be revealed to the self and other' (Bakhtin, 1988, p. 343).

There are other intellectual resources from different cultures that nurture the dialogical communicator. Among these are Confucian principles such as 'Sage within and king without' and 'cultivate the self, harmonize the family, govern the state, and bring peace to the world', Erich Fromm's 'productive orientation', Abraham Maslow's 'self-actualization', to name a few. Though from different perspectives and located in different cultures, they all favor transcendence of dichotomies, most notably between 'self' and 'other'.

Based on critique of previous social theories, contemporary sociologist Margaret Archer (2000, 2003) offers her social realist theory to the tension between social structure and individual agency, focusing on 'internal conversation'. Distinct from social determinism, individualism and what she calls 'central conflation' of structure and agency (e.g. Giddens), Archer finds 'internal conversation' a missing link between the two. Through such an inner dialogue, individuals reflect upon their social situation in the light of current concerns and projects. This theory has obtained attention in applied

INTERCULTURAL DIALOGUE

linguistics and intercultural communication research (Block, 2013). The idea of 'internal conversation' between structure and agency, society and individual, other and self, may provide further theoretical nurturance to the growth of the dialogical communicator.

Constraints

At the social level, a nurturing environment for the dialogical communicator is not always granted in reality. Paradoxically, only with more dialogical communicators can the soil for their growth be fertilized. It is very difficult to develop love if one lives in an environment full of hatred, sadness, and frustration. At the individual level, when deficient basic needs – physiological needs, safety, belonging, and esteem – are not substantially satisfied, it is very hard to achieve the merge of 'specieshood' and 'selfhood' (Maslow, 1971, p. 187). In addition, from an educational perspective, the growth of the dialogical communicator does not lend itself easily to programmed training or testing (cf. Kramsch, 1993). It relies essentially on sustained personal commitment and gradual maturation in a nurtured environment. This may disappoint eager educators and learners driving at fast and immediate outcomes.

Conclusion

In this paper, I have presented my viewpoint that, over the past half century, the model L2 learner/user of English has undergone a development through several prototypes – the faithful imitator, the legitimate speaker, the playful creator, and the dialogical communicator. Along with the shift is the sociohistorical change – the collapse of colonialism, the increased impact of globalization, the increased call for intercultural dialogue amidst clash and conflicts. The development of intellectual resources has also contributed to the formation of the prototypes.

I will further venture to convey my perception that the prototypes can be roughly paralleled to stages of individual psychological development. The faithful imitator resembles a small child without a 'self', eager for identification with parents. The total integration or merging with parents provides a sense of badly needed security. The legitimate speaker and playful creator resemble an adolescent or young adult, striving to develop a distinct self-identity by making loud (resistant) voices or performing 'peculiar' acts. The need for autonomy, recognition, and esteem has surpassed that for parental affiliation and security. The dialogical communicator is like a mature adult in productive love (Fromm, 1948). It is based on ample sense of security and esteem that one can readily opens up to the exploration of simultaneous deepening of specieshood and selfhood (Table 1).

It should be noted, however, that these L2 identity prototypes are not rigidly positioned on a linear evolutionary continuum, socially or psychologically. In my perception, sociohistorically they peak in different times – the faithful imitator in the 1970s, the legitimate speaker in the 1980s and 1990s, the playful creator is now undergoing its high time in the first two decades of the new millennium, and the full development of the dialogical communicator is yet to come. Their general waves overlap; an old prototype may ebb but continue to exert influence when a new one's tide is high. The faithful imitator has continued to function, for instance, though its golden time as the dominating prototype has long passed. Different prototypes may also exist within the same individual, and have variations and combinations for different situations. It is also clear that L2 identities are not determined by social or individual factors alone; they

INTERCULTURAL DIALOGUE

Table 1. Summary of four L2 learner/user prototypes.

	Faithful imitator	Legitimate speaker	Playful creator	Dialogical communicator
Characteristics	L2 and cultural conduct strictly modeled on NS	Claims equal standards and rights with NS	Creates hybrid language use for self-expression	Converses on the basis of mutual respect; reflectivity
Contexts	Modernism; influence of colonialism	Fall of colonialism; postcolonialism	Postmodernism and globalization	Clash and dialogue among civilizations; dialogism
Constraints	Identity conflicts; loss of L1/C1	Paradoxical marking and strengthening of lower position	Constrained in domains of influence	Lack of nurturing environment; unsatisfied deficiency needs
Bilingualism	Subtractive	Additive	Hybrid	Productive
Psychological stage parallel	Small child	Adolescent; young adult	Adolescent; young adult	Mature adult

emerge in the interaction between the two. Therefore, it is not contradictory to examine at the same time individual learning 'motivation', 'orientation', or 'investment', how the contexts fosters them, and how they serve to constitute the changing context. It also follows that in constructing L2 identity models, researchers are constructing social and psychological spaces for further practice.

The above portrayal is primarily descriptive rather than normative, and the choice and evaluation of prototypes will depend on specific contexts and individuals. I hope the conceptualization of embodied persons will offer alternative targets for L2 learners, educators, and researchers in their own situations. Nevertheless, I have my own perception that the model L2 learner/user of English has undergone a marked development, on a general path from innocence to maturity. The dialogical communicator prototype, which remains to be fully developed, has particular implication for future English education targeted at intercultural competence and intercultural citizenship.

Acknowledgements

The author would like to extend her thanks to the two anonymous reviewers who have offered helpful comments and suggestions in the revision of this paper, to Dr John O'Regan who has helped on language improvement, and to Dr Prue Holmes who has provided continuous moral support.

Notes

1. http://huati.weibo.com/29836?order=time
2. For example: 'Leaves are dripping down like the spray of a waterfall, While I watch the long river always rolling on'. – Witter Bynner.

References

Anderson, B. (1983/1991). *Imagined communities*. London: Verso.

Archer, M. (2000). *Being human: The problem of agency*. Cambridge: Cambridge University Press.

Archer, M. (2003). *Structure, agency and the internal conversation*. Cambridge: Cambridge University Press.

Bakhtin, M. M. (1988). *Problems of Dostoevsky's poetics*. (Chinese translation by C. R. Bai & Y. L. Gu). Beijing: Sanlian Shudian.

Bauman, Z. (2005). *Liquid life*. Cambridge: Polity.

Block, D. (2007). *Second language identities*. London: Continuum.

Block, D. (2013). The structure and agency dilemma in identity and intercultural communication research. *Language and Intercultural Communication*, *13*(2), 126–147. doi:10.1080/14708477.2013.770863

Blommaert, J. (2005). *Discourse*. Cambridge: CUP.

Blommaert, J. (2010). *The sociolinguistics of globalization*. Cambridge: Cambridge University Press.

Bolton, K. (2003). *Chinese Englishes: A sociolinguistic history*. Cambridge: Cambridge University Press.

Bourdieu, P. (1977). The economics of linguistic exchanges. *Social Science Information*, *16*, 645–668. doi:10.1177/053901847701600601

Bourdieu, P. (1990). *In other words*. (translated by M. Adamson). Stanford, CA: Stanford University Press.

Bucholtz, M., & Hall, K. (2005). Identity and interaction: A sociocultural linguistic approach. *Discourse Studies*, *7*, 585–614.

Butler, J. (1997). *Excitable speech: A politics of the performative*. London: Routledge.

Byram, M. (2008). *From foreign language education to education for intercultural citizenship*. Clevedon: Multilingual Matters.

Davies, A. (2004). The native speaker in applied linguistics. In A. Davies & C. Elder (Eds.), *The handbook of applied linguistics* (pp. 431–450). Malden, MA: Blackwell.

Ding, J. X., & Shen, W. J. (Eds.). (2013). *Marginal discourse analysis* [丁建新、沈文静主编，《边缘话语分析》]. Tianjin: Nankai University Press.

Dörnyei, Z., Csizér, K., & Nemeth, N. (2006). *Motivation, language attitudes and globalization*. Clevedon: Multilingual Matters.

Fromm, E. (1948). *Man for himself*. London: Routledge and Kegan Paul.

Gao, Y. H. (2001). *Foreign language learning: '1+1>2'*. Beijing: Peking University Press.

Gao, Y. H. (2002). Productive bilingualism: 1+1>2. In D. W. D. So & G. M. Jones (Eds.), *Education and society in Plurilingual contexts* (pp. 143–162). Brussels: VUB Brussels University Press.

Gao, Y. H. (2010). Speaking to the world: Who, when and how? An ethnographic study of slogan change and identity construction of Beijing Olympic Games volunteers. *Asian Journal of English Language Teaching*, *20*, 1–26.

Gardner, R. C., & Lambert, W. E. (1972). *Attitudes and motivation in second language learning*. Rowley, MA: Newbury House.

Giddens, A. (1984). *The constitution of society*. Berkeley: University of California Press.

Giddens, A. (1991). *Modernity and self-identity*. Cambridge: Polity Press.

Giles, H., & Johnson, P. (1987). Ethnolinguistic identity theory: A social psychological approach to language maintenance. *International Journal of the Sociology of Language*, *68*, 69–99.

Holliday, A. (2013). *Understanding intercultural communication: Negotiating a grammar of culture*. London: Routledge.

Huntington, S. (1996). *The clash of civilizations and the remaking of world order*. New York, NY: Simon & Schuster.

Jenkins, J. (2007). *English as a Lingua Franca: Attitudes and identity*. Oxford: OUP.

Joseph, J. (2004). *Language and identity*. London: Palgrave.

Kachru, B. B. (1982/1992). *The other tongue*. Urbana: University of Illinois Press.

Kramsch, C. (1993). *Context and culture in language teaching*. Oxford: Oxford University Press.

Kramsch C., & Whiteside, A. (2008). Language ecology in multilingual settings: Towards a theory of symbolic competence. *Applied Linguistics, 29*, 645–671. doi:10.1093/applin/amn022

Lambert, W. E. (1974). Culture and language as factors in learning and education. In F. E. Aboud & R. D. Meade (Eds.), *Cultural factors in learning and education* (pp. 91–122). Bellingham: Washington Stage College.

Li, S. H. (2006). *China English in perspective of English globalization and localization* [李少华, 《英语全球化与本土化视野中的中国英语》]. Yinchun: Ningxia People's Press.

Li, W. Z. (1993). China English and Chinglish [李文中,中国英语和中国式英语, 《外语教学与研究》]. *Foreign Language Teaching and Research, 1993*, 18–24.

Liu, L., & Gao, Y. H. (2013). Report of the comprehensive university sample. In Y. H. Gao & Project Group, *English learning motivation and self-identity development among Chinese University Students – A four-year longitudinal study in 5 universities* [刘璐、高一虹, 综合性大学样本报告, 高一虹等, 《大学生英语学习动机与自我认同发展—— 四年五校跟踪研究》] (pp. 51–80). Beijing: Higher Education Press.

Makoni, S., & Pennycook, A. (Eds.). (2007). *Disinventing and reconstituting languages*. Clevedon: Multilingual Matters.

Maslow, A. H. (1971). *The farther reaches of human nature*. New York, NY: The Viking Press.

New Weekly. (2013). *Biographies of diors – Best publications of* New Weekly *2012* [《屌丝传—<新周刊>2012年度佳作》]. Guilin: Lijiang Press.

Norton, B. (1995). Social identity, investment, and language learning. *TESOL Quarterly, 29*(1), 9–31. doi:10.2307/3587803

Norton, B. (2000). *Identity and language learning*. Harlow: Harlow Pearson Education.

Norton, B. (2001). Non-participation, imagined communities, and the language classroom. In M. Breen (Ed.), *Learner contributions to language learning: New directions in research* (pp. 159–171). Harlow: Pearson Education.

Pennycook, A. (2007). *Global Englishes and transcultural flows*. London: Routledge.

Rodriguez, R. (1982). *Hunger of memory*. New York, NY: Bantam Books.

Schumann, J. (1978). The acculturation model for second language acquisition. In R. C. Gingras (Ed.), *Second language acquisition and foreign language teaching* (pp. 27–50). Arlington, VA: Center for Applied Linguistics.

Shi-xu. (2009). Reconstructing Eastern paradigm of discourse studies. *Journal of Multicultural Discourses, 4*, 29–48. doi:10.1080/17447140802651637

Song, Y. W., & Xiao, L. F. (2009). The present situation of Chinese cultural aphasia in College English teaching in China [宋伊雯, 肖龙福, 大学英语教学'中国文化失语'现状调查, 《中国外语》]. *Foreign Language in China, 2009*, 88–92.

Tajfel, H. (1982). Social psychology of intergroup relations. *Annual Review of Psychology, 33*(1), 1–39. doi:10.1146/annurev.ps.33.020182.000245

Tian, H. L., & Cao, Q. (Eds.). (2012). *Reinventing identities: The poetics of language use in contemporary China*. Tianjin: Nankai University Press.

Wen, Q. F., & Gao, Y. H. (2007). Dual publication and academic inequality. *International Journal of Applied Linguistics, 17*, 221–225. doi:10.1111/j.1473-4192.2007.00147.x

Wenger, E. (1998). *Communities of practice*. Cambridge: Cambridge University Press.

Wu, D. (Ed.). (2008). *Discourses of cultural China in the globalizing age*. Hong Kong: Hong Kong University Press.

Wu, Z. J. (2009, March). *'China study' from an intercultural perspective* [吴宗杰, 跨文化视角下的'中国学研究']. Paper presented at Annual Conference of Zhejiang Association of Foreign Languages, Ningbo. Retrieved from http://wenku.baidu.com/view/91fa253731126edb6f1a10f2.html

Ye, H. (2012). *A critical intercultural approach to empowering Chinese learners as English writers*. Changsha: Hunan People's Press.

Interreligious dialogue in schools: beyond asymmetry and categorisation?

Anna-Leena Riitaoja[a] and Fred Dervin[b]

[a]Institute of Behavioural Sciences, University of Helsinki, Helsinki, Finland; [b]Department of Teacher Education, University of Helsinki, Helsinki, Finland

> Interreligious dialogue is a central objective in European and UNESCO policy and research documents, in which educational institutions are seen as central places for dialogue. In this article, we discuss this type of dialogue under the conditions of asymmetry and categorisation in two Finnish schools. Finnish education has often been lauded for its successful implementation of equity and equality by the thousands of 'pedagogical tourists' who visit the country's schools to witness the so-called miracle of Finnish education due to Finland's excellent results in the OECD Programme for International Student Assessment (PISA) study. Through theoretically informed reading of ethnographic data, we examine how Self and Other are constructed in everyday encounters in school and how religions, religious groups and individuals become regarded as Others. We also ask whether the aims of interreligious dialogue in schools represent a viable way to learn about each other and to increase mutual understanding. The theoretical and methodological approaches derive from post-colonial, post-structural and related feminist theories as well as from recent research on intercultural education and communication.

> Uskontojenvälistä dialogia pidetään keskeisenä tavoitteena monissa eurooppalaisissa ja UNESCOn poliittisissa dokumenteissa ja tutkimusasiakirjoissa, joissa koulutusinstituutiot esitetään näissä usein keskeisiksi dialogin paikoiksi. Artikkelissamme tarkastelemme arjen kohtaamisiin liittyvää uskontodialogia sekä kohtaamisissa läsnä olevaa epäsymmetriaa ja kategorisointia kahdessa suomalaisessa koulussa. Suomalaisten koulutusjärjestelmän yhdenvertaisuutta ja tasa-arvoisuutta ovat kehuneet ne tuhannet 'koulutusturistit', jotka ovat vierailleet Suomen kouluissa tutustumassa OECD: n Programme for international student assessment (PISA) - arvioinnin erinomaisiin tuloksiin perustuvaan suomalaisen koulutuksen menestystarinaan. Tarkastelemme etnografista aineistoamme teoriasta ammentavan etnografisen luennan avulla analysoiden sitä, kuinka itse ja toinen rakentuvat koulun arjen kohtaamisissa ja kuinka uskontoja, uskonnollisia ryhmiä ja yksilöitä pidetään toisina. Pohdimme, pystyykö kouluihin sijoittuva uskontodialogi edistämään tavoitteidensa mukaisesti keskinäistä oppimista ja lisäämään keskinäistä ymmärtämistä. Artikkelimme teoreettiset ja metodologiset näkökulmat perustuvat jälkikoloniaalisiin ja jälkistrukturalistisiin feministisiin teoretisointeihin sekä viimeaikaiseen interkulttuurisen kasvatuksen ja vuorovaikutuksen tutkimukseen.

Introduction

Interreligious dialogue together with intercultural dialogue is a central objective of European and UNESCO educational and policy documents (Council of Europe, 2005,

2007, 2008, 2011; Jackson, 2009; UNESCO, 2006; Rec. 1720, 2005; Rec. 1804, 2007; Rec. 12, 2008). While researchers of religious education have written extensively about the links between intercultural and interreligious education (see e.g. Jackson, 2004a; Jackson, Miedema, Weiße, & Willaime, 2007) the fields of multicultural/intercultural education/ communication have been hesitant to tackle the theme (exceptions: Riitaoja, Poulter, & Kuusisto, 2010; Wolf, 2012). In both policy and scholarly texts, educational institutions are considered to be central places for such dialogue. The main goal is to foster a sense of equal togetherness and discussions between people or groups representing 'different' faiths, religions and even 'cultures'. The overarching goals consist in learning about diversity and increasing mutual understanding, respect and tolerance but also social cohesion and the integration of religious minorities into the society (see Jackson, 2004a). The controversial notion of citizenship is also often used in that regard.

In this article, we discuss the conditions of and the possibilities for interreligious dialogue in a school context, taking Finland as an illustration. Finland, a country 'new' to mass immigration represents an interesting case, especially as the Finnish system of education has been the centre of world attention due to its excellent results in the OECD Programme for International Student Assessment (PISA) studies. Our interest lays in how self and the other are constructed in everyday encounters in schools (Dervin, 2012). What modes of identification are available for different groups of students and staff in the school space? What and who seems to enable and disable the 'possibilities of becoming' (Butler, 1993, p. 10; Youdell, 2003), that is to say the possibilities to identify in a way one hopes to be identified, seen and heard as a subject and not as an object in interreligious encounters? Finally, we also examine how the ideas of 'religions', religious groups and persons are constructed through discourses and practices of schooling.

Based on theoretically informed reading of our ethnographic data, we suggest that some students and staff members are Otherised in the interreligious encounters in schools. We also argue that the conditions of dialogue are different for those who are constructed as Others. Finally, such Othering that is related to unproblematised notions about religion and dialogue works against the aims of togetherness and mutual learning of interreligious dialogue.

Background and theoretical and methodological considerations

This paper derives from the observations that discussion on religion and interreligious dialogue in intercultural/multicultural educations studies has been mainly lacking or it has been problem-centred: the presence of religion is considered as problematic in the school space and as a potential risk for the coherence of societies (for an example see Coulby & Zambeta, 2008; see critique in Modood, 2007; Riitaoja et al., 2010; Salili & Hoosain, 2006). Although intercultural studies have discussed Othering and prejudices related to religious minorities (especially Muslims) in European societies and schools (Dhamoon, 2009), there has been less discussion on how the notions of religion and religion as a social category may contribute to the process of Othering. Religion as a social category has, therefore, been lacking theoretical and methodological analyses. In intercultural education studies interreligious dialogue, and its related terms – mutual learning and respect – have been offered as solutions for such asymmetry (e.g. Jackson, 2004b). Along with European policy documents, some intercultural education studies have also considered interreligious and intercultural dialogue as a tool of integration for minorities in society (Arthur, 2011; Hodgson, 2011). We argue that the conditions under which the assumedly equal dialogue takes place, and the positions of the self and the other (asymmetrically) constructed in such encounters, are not sufficiently problematised. Moreover, discussions on how the problem-oriented aim of integrating religious minorities may contribute to Othering and how integration may work as a tool for domesticating the Other are lacking (exceptions: Hoskins & Sallah, 2011; Riikonen & Dervin, 2012).

Our theoretical approach derives from post-colonial philosophy that problematises the concept of religion (e.g. King, 2009; Mignolo, 2009; Nandy, 2002), from post-structural feminist studies that analyse the discursive construction of the Self and social categories (e.g. Butler, 1993; Youdell, 2003), and from post-colonial and feminist studies that analyse the construction of the privileged subject and the subaltern Other through knowledge, discourses and social and institutional practices (e.g. Ahmed, 2012; Andreotti, Ahenakew, & Cooper, 2012; Spivak, 2004). We combine these theoretical approaches with recent research on intercultural education and communication aiming to deconstruct the solid and fixed notions of culture and identity (see Dervin, 2010, 2011; Gillespie, Howarth, & Cornish, 2012; Holliday, 2011). We intentionally discuss interreligious dialogue in relation to interculturality. Although these notions are not the same, they are very much related. For example, problems related to the solid and static social category of 'culture' (often considered as national culture) but also gender or social class (Gillespie et al., 2012; Holliday, 2011) are also applicable to the discussions of religion and cannot be separated.

Along with post-colonial and post-structural feminist school ethnographies, the focus is on social positions and spaces that are constructed through institutional and social practices (Gordon, Holland, & Lahelma, 2000; Lappalainen, 2006). As such we are not analysing the experiences of Othering of the other (although such experiences are also expressed in our interview data). We are analysing how asymmetries, categorisations and otherness are constructed in relation to knowledge, language, social actions and material–physical distinctions (Riitaoja, 2013). In this kind of ethnographic research, the positions and subjectivities of the researcher and the researched are understood as contextual and intersubjectively constructed (Dervin & Risager, 2014).

The research data come from an ethnographic study on the construction of Otherness in schools (Riitaoja, 2013). The data were collected in two primary schools (with children aged 7–13) in Helsinki in 2008 and 2009 (Riitaoja, 2013). One of the schools is considered more 'diverse' in terms of race, religion and social class than the other (white, middle class, Lutheran-oriented) school. The data consist of interviews of the school staff ($n = 27$, interviewed individually, in small groups, or both) as well as field notes about lessons and other school activities. For this article, we have selected excerpts that best illustrate the idea of interreligious dialogue in the schools under scrutiny. The original language of the excerpts is Finnish and they were translated in English for this article.

Othering the Other in interreligious encounters

Who wears the trousers?

We start by analysing the othering of the Other in interreligious encounters. In the schools under scrutiny, white secular Lutheranism constituted the unproblematised, and therefore, the 'invisible' norm of schooling (Riitaoja, 2013). In this context, certain bodily characters represent 'difference' and they become the marks of religiosity, resulting in othering. The data reveal that this process of othering can apply to both students and staff members. In this process, the intersection of religion, race, nationality and gender is an essential tool for analysing what is happening:

INTERCULTURAL DIALOGUE

It's recess, I am in the teachers' room. A young Somali-born girl enters the room. Her clothes are wet because of playing outside. Her teacher goes to another room to find dry clothes for her. At the same time two other staff members are talking to the girl.

Staff member 2: Can you use trousers?

Girl: No.

(Staff members 2 and 3 are watching each other for a moment in a specific way).

Staff member 3: Well, should you go home, how long is your school day today?

Girl: Until 12.

Staff member 2: Well, you will survive then as you are. (Fieldnotes, 27 February 2008)[1]

The exchange of glances between the two staff members is interesting as it seems to connote potential frustration or/and compassion towards the girl. The girl's religion and 'culture' (Somali) seem to be seen to prevent her from acting in a 'reasonable' way, in other words to change into dry clothes. In this situation, the normative 'right' and 'reasonable' way of acting would be to dress 'according to the given situation', where 'practical clothing' and dry clothes would be prioritised over other principles.

The trousers are an insignificant side issue but at the same time a meaningful symbol representing equality. They are also used in a way to categorise people. On the one hand, trousers are ordinary pieces of clothing. The 'Finnish' gendered way of dressing and the notion of 'situation-specific dressing' become normal and unproblematised. Implicitly, the girl's refusal to wear trousers seems to be read as an overreaction: it becomes an insurmountable issue for the girl who is seen as a victim of the gendered practices of her religion and culture. On the other hand, the act of wearing trousers significantly symbolises equality between men and women. It symbolises the fact that a woman is free and equal; she is – in the context of Finnish gender and related equality debates – *like a man* in a sense.

From the staff members' perspective, it could be perceived that the problem is not the lack of proper extra clothes but the gendered, religion- or culture-related clothing of the girl that represents a sign of inequality. One could ask what if the child with wet clothes had been a white Finnish boy and the only extra piece of clothing available had been a skirt? Would the staff have offered him a skirt or would they have felt sorry for not having 'proper' clothes for the boy? And, if the boy had refused the skirt, would he have been considered as a victim of the gendered practices of his 'Finnish' culture and religion? Women are expected to become man-like, which would prove their equality. Such logic does not seem to work in reverse.

The notion of equality is closely linked to the idea of free will and choice. A white European liberal secular educated male person is considered to be free and independent (Spivak, 1999). A subject making choices is considered as a free subject. Only certain types of choices, however, are seen as 'right' choices that 'prove' the freedom of the individual. A 'wrong' choice, like refusing to wear trousers, indicates that there is no freedom of choice or that this choice is not an autonomous act (Laws & Davies, 2000; Youdell, 2003).

INTERCULTURAL DIALOGUE

From the 'real' other to the 'same-other'

The superiority of the so-called secular subject is also evident in the following excerpt taken from the interview of a white Finnish-born teacher who converted to Islam and wears a veil. Finnishness and Muslim identity are in tension with each other:

> Interviewer (relates to a wider discussion on the experiences of being different): Well, are there moments or situations that have caused you to think about life differently?
>
> **'Sara' [teacher]:** Well, I think that changing my religion and … what it means is surprising. When you become part of a minority, a Muslim in Finland, you find out that while legally you can practice any religion, according to the law, in practice Finnish culture is not very tolerant.
>
> **Interviewer:** In what kind of situations do you see this?
>
> **Sara:** Mm, what I said before, indirect discrimination, there is not so much direct discrimination … sometimes of course … (…) when somebody … talks to me like I was inferior to them there is an assumption that you cannot be reasonable or grown up, no matter how old you are, if you are a Muslim. You feel you are like someone to be watched after. I think they would never talk to me in this way if I did not wear a veil, because they would not see that I am a Muslim without the veil.
>
> **Interviewer:** Is there any difference between the two, being an immigrant and a native Muslim?
>
> **Sara:** Yes, mm, there are prejudices really towards, especially towards Somali people, because of their ethnic background. But, on the other hand, when they come from elsewhere it is more easily accepted that you are a Muslim compared to if a Finn is a Muslim. Ok, there are also situations that being a Muslim is an advantage, that people [the non-Muslim majority] will listen to you much better for certain issues, what I say about religion as a Finnish Muslim. For example, let's take a simple example that circumcision does not belong to Islam. And sometimes you can build bridges but occasionally it is the most terrible thing that there can be, not from my perspective but meaning how the people around me are thinking about me. So, in such situations you do feel different. ('Sara', Islamic studies in 2009)

Here the teacher describes how her position as a reasonable, grown-up person, who used to be part of the white Finnish majority (the 'same'), was altered due to her conversion (same-other). As such, she became a 'same' who is an 'other', in other words, a 'same-other'. Her veil becomes a bodily mark that signals her being a Muslim and thus a 'subordinate Other' potentially oppressed by her religion. This is because wearing a veil is not always perceived as a sign of free choice in Finland and in many other 'Western' countries (see Bilge, 2010; also Yang, 2009). Her conversion to Islam is seen as an unreasonable and deplorable choice that also 'shows' her to be, as she describes, an unreasonable person (an unreasonable 'same' who turns into a same-other). Due to wearing of the veil she is not seen to belong to the group of autonomous, reasonable, wise and rational adults anymore (the 'same'). This could be related to the idea that identities and positions are not stable but continuously reconstructed through repetitive 'right' actions (see Butler, 1993; Youdell, 2003).[2] Here some choices are seen as 'free' and 'reasonable' choices that reconstruct the identity of a person as an autonomous and a reasonable subject while some actions become 'wrong' choices indicating the lack of reason and choice and therefore the lack of autonomy and reason of that person.

80

INTERCULTURAL DIALOGUE

The status of same-other that she describes in the excerpt seems to derive from the latter. According to Mignolo (2009), on the continuum of the temporal development of people, nations and ideas, the liberal secular individual represents 'progress' while Muslims represent temporal 'backwardness':

> In 'modern space', epistemology was first Christian and then White. In 'enchanted places', 'wisdom' (and *not* epistemology) was, to begin with, non-Christian (one of the reasons why Christianity remained complicit with secular philosophical critics) and also, later on, 'colored'. Islam, for instance, became a colored religion. Christianity, particularly Protestant Christianity, became whiter after the reformation. (...). (Mignolo, 2009, p. 278)

The position of the veiled Finnish teacher as a white European Muslim, a 'same-other' is, however, different from the position of the 'real' Other. This is seen in the opportunity of the teacher to speak on behalf of the 'real' Other (e.g. in the case of circumcision). Her whiteness and Finnishness offers her the position to speak and to be heard among the white secular Lutheran Finns. The 'real' Other, instead, is often thought of as profoundly 'lacking' the virtues of the liberal secular individual. This Other is yet an Otherised Other seen to be without free will and freedom of choice. Because of such an Otherising lens her actions are not considered as choices or 'proofs' of autonomy. Instead they are seen to be the result of 'socialization' caused by her 'cultural' or religious background: she was born in an 'inferior' religion or 'culture'. The 'real' Other is not considered to have the capacity to distance herself from her traditions nor to take an 'objective' position. In popular doxa she is not expected to make reasonable choices. It is thus more 'excusable' for her to be a Muslim than for a white Finn who is considered as capable to make reasonable choices.

In the following section, we examine how the construction of the 'subaltern' Other prescribes the positions the Other has at her disposal in interreligious negotiations in the school context.

'Negotiating' with the Other in a school context

The everyday life in a school with students from different religious backgrounds requires accepting 'exceptions' to the general rules but also structural changes to the secular Lutheran school culture typical of Finnish institutions. In our data, school staff told how they aimed to take 'different' cultures and religions into account in the everyday life of a school. Structural changes such as changes in the traditions, routines and rules of schooling as well as changes in the contents and practices of teaching were, however, more difficult to execute than individual exceptions to these orders (Riitaoja, 2013). We consider these situations to be 'negotiations' with the Other. Such situations were considered by staff members to include a risk of renunciation of the 'Finnish' traditions in favour of the Other's. Because such acts of tolerance and flexibility were not always desirable, the precondition of the negotiation was that, along with the suggested structural changes to Finnish practices and traditions, the Other would also give up some of her traditions. This appears clearly in a teacher's comments in the following excerpt:

> Yes, I think that we can't think of this as a one-way process that we have to be flexible but then ... I think this is both a challenge and an opportunity that we learn to live together respecting each other. And this is why, it's not just from our side but it depends on all the oth [ers], different cultures too. And one needs to make some kind of compromise. But what is not a solution is a kind of flexibility that the Finnish school- or cult[ure], that we start to change our habits a lot, but it depends also on everybody else to [move on] in such a

direction. So we will go towards them but they should come towards us and then we will find each other … ('Lisa' in 2009)

What is considered as flexible and negotiable in general appears to be defined by the 'locals', i.e. Finns in our context (see also Lappalainen, 2006). Here the preconditions, options and positions of the negotiators seem to be already prescribed and evaluated and the seats for negotiators already arranged in the negotiation room. The Other who is seated at the negotiation table is, however, the *representation* of an Other constructed by the school actors. The figure of the Other is their own reflection and the voice of the Other is the echo of their voice. The subaltern Other cannot speak because the only voice heard is the echo of the subject's own voice (Spivak, 1988). She can 'speak' and make her 'choice' only within the logic and under the conditions predetermined by the 'locals'. If the Other chooses 'right' she will have a temporary position as a reasonable and flexible subject. Denial or 'wrong' choice can be interpreted as unwillingness to be flexible.

In the following section, we discuss how the unproblematised norms of the educational space and the asymmetric positions between the secular Lutheran subject and the Otherised Other influence the possibilities and conditions of interreligious dialogue.

Power relations in interreligious dialogue and in the educational space

In scholarly discussions on religious education, the space of dialogue is often considered as neutral and equal for all participants (see Riitaoja et al., 2010). Besides, the people participating in interreligious dialogue are often considered as pre-existing essentialist entities and not intersubjectively and discursively constructed (Dervin, 2010). The space of dialogue is not a fixed room where dialogue is going to take place. Instead, the space and the subjects are socially constructed in relation to each other: we construct the space but it also constructs us as subjects (e.g. Massey, 2005). It also constructs meanings and power relations related to our bodily characters (Young, 2005). The following excerpt reflects the interrelation of the researcher and the researched, but also, it shows how the space of dialogue in a lesson of Islamic studies changes along with the bodies and related power relations present in the classroom:

It is a lesson in Islamic studies (pupils' age: 7–8). The teacher is going through the most important things in the curriculum, right before the exam.

Teacher: What does Islam mean? What does Muslim mean? If your Finnish friend, a Christian, asks this from you, what would you say?

The teacher writes on the board: 'Islam is a religion'.

Teacher: A Muslim believes in Allah. And then, who is our prophet?

(…)

After the lesson the teacher comes to me and asks: 'Are you a Christian? I am sorry, please do not feel offended. The law of Islam is very strict sometimes'. (Fieldnotes, 7 March 2008)

INTERCULTURAL DIALOGUE

The presence of one of us in the class changes something: from the minority's point of view it is not a lesson 'among us' anymore. The teacher, a non-European immigrant and Muslim herself, has to take into consideration the white, European and presumably Christian researcher in her classroom and possibly adapt her teaching accordingly.

Post-colonial and feminist researchers have paid attention to the altered positions of the Other in the spaces dominated by hegemonic groups. In New Zealand, Jones (1999) analyses the limits of cross-cultural dialogue by making visible how, for example, Maori students preferred to study among themselves and without white Pākehā (New Zealanders of European descent) students, and to be able to talk about their issues without being dominated by the Pākehā framework. For Pākehās, the separated lessons meant a missed opportunity for learning about the other and to access their knowledge. Fraser (1995) talks about the relevance of alternative spaces for sexual minorities. Ahmed (2012) examines the meaning of queer and black spaces outside straight and white spaces. All of these scholars point out that the presence of representatives of the hegemonic group excludes other voices and ways of being. In this sense, the common space, togetherness and dialogue can actually be harmful for those who are constructed as Others. Furthermore, dialogue may not offer any mutual opportunities to learn because it does not offer extra knowledge for the Others about the hegemonic group: in order to survive in the unfamiliar spaces the Others have yet to learn the 'culture' of that group. The Others only become the objects or tools of learning for the hegemonic group in order for them (the Others) to be heard in their (the hegemonic groups') terms and understood through their framework. In this way, interreligious dialogue does not increase equality, respect and mutual understanding. Instead, it becomes a tool of dominating and domesticating the Other.

Pause: are religious staff and students the Other par excellence?

In the dichotomy religion/secularism, religion is often considered monolithic with authoritative ideology essentially controlling individuals, while secularism, a state 'without religion', is considered to be neutral and equal, offering freedom for people. The following excerpt with a Finnish teacher illustrates this logic:

> One thing I've recently realised is that all religions, ideologies, fundamentalisms, if we take them literally … they may lead to terrible things. When we interpret the Old Testament there are really awful events there and probably we would find out, I am not sure, from the New Testament too. We don't realise the basic connections among people because we focus on differences. These differences are, after all, related to different interpretations. Obviously there are different interpretations in different parts of the world. But I don't know whether people will ever be able to [find a connection], because religion and culture are used as tools of power … it's possible that a person is good even if s/he had killed someone. I don't know if this means we must take our distance or that one must look from the outside inwards. (teacher 'Lisa' in 2009)

In this excerpt, religious people are constructed as victims with limited opportunities to think and act independently. Opposed to this victimised Other is the free and independent, enlightened secular or secular Christian subject who is able to 'step outside' of his own framework and to think objectively. Adopting such an 'objective' standpoint means to become an autonomous subject and to break away from the authoritarian power (Andreotti et al., 2012; Hoskins & Sallah, 2011).

In the context of schooling, one of the main goals is to help students to become autonomous. According to Popkewitz (2001, p. 180) 'the object of pedagogical reflection

INTERCULTURAL DIALOGUE

and action in modernity is an individuality that is systematically calculated and rationalized in the name of freedom'. The values and beliefs that direct the Other are considered as restrictive:

> I've also had a student from a very strict Pentecostal family, and there were very strict orders [by the family] that s/he cannot do this or that. Then you just tried, you had to accept that there are things that you could not do within the curriculum. ('Karen', 2009)

The normalising discourses and practices of schooling are often considered as emancipatory. Yet the fact that one disregards that such discourses and practices are related to power differentials is problematic (Popkewitz, 2001).

Religions at school: explaining categories or the categories as explanations?

The necessity to problematise categories in interreligious dialogue

In the previous sections, we have seen how the religious other is othered in the Finnish school contexts where we collected data. We saw that both students and staff members can be othered depending on what they represent through certain bodily markers (veil, skirt instead of trousers) amongst others. In this section, we explore the role of teachers in interreligious dialogue. School leadership and teachers play an important (powerful) role in creating discourses and practices in schools. We start with an excerpt from ethnographic field notes:

> … It was very interesting when we studied and discussed practices of Islam in the lessons. The [Muslim] students mentioned how funerals and weddings are celebrated. The teacher whispered to me: 'It is a surprise how diverse the traditions are because of different Imams. I expected Muslim traditions to be the same'. (Fieldnotes, 25 March 2008)

In this excerpt, the teacher tells us how she assumed that all the Muslim (Somali) students in her class would have similar wedding or funeral traditions. Religion (Islam) and ethnicity (Somali) are markers that have made the teacher assume consistency among the students. Islam is considered as a monolithic tradition and the Somali-born Muslims as a homogenous group who share similar celebrations. Similar assumptions also appeared elsewhere in the data: another staff member told us how he assumed that all 'multicultural students' (meaning Muslim immigrants in his case) would share a similar worldview. He was also very surprised by the disagreements among Muslim students in his class.

Social categories are increasingly considered as problematic in research (Gillespie et al., 2012). Yet in the school context, discourses and practices are based on categories and categorisation. One aim of (national) education is to order unclassified differences to provide information on how they could be used in the labour market (Foucault, 1995; Popkewitz, 1998). From this approach, categories and categorisation processes could be considered as a crucial and inherent part of schooling and the making of nation, workers and labour force.

It is important to keep in mind the contextual nature of categories. As Gillespie et al. (2012, p. 392) write 'the process of categorization always stems from a social position, a historical way of seeing and particular interests'. Moreover, 'the social categories we use to conceptualize groups are also changing' and 'all human groups are historical and changing' (Gillespie et al., 2012, p. 393). This is obvious if examining the historical and geographical context where the term religion emerged: the term religion has its roots in Christian theology and the secular sociology of religion in Christian Europe (e.g. King,

INTERCULTURAL DIALOGUE

2009; Mignolo, 2009). Using 'religion' for non-Christian-secular worldviews implicitly (or explicitly) assumes that similar kinds of structures, epistemologies and meanings exist outside of the West[3] (Andreotti et al., 2012; King, 2009).

The concept of religion also has a very particular connection to the modern nation state that is closely linked to Christian-secular epistemology (e.g. for discussion of Christianity and secularity and the citizen-subject, see Mignolo, 2009; Popkewitz, 2008; Spivak, 1999; and for discussions of modernity and the modern nation state as colonial projects, see Mignolo, 2009; Santos, 2007). Nandy (2002, p. 62) differentiates religion as a plural tradition (religion-as-faith) from religion as monolithic political tool (religion-as-ideology). His differentiation associates faith with 'a way of life, a tradition that is definitionally non-monolithic and operationally plural', while religion-as-ideology is defined as:

> a sub-national, national or cross-national identifier of populations contesting for or protecting non-religious, usually political or socioeconomic, interests. Such religion-as-ideologies usually get identified with one or more texts, which, rather than the ways of life of believers, then become the final identifiers of the pure forms of religions. The texts help anchor the ideologies in something seemingly concrete and delimited and, in effect, provide a set of manageable operational definitions. (Nandy, 2002, p. 62)

Religion, therefore, takes the modern notion of the institutional faith system and the nation state as its basis and tries to explain the rest of the world through its own framework. This framework denies the particularity of the Other and the existence of different epistemologies that are not reconcilable with modern 'Western' thinking. One could also ask, to what extent is the religion-as-national-political-ideology adequate to explain the variety of faiths or worldviews even within the modern Western context? Can we assume that everything that may or may have existed in this context is the religion–nation state combination? The goal here is to use the answers to these questions to explain how some histories and notions of the self are denied within the modern Western context. We question whether social categories can be used to explain people and their behaviour or if the categories themselves should be explained in the school context. As Gillespie et al. (2012, p. 399) write '[n]ot to problematize social categories, especially when they are used to explain behaviour, is to undermine human agency'.

When categories related to religion become confusing ...

In the schools we visited, religious categories were used to organise different activities for different groups of students. Students were divided into groups depending on the religion of their families, i.e. during religious education and so-called secular ethics lessons. 'Exceptions' to the general order of schooling were made for those students who did not represent the secular Lutheran norm (Riitaoja, 2013). Such exceptions meant opportunities of dropping out from the Christian-based events or from specific gym or craft activities and to opt for alternative programmes during the events or alternative ways of passing the course.

The perceptions of inner-group diversity among the assumed homogenous religious minorities generated confusion and irritation among school staff. Such irritation stems from the realisation that previous categories and practices of the 'main rule' and 'exceptions' did not work anymore. Instead, the staff had to rethink categories and practices regarding the minority groups and their values. A teacher described how she familiarises herself with every group of first graders in order to determine her role with 'immigrant students' (meaning, in her context, black Muslim students):

> ... one thing that is challenging – a few years ago with the immigrant first-graders, parents were different from the immigrant parents of first-graders this year. (Sigh) Every time you start from scratch with a new group of students you must carefully familiarize yourself with the [immigrant] families and their principles. And when you find these things out during the first year ... the second grade is much easier ... Although they have the same religion, when they come from different countries, they have very different practices and levels of tolerance ... ('Sharon', 2009)

Starting over with a new group of students and with new categories was challenging for Sharon. The teacher could not consider her students as part of previously identified groups. Instead, she had to create new rules and practices for every new student and family 'different' (deviant) from the norm. The instability of categories also meant that staff faced unanticipated changes to the school activities. The following excerpt from the fieldnotes serves as an illustration:

> It's recess; I am in the teachers' room. A teacher says the Muslim students in a class will not participate in dancing (refers to school disco before May day). 'So you have to keep figuring out something else'. A school assistant adds that another [Muslim] student in another class could not participate in craft activities related to Easter. The assistant says students coming from Iran, instead, can participate. There is variation among the [Muslim] families. 'That [Iranian] student participates in everything and is the best [the most skilful student]', she says.

> **Teacher:** Is it so that if you are a true believer you cannot participate?

> The teacher tells about a Jehovah's Witness student that was in her class. 'S/he did not participate in a birthday party [in the class] but the candies were ok'.

> The staff discuss Christmas biscuits, whether you can bake them in the school or not. (Fieldnotes, 20 March 2009)

This episode is representative of a situation where the school staff tried to grasp different convictions and rules of behaving from the viewpoint of students and their families. They tried to create some kind of logic of categorisation that would make the differences among families of the 'same' group understandable and the 'illogical' rules of the families reasonable. The situation is confusing for the staff: on the one hand, the convictions appear not to be negotiable, but on the other they may be flexible in certain (unexpected) situations. The aforementioned staff member considers active participation and skills of the Iranian [Muslim] student confusing. In the case of the Jehovah's Witness student, her/his decision not to participate in birthday celebrations but her/his willingness to eat the birthday candies seems illogical from the teacher's point of view. The (ir) rationality of the student's behaviour is justified by the logic of the teacher and not by the logic of the student's family and their value system.

Conclusion

In this article, we have discussed the conditions of interreligious dialogue in the Finnish context. Our data and analysis suggest that the Other was constructed against the white, middle class and secular-Lutheran normal subject of schooling.

INTERCULTURAL DIALOGUE

Based on these findings, one can ask whether the aims to foster interreligious (but also at the same time intercultural) dialogue in the school context are credible. The following questions then become essential: Who is going to learn about whom, and whose knowledge is to be learnt? Does the Other have an opportunity to be seen and heard as a subject or relegated to a subaltern position? Are knowledge and understanding about her constructed *with* her and in her own terms? Will a religious 'subaltern' ever be equal to the majority in (Finnish) schools?

Arthur (2011, p. 76) notes that the 'religious dimension of dialogue for the Council (of Europe) is effectively a political mechanism and response to any perceived Islamic threats to Western democratic laws and European stability'. Even more '[t]he Council believes that the religious dimension of intercultural dialogue can only be approached from the standpoint of shared values of democratic humanism' that are 'largely secular constructions'. Therefore, 'the European Council's aim of intercultural dialogue can be seen as the neutralization of difference that means erosion of the particularity that distinguishes one religion from other' (Arthur, 2011, p. 76, see also Poulter, 2013; Riitaoja, 2013; Riitaoja et al., 2010).

The aims of togetherness, dialogue and understanding may thus become tools for domesticating and mainstreaming the minority students as secular liberal citizens. Togetherness and dialogue could be, first of all, seen as ways to nurture the common secular public space that is a key structure of the modern liberal secular state (Fraser, 1995). The aim of such space is to keep the citizens under surveillance, maintain cohesion and prevent fragmentation and open confrontations (Ahmed, 2012; Foucault, 1991, 1995; Fraser, 1995; Hodgson, 2011; Hoskins & Sallah, 2011).

Without careful deconstruction, the discussion on religions and religious groups in schools could contribute to preserve the division between the 'religious' as subjective and positional and the 'secular' as objective and neutral. Behind these categories lie individuals and thus asymmetries between them. We see the term religion as somehow problematic and suggest that the term worldview (in its ontological, epistemological and ethical meaning) emphasises the idea that positionality, particularity and partiality are elements related to every worldview. Although the term 'worldview' does not go without problems either (e.g. the possibility of conceptual ambiguity), it still enables different discursive and social spaces and construction of alternative positions. Better than 'religion' 'worldview' would stress the fact that every person positions herself, and not just the Other, in the inescapable interrelatedness of self and other when discussing identity.

Notes

1. Translated from Finnish.
2. Butler (1993) and Youdell (2003) talk about subjectivities. For the purposes of this article, we talk about positions and identities.
3. The West here refers to an epistemological and geographical space of Modernity (see Santos, 2007).

References

Ahmed, S. (2012). *On being included. Racism in institutional life.* Durham, NC: Duke University Press.

Andreotti, V. de O., Ahenakew, C., & Cooper, G. (2012). Equivocal knowing and elusive realities: Imagining global citizenship otherwise. In V. Andreotti & L. M. De Souza (Eds.), *Postcolonial perspectives on global citizenship* education (pp. 221–237). New York, NY: Routledge.

Arthur, J. (2011). Intercultural versus interreligious dialogue in a pluralist Europe. *Policy Futures in Education, 9*(1), 74–80. doi:10.2304/pfie.2011.9.1.74

Bilge, S. (2010). Beyond subordination vs. resistance: An intersectional approach to the agency of veiled Muslim women. *Journal of Intercultural Studies, 31*(1), 9–28. doi:10.1080/07256860903477662

Butler, J. (1993). *Bodies that matter: On the discursive limits of 'sex'.* New York, NY: Routledge.

Coulby, D., & Zambeta, E. (2008). Intercultural education, religion and modernity. *Intercultural Education, 19*, 293–295. doi:10.1080/14675980802376812

Council of Europe (Ed.). (2005). *The religious dimension of intercultural education.* Strasbourg: Author.

Council of Europe (2007). *Religious diversity and intercultural education: A reference book for schools.* Strasbourg: Author.

Council of Europe (2008). *White paper on intercultural dialogue 'living together as equals in dignity'.* Strasbourg: Author. Retrieved from http://www.coe.int/t/dg4/intercultural/source/white%20paper_final_revised_en.pdf

Council of Europe (2011). *Living together. Combining diversity and freedom in 21st century Europe – Report of the Group of Eminent Persons of the Council of Europe.* Strasbourg: Author.

Dervin, F. (2010). Assessing intercultural competence in Language Learning and Teaching: A critical review of current efforts. In F. Dervin & E. Suomela-Salmi (Eds.), *New approaches to assessment in higher education* (pp. 157–173). Bern: Peter Lang.

Dervin, F. (2011). A plea for change in research on intercultural discourses: A 'liquid' approach to the study of the acculturation of Chinese students. *Journal of Multicultural Discourses, 6*(1), 37–52. doi:10.1080/7447143.2010.232218

Dervin, F. (2012). *Impostures interculturelles.* Paris: L'Harmattan.

Dervin, F., & Risager, K. (2014). *Researching identity and interculturality.* New York, NY: Routledge.

Dhamoon, R. (2009). *Identity/difference politics: How difference is produced, and why it matters.* Vancouver: UBC Press.

Foucault, M. (1991). Governmentality. In G. Burchell, C. Gordon, & P. Miller (Eds.), *The Foucault effect: Studies in governmentality* (pp. 87–104). Hemel Hempstead: Harvester Wheatsheaf.

Foucault, M. (1995). *Discipline and punish: The birth of the prison* (A. Sheridan, Trans.). New York, NY: Second Vintage Books.

Fraser, N. (1995). Politics, culture, and the public sphere: Toward a postmodern conception. In L. Nicholson & S. Seidman (Eds.), *Social postmodernism: Beyond identity politics* (pp. 287–312). Cambridge: Cambridge University Press. [Originally published in Critical Inquiry 18 (Spring 1992)].

Gillespie, A., Howarth, C. S., & Cornish, F. (2012). Four problems for researchers using social categories. *Culture & Psychology, 18*, 391–402. doi:10.1177/1354067X12446236

Gordon, T., Holland, J., & Lahelma, E. (2000). *Making spaces: Citizenship and difference in schools.* Houndmills: Macmillan.

Hodgson, N. (2011). Dialogue and its conditions: The construction of European citizenship. *Policy Futures in Education, 9*(1), 43–56. doi:10.2304/pfie.2011.9.1.43

Holliday, A. (2011). *Intercultural communication and ideology.* London: Sage.

Hoskins, B., & Sallah, M. (2011). Developing intercultural competence in Europe: The challenges. *Language and Intercultural Communication, 11*(2), 113–125. doi:10.1080/14708477.2011.556739

Jackson, R. (2004a). Intercultural education and recent European pedagogies of religious education. *Intercultural Education, 15*(1), 3–14. doi:10.1080/1467598042000189952

Jackson, R. (2004b). *Rethinking religious education and plurality: Issues in diversity and pedagogy.* London: Routledge.

Jackson, R. (2009). Editorial: The Council of Europe and education about religious diversity. *British Journal of Religious Education, 31*(2), 85–90. doi:10.1080/01416200802663825

Jackson, R., Miedema, S., Weiße, W., & Willaime, J. P. (Eds.). (2007). *Religion and education in Europe: Developments, contexts and debates.* Verlag: Waxmann.

Jones, A. (1999). The limits of cross-cultural dialogue: Pedagogy, desire, and absolution in the classroom. *Educational Theory, 49*, 299–316. doi:10.1111/j.1741-5446.1999.00299.x

King, R. (2009). Philosophy of religion as border control: Globalization and the decolonization of the 'love of wisdom' (philosophia). In P. Bilimoria & A. Irvine (Eds.), *Postcolonial philosophy of religion* (pp. 35–54). New York, NY: Springer.

Lappalainen, S. (2006). Liberal multiculturalism and national pedagogy in Finnish preschool context: Inclusion or nation making? *Pedagogy, Culture and Society, 14*(1), 99–112. doi:10.1080/14681360500487777

Laws, C., & Davies, B. (2000). Poststructuralist theory in practice: Working with 'behaviorally disturbed' children. *International Journal of Qualitative Studies in Education, 13*, 205–221. doi:10.1080/09518390050019631

Massey, D. (2005). *For space.* London: Sage.

Mignolo, W. (2009). The enduring enchantment: Secularism and the epistemic privileges of modernity. In P. Bilimoria & A. Irvine (Eds.), *Postcolonial philosophy of religion* (pp. 279–294). New York, NY: Springer.

Modood, T. (2007). *Multiculturalism: A civic idea.* Cambridge, MA: Polity Press.

Nandy, A. (2002). *Time warps: Silent and evasive pasts in Indian politics and religion.* London: Hurst & Company.

Popkewitz, T. (1998). *Struggling for the soul. The politics of schooling and the construction of the teacher.* New York, NY: Teachers College Press.

Popkewitz, T. (2001). Rethinking the political: Reconstituting national imaginaries and producing difference. *International Journal of Inclusive Education, 5*, 179–207. doi:10.1080/13603110010028707

Popkewitz, T. (2008). *Cosmopolitanism and the age of school reform. Science, education, and making society by making the child.* New York, NY: Routledge.

Poulter, S. (2013). Uskonto julkisessa tilassa: koulu yhteiskunnallisuuden näyttämönä [Religion in the public space: School as a scene of the public]. *Kasvatus, 44*, 162–176.

Rec. 1720 = Recommendation 1720 (2005) on education and religion. Council of Europe.

Rec. 12 = Recommendation 12 (2008) on the dimension of religions and non-religious convictions within intercultural education. Council of Europe.

Rec. 1804 = Recommendation 1804 (2007) on state, religion, secularity and human rights. Council of Europe.

Riikonen, T., & Dervin, F. (2012). Multiculturalism as a Foucauldian technology of power: Constructing of Muslim religious identity online in Finland and the Quebec province (Canada). *Nordic Journal of Migration Research, 2*(1), 35–44. doi:10.2478/v10202-011-0025-x

Riitaoja, A. L. (2013). *Constructing Otherness in school: A study of curriculum texts and everyday life of two primary schools in Helsinki* (Research reports 346). Helsinki: University of Helsinki, Department of Teacher Education.

Riitaoja, A. L., Poulter, S., & Kuusisto, A. (2010). Worldviews and multicultural education in the Finnish context – A critical philosophical approach to theory and practices. *FJEM, 3*, 87–95.

Salili, F., & Hoosain, R. (2006). *Religion in multicultural education.* Greenwich: Information Age.

Santos, B. de S. (2007). Beyond abyssal thinking: From global lines to ecologies of knowledges. *Revista Critica de Ciencias Sociais, 80*, 1–33. Retrieved from http://www.eurozine.com/articles/2007-06-29-santos-en.html.

Spivak, G. C. (1988). Can the subaltern speak? In G. Nelson & L. Grossberg (Eds.), *Marxism and the interpretation of culture* (pp. 24–28). London: Macmillan.

Spivak, G. C. (1999). *A critique of postcolonial reason: Toward a history of the vanishing present.* Cambridge, MA: Harvard University Press.

Spivak, G. C. (2004). Righting wrongs. *The South Atlantic Quarterly, 103*, 523–581. doi:10.1215/00382876-103-2-3-523

UNESCO. (2006). *UNESCO guidelines on intercultural education*. Paris: Author.

Wolf, A. (2012). Intercultural identity and inter-religious dialogue: A holy place to be? *Language and Intercultural Communication, 12*(1), 37–55. doi:10.1080/14708477.2011.626860

Yang, C. L. (2009). Whose feminism? Whose emancipation? In S. Keskinen, S. Tuori, S. Irni, & D. Mulinari (Eds.), *Complying with colonialism: Gender, race and ethnicity in the Nordic region* (pp. 241–256). Farnham: Ashgate.

Youdell, D. (2003). Identity traps or how black students fail: The interactions between biographical, sub-cultural and learner identities. *British Journal of Sociology of Education, 24*(1), 3–20. doi:10.1080/01425690301912

Young, I. M. (2005). *On female body experience: "Throwing like a girl" and other essays*. New York, NY: Oxford University Press.

Capabilities for intercultural dialogue

Veronica Crosbie

School of Applied Language and Intercultural Studies, Dublin City University, Dublin, Ireland

The capabilities approach offers a valuable analytical lens for exploring the challenge and complexity of intercultural dialogue in contemporary settings. The central tenets of the approach, developed by Amartya Sen and Martha Nussbaum, involve a set of humanistic goals including the recognition that development is a process whereby people's freedoms are expanded, and in so doing, increasing the capabilities of individuals to lead valuable lives. How the construct of capabilities can be seen to work in practice is demonstrated here through a description and presentation of findings from an insider-practitioner case study concerning the teaching and learning of English to Speakers of Other Languages (ESOL) in higher education and based on a critical cosmopolitan pedagogical approach. Evidence from the study indicates that cosmopolitan citizenship learning has a valued place in an ESOL multicultural classroom in which intercultural dialogue is fostered. A proposal is made to use the capabilities approach as a normative framework for social justice in the field of foreign language and intercultural education.

潜在能力アプローチは現代の異文化間対話が直面する問題やその複雑な構造を分析するための切り口を提供する。センとM.ヌスバウムの提唱したこのアプローチは、発見的ゴールを中心にしている。その発見的ゴールに含まれるものは、発展が人間の自由の拡大であり、それによって自己の潜在能力が増加する認識することなどである。本稿では、現実には潜在能力がどのように構築されるのかを大学での英語教育関係者および批評的国際教育アプローチの知見を元に論証した。その結果、世界的シティズンシップへの学習法は、異文化間の対話が発生する多文化教室で行われる英語教育にも応用されうることが明らかになった。本稿は外国語および異文化教育において社会正義に関する規範的枠組みを潜在能力アプローチとして使用することを提言する。

Introduction

Higher education is viewed by many as a resource that is vital to the sustainability of democratic and civic life of the nation. Giroux (2002) points out that this democratic imperative is vital:

> because it is one of the few public spaces left where students can learn the power of questioning authority, recover the ideals of engaged citizenship, reaffirm the importance of the public good, and expand their capacities to make a difference. (Giroux, 2002, p. 450)

However, if we look at the activities and manifestations emanating from institutes of higher education today, what we see, more often than not, are demand-led curricula, responding to neoliberal imperatives, that focus on the instrumental dimension of education. Skills and learning outcomes take precedence over activities that engage with the heart, the senses and the imagination; in other words, the 'cultivation of humanity' (Nussbaum, 1997).

In this paper, I argue that the capabilities approach (Nussbaum, 2000; Sen, 1999) offers a valuable analytical lens for countering the neoliberal hegemonic turn and for exploring the challenge and complexity of intercultural dialogue. The central tenets of the approach involve a set of 'humanly rich goals' (Nussbaum, 2006b), which include the recognition that development is a process of 'expanding the real freedoms that people enjoy' (Sen, 1999, p. 3), and in so doing, thus expanding the capabilities of individuals 'to lead the kind of lives they value – and have reason to value' (Sen, 1999, p. 18). This is done by focusing on capabilities, otherwise known as valued beings and doings, for a life of flourishing. Lozano, Boni, Peris, and Hueso (2012), in an investigation of the differences between a 'skills' or 'competence' based approach with that of capabilities, highlight the fact that the former focus on the results or ends that an individual can achieve, whereas the capabilities approach places an emphasis on the freedom and agency that an individual has to be and to act. From this perspective, specific problems and demands of a given context (for example, responding to an economic crisis) are replaced by a more holistic approach in which ethically informed individual choice is paramount.

Nussbaum has written about the capabilities approach in conjunction with democratic citizenship in education (Nussbaum, 1997, 2006b), and in this context she advocates three main capabilities that inform human development: critical examination, affiliation and narrative imagination. Sen (2006) encourages intercultural dialogue that precludes the essentialising of individuals on ethnic or religious grounds but rather celebrates the multiplicity of identities (cf. Holliday, 2010). Sen (2006) also argues that multiculturalism that becomes in practice 'plural monoculturalism' poses challenges to intercultural dialogue and should be replaced by policy that 'focuses on the freedom of reasoning and decision-making, and celebrates diversity to the extent that it is as freely chosen as possible by the persons involved' (p. 150).

Cosmopolitanism posits a particular notion of global citizenship; as a means of 'building an ethically sound and politically robust conception of the proper basis of political community, and of the relations among communities' (Held, 2005, p. 10). It could be argued that cosmopolitanism, given its focus on democratic equality (Bertram, 2005), is closely related to the capabilities approach concerning issues pertaining to diversity, equality and justice. As such, the cosmopolitan construct, when used in conjunction with the capabilities approach, can offer more nuanced ways of analysing instrumental freedoms in spheres related to global citizenship.

Central tenets of the capabilities approach

The capabilities approach, as conceived by Sen (1999), sees development in terms of freedom. This freedom, it is suggested, has at its heart human agency, that is, an ability to act as an individual and bring about change based on one's own values and objectives (p. 19). According to Sen, agency work cannot be perceived in isolation. It is constrained by social, political and economic factors and these factors must be borne in mind when looking to develop and support agency. Walker and Unterhalter (2007) call this construct 'ethical individualism' (p. 2).

As capabilities are theoretical or 'counterfactual' constructs (Walker & Unterhalter, 2007, p. 16) and not directly or easily assessed, Sen introduces the term *functioning* to describe the valuable beings and doings that are made possible through the availability of a capability or set of capabilities. Thus, according to Sen, a 'person's capability refers to the alternative combinations of functionings that are feasible for her to achieve' (Sen, 1999, p. 75). An example that he gives, and is often quoted (Alkire & Deneulin, 2009; Robeyns, 2003) is that of two people who are starving. Person 'a' might choose to starve as a form of religious or political fasting, whereas person 'b' might starve because of a lack of access to food. While both persons experience the same deprivation, only in the case of the latter can it be said that there is capability deprivation, as 'b' does not have the freedom to choose. This notion of freedom and choice is central to all Sen's concerns around capability enhancement and functioning and the opportunity to live a life in the fullest possible way.

Nussbaum's capability lists

Sen and Nussbaum's ways of interpreting the capabilities approach diverge when it comes to an iteration of capabilities and functionings. Sen (1999) describes the development of capabilities in terms of the expansion of freedoms and, while he does give examples of functionings to illustrate a point, he prefers to leave the approach as broadly framed as possible so that those who work with it can have greater scope to make it their own, in the light of their own context. The means for arriving at such specification are through public reasoning and democratic deliberation.

Nussbaum, however, favours the creation of a list of central capabilities so that individuals, groups, organisations and governments can use it to evaluate their norms and practices accordingly. Nussbaum advocates that a list, or set of universal political principles, be underwritten by constitutions (Nussbaum, 2000), akin to the referencing of the Universal Declaration of Human Rights for moral guidance by many nation states. She thus aims to develop 'a partial theory of justice' (Robeyns, 2003, p. 24). This is underpinned by the question 'What does a life worthy of human dignity require?' (Nussbaum, 2011, p. 32).

Nussbaum emphasises the fact that her list is provisional and subject to change through debate and rational consideration, and also that it had evolved through a process that involved consultation with many people. The list is based on a 'political overlapping consensus' (Nussbaum, 2000, p. 14) and should continue to do so.

Before looking at the list, it should be pointed out that all the capabilities listed are based on two overarching capabilities that suffuse the rest. These are 'practical reason' and 'affiliation', and Nussbaum explains that, following Aristotelian, Kantian and Marxist philosophies, these capabilities set individuals apart from animals and mark them as being truly human. Nussbaum's list of central capabilities (Figure 1), expressed as functionings, is useful to begin to see what a capabilities rich landscape might look like.

Although Sen (2005) does not advocate a central list of capabilities, he does, however, refer to a set of 'basic' capabilities for survival. His work on the Human Development Index (HDI) with Mahbub ul Haq is a case in point. Sen points out that he is not against lists per se; he has, in fact, drawn up lists for the HDI, for example, but that he 'must stand up against a grand mausoleum to one fixed and final list of capabilities' (p. 337). He also says that the hierarchical nature of a list can be misleading, giving prominence to some capabilities over others.

When we take both Sen's and Nussbaum's theoretical views together, they can be seen as a complementary set of constructs that provide a framework of evaluation for an

INTERCULTURAL DIALOGUE

Central Human Functional Capabilities

1. Life
2. Bodily Health
3. Bodily Integrity
4. Senses, Imagination, and Thought
5. Emotions
6. Practical Reason
7. Affiliation
8. Other Species
9. Play
10. Control over One's Environment

Figure 1.   Nussbaum's list of central human functional capabilities.

enriched quality of life. Freedom, agency and capabilities work together in multi-dimensional ways to inform how the lives of individuals and, by extension, of society can be enhanced.

Three central capabilities for education

Nussbaum has written widely about the capabilities approach in conjunction with democratic citizenship in education (Nussbaum, 1997, 2002b, 2006b, 2011). In this context, she advocates three main capabilities that inform human development: (1) critical examination, (2) affiliation and (3) narrative imagination.

The first, the capacity for *critical examination* is in the spirit of Socrates' 'The examined life'. This concept is present in pedagogical approaches that engage with critical theory (e.g. Barnett, 1997; Freire, 2005; Giroux, 1992; Guilherme, 2002; Pennycook, 2001; Phipps & Gonzalez, 2004), where educators are called on to move beyond recognition to action.

The second capability for democratic or world citizenship is that of *affiliation*, which Nussbaum describes as 'human beings bound to all other human beings by ties of recognition and concern' (Nussbaum 2006b, p. 389). This capability is central to intercultural studies and cosmopolitan citizenship.

The third capability is *the narrative imagination*. It refers to the capacity to walk in other people's shoes, imagining how they live and is ideally cultivated through literature and the arts, which both Dewey and Tagore advocated. Nussbaum says that freedom is at the heart of these three 'Tagorian capacities' (p. 392). This claim brings her more strongly in line with Sen's approach. Narrative accounts are used widely in intercultural education to elucidate the 'transcultured self' (Parry, 2003), for example, Kramsch (2009) and Ros i Solé (2004).

Together, these three capabilities can be seen to have a direct relevance to the field of education, and resonate particularly well with the field of foreign language pedagogy, given its concern with the exploration of self and otherness through language, literature, interculturality and translation.

The capabilities approach and interculturalism

I turn, now, to examine Sen and Nussbaum's exposition of the capabilities approach pertaining to culture, in particular, to interculturalism. Sen's contribution rests firmly on the belief that, while there are different norms and practices in a diverse range of settings across the globe, it is 'dangerous' and 'fallacious' (Sen, 1999, p. 232) to make cultural claims for a given region. All cultures have been influenced from elsewhere. For example, if one looks at ancient philosophies and writings, one can see echoes of the same sentiments regarding citizenship values and leading the good life in both the east and the west. Sen thus affirms the validity of cultural diversity, a value that Nussbaum also strongly shares, as is manifest in her writings on the cultivation of humanity, capabilities and social justice (Nussbaum, 1997, 2000, 2002c, 2006a, 2006b, 2011).

In defence of her list of 10 central capabilities for the construction of a theory of basic social justice, Nussbaum (2011) focuses on constructs such as 'human dignity', 'threshold' and 'political liberalism' to support her approach. She rebuts claims of cultural imperialism in relation to her list, saying that, to begin with, the CA comprises scholars from all over the world and that the two founding figures come from different cultural traditions (Sen from India and she from the USA). Like Sen, she underlines the heterogeneity inherent in cultures and societies thus:

> More generally, as we ponder the whole issue of pluralism and cultural values, we should bear in mind that no culture is a monolith. All cultures contain a variety of voices, and frequently what passes for 'the' tradition of a place is simply the view of the most powerful members of the culture, who have had more access to writing and political expression… Once we understand this point, it is very difficult to think of traditional values as having any normative authority at all: tradition gives us only a conversation, a debate, and we have no choice but to evaluate the different positions within it. The Capabilities Approach suggests that we do so using the idea of human dignity for all as our guide. (Nussbaum, 2011, p. 107)

Sen and Nussbaum's elaborations of the CA, while they might diverge at certain points, offer a rich paradigm and set of analytical tools for the development of capabilities for intercultural dialogue, centred on notions of freedom, agency, opportunities and valuable 'beings and doings' that individuals, wherever they live, can aspire to for a life worthy of living. As the approach is underpinned by ethical individualism, there is a strong connection here with theories of cosmopolitan citizenship, which Nussbaum also advocates in her writings, as discussed in the next section.

Cosmopolitan citizenship

The Greek philosopher, Diogenes, alleged founder of the Cynic movement, when asked where he came from, replied, 'I am a *kosmou politês*' (world citizen) (Nussbaum, 2002b, p. 6). In this account, he thus appears to eschew local familial and civic bonds in favour of a bond with humanity. A century later, in ca. 300 BC, the Stoics were the first to develop a comprehensive cosmopolitan philosophy which continues to influence cosmopolitan thinking today (Papastergiadis, 2012). They put forward the following four principles: (1) the polis should be replaced by the whole of humanity as a community to which the individual belongs, (2) human rights should not be bounded by geopolitical spheres, (3) a non-hierarchical vision of cultural value should be promoted and (4) reflexivity should be encouraged through an engagement and open exchange with cultural others.

Nussbaum (2002b), in her study of Stoic philosophy, cautions that to be a citizen of the world does not mean one should give up allegiance to local ties; such identifications are a great source of richness in life and are to be upheld and cherished. She demonstrates this through a schema developed by the Stoics to show the relationship between the individual and different allegiances (See Figure 2), which places the individual in the centre of a set of concentric rings. Each ring represents affiliations, e.g. immediate and

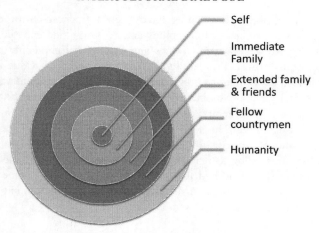

Figure 2. Stoic vision of cosmopolitanism (my interpretation).

extended family, neighbours, local groups, etc., in ever widening circles. The final circle represents humanity as a whole. The task, as citizen of the world, is to draw these circles towards the centre, and through the overlapping of rings, to show that humans living on our periphery should be accorded the same respect and compassion as those close by (Hierocles, cited Nussbaum, 2002b, p. 9).

Nussbaum (2002a, 2002b), basing her arguments on the Graeco–Roman scholars and the Kantian legacy the Western world has inherited, advocates a broadening of school curricula to reflect global as well as local concerns. Her call for a move to a cosmopolitan mind-set is based on a premise that national boundaries are arbitrary and exclude those natural ties and bonds that exist on other levels of society; she cites examples of religious, linguistic, ethnic, gender and race affiliations in this context. Nussbaum argues that it does not make sense to identify oneself solely with national or patriotic narratives, especially as they can result in a type of 'jingoism' that is detrimental to the human condition.

The field of second language learning does not abound with examples of global citizenship learning; however, there are some notable exceptions (Starkey, 2011). The fact that second language pedagogy has moved to embrace cross-cultural and intercultural communication in later years means that it plays an increasingly important role in promoting understanding of people from different ethnic and linguistic backgrounds, as well as fostering a greater awareness of learners' own culture and identity.

Other dimensions of global citizenship learning, such as those put forward by Noddings (2005) including economic and social justice, well-being of the physical environment, social and cultural diversity (including intellectual) and educating for peace are addressed, to some extent, by Pennycook (2001), Guilherme (2002, 2007) and Byram (2008) but are otherwise largely absent from much of the foreign language pedagogy literature. Guilherme (2002) advocates a multi-perspective approach to language teaching and learning, one that includes human rights education and education for democratic citizenship. She points out that language educators need to be educated about human rights and democratic citizenship themselves if they are to be seen as responsible, in part, for the preparation of democratic global citizens and intercultural speakers. Guilherme's work is complemented by a study undertaken by Jackson (2011), indicating that the development of cosmopolitan subjectivities can be transformative for the individuals concerned.

How the constructs of capabilities and cosmopolitan citizenship can be seen to work in practice is demonstrated in the next part of this paper, through the description and presentation of findings from an insider-practitioner case study concerning the teaching and learning of English to Speakers of Other Languages (ESOL) in higher education in which the following research question is posited; 'In what ways can the language classroom be seen to contribute to the formation of learners' cosmopolitan and learning identities, which affect their capability to live and act in the world?' Evidence from the study indicates that cosmopolitan citizenship learning has a valued place in an ESOL multicultural classroom and a proposal is made to use the capabilities approach as a normative framework for social justice in the field of foreign language and intercultural education.

The study

The research inquiry at the centre of this study, based on critical theory, could be viewed as a quest for social transformation in that it begins with a language-learning classroom in which students are encouraged to deal with cosmopolitan ideals, giving rise to a possible scenario where engagement with the world is shaped by social justice. These aims are underpinned by notions of power, participation and pedagogy (Crosbie, 2013).

The study is a form of critical participatory action research (CPAR) or, equally, *interrupted* critical action research, in that one particular cycle in an action research model (constituting a teaching semester) is foregrounded for analysis. As I have continued to teach the module on an annual basis since data were collected in 2006, I continue the analysis, albeit in a less rigorous way, and make incremental adjustments accordingly.

Research was conducted over the course of the spring semester. I adopted the role of 'Researcher as *Bricoleur*' (Denzin & Lincoln, 2005, p. 4), a metaphor that refers to the creation of a patchwork quilt from different materials; in the case of qualitative research, of drawing together different, eclectic texts to create a unified whole. In my case I draw on a range of methods that add 'rigour, breadth, complexity, richness and depth' (Denzin & Lincoln, 2005, p. 5) to the study. Rather than seeing the use of diverse methods as a means of achieving triangulation, or fixed validity, I favour the concept of *crystallisation*, put forward by Richardson and Adams St. Pierre (2005), with its connotations of prisms, layers, multidimensions and diverse perspectives. With this in mind, I studied 'texts' (or data) via four main sets of methods: focus groups, participant observation, questionnaires and document analysis.

When participant observation happens in classroom settings, as opposed to more exotic locations often associated with anthropology, there is a shift in the balance and focus. The teacher–researcher is not a 'visitor' but an intrinsic member of the learning community, which can have both positive and negative repercussions. The familiarity with the context means that the research practitioner is not a stranger, and positive attributes that Denscombe (2010) lists, such as ecological validity and the study being holistic in nature are valid for this type of research. However, there are drawbacks in relying on the teacher's self for interpretation that needs to be considered. The researcher–practitioner needs to be mindful of her own values and ways of interpreting. However, much of the qualitative literature, while acknowledging validity is an issue, suggests that all research is socially constructed. As long as possible biases and ways of seeing and being in the world are acknowledged, then the research in question can be considered valid, albeit under different conditions (cf. Denzin & Lincoln, 2005; Holliday, 2007; Lather, 1993; Piantanida, Tananis, & Grubs, 2004; Somekh, 2005; Walker, 1995).

The module of learning

The module of learning that is central to this study, ENG06, *English and Globalisation*,[1] was originally designed for a Business Studies programme in an institute of higher education in Ireland, and included learning aims such as Curriculum Vitae (CV) writing, preparing for interviews and report writing. As module coordinator, I was in the position to make changes to the course content and learning outcomes and I chose to redesign the module, placing an emphasis on critical pedagogy and globalisation over a more instrumental, skills focused approach, using a Content and Language Integrated Learning (CLIL)[2] approach. The module aims were thus changed to include the following:

- To develop a deeper understanding of processes and issues concerning globalisation;
- To develop fluency and accuracy in the four language skill domains of listening, speaking, reading and writing in the context of the topics: (1) globalisation and (2) language and intercultural learning; Common European Framework of Reference (CEFR level B2-C1)[3];
- To foster group work by identifying common goals and working towards individual & group aims;
- To work with an electronic version of the European Language Portfolio (ELP),[4] Language On-Line Portfolio Project (LOLIPOP)[5] and thus to assist learner autonomy by conducting self-assessment and goal-setting exercises, as well as reflecting on the language and intercultural learning process.

In keeping with a cosmopolitan perspective, one of the underlying aims was to bring social justice and agency to the forefront of the curriculum, fostered through the development of a set of capabilities (see below). There was also a desire to create a multi-perspective rationale, in which human rights education, democratic deliberation and agency coexisted with language studies, values and reflexivity (cf. Byram, 2008; Guilherme, 2002).

The cohort for the study comprised a set of 29 international students from diverse national backgrounds, including Austria, France, Germany, Japan and Spain; ranging in age from 19 to 25; and with a gender ratio of 21 females to 8 males. The students displayed heterogeneity of academic disciplines, including anthropology, business, communications, law, linguistics and literature. Their level of English ranged from B2–C1 on the whole.

The learners were called on to be active learners, developing agency with their peers in the classroom through such activities as negotiating syllabus content, designing and teaching content and conducting self- and peer-evaluation, as well as contemplating their differing roles in society from a cosmopolitan perspective.

Some of the teacher-led components included: an overview of the different dimension of globalisation, including political, economic and social affairs; fair versus free trade; ethnic identity; and intergroup theories. There were also a number of ice-breakers including scanning newspapers for themes linked to globalisation, drawing pictures of rooms in their family homes, indicating local and global objects and activities and depicting social and individual values, again through drawings which were shared within groups. Peer-presentations were conducted in two different ways: (1) initially, in the form of short presentation-based group work, with students discussing global bodies such as

INTERCULTURAL DIALOGUE

the International Monetary Fund (IMF), the United Nations (UN) and Amnesty International (AI) and (2) longer 50' peer-teaching sessions based on themes addressing globalisation. The students were placed in multinational groups and selected topics of their own choosing, including: child labour, drugs, ethnicity, fairtrade, Mcdonaldisation, sport, and world music.

Sample teacher-led lessons

Teacher-led classes were conducted in the first half of semester and students engaged actively in tasks, in the L2, through various media including video, audio recordings, website and journal article research, and lively class discussion. An activity that had a strong impact on the students was the viewing of the BBC 1 television programme, *Horizon*, devoted to Fair Trade, called '*The Dollar a Day Dress*' (British Broadcasting Corporation, 2005). The programme tracks the footsteps of a tutor from a London Fashion school as he travels to different parts of the world to source ethically produced fabric for his students, in so doing uncovering ways in which unfair global trade practices keep many producers in poverty. The film draws the viewer into the debate on fair versus free trade as the tutor engages with local producers and discusses their critical situations, raising awareness of inequities in the trade. The accompanying visuals and soundtrack create a powerful sensory stimulus to underscore the message.

Students' responses to the video were manifold: Hiroko (Oral E, p. 1) found the programme very interesting; it opened her eyes to the negative aspects of globalisation in developing countries. Aiko (Focus 2b, p. 7) said that she was so interested in the plight of the people depicted, it led her to choose fairtrade as a topic to research for her peer-teaching session, and Mayuko's response (Focus group 1a, p. 6) was to lead her to want to buy fairtrade items in future.

Another theme developed concerned ethnic and global identities. As the class was composed of students from ethnically diverse backgrounds, there was a lot of interest in ethnicity studies, especially as the students were on a Study Abroad Programme, which gave them the opportunity to view their own ethnic identity, in many cases, for the first time, in a tangible manner. The students listened to a radio documentary about ethnicity and a post-listening task included a discussion of their own ethnicity and whether they could identify ethnic markers in terms of values, customs and beliefs. This led on to an 'Ethnic Identity Development' exercise (Yeh, 1998) in which they were grouped according to their ethnic affiliations to discuss commonalities.

In another activity, based on the development of intercultural understanding, students were asked to read an article by Worchel (2005) that addresses the issue of in-group/out-group binary divisions based on social-identity theory (Tajfel & Turner, 1979). As the article is quite long and potentially challenging for non-native speakers, it was divided into five sections, and students were given one section each to read and summarise and discuss in groups with colleagues who had read the other sections.

Afterwards, the students were invited to relate the article to local and global contexts, to see how social-identity theory worked in practice. In the final focus group interview, one of the students, Hiroko, referred to the article and how it had pushed her to think more deeply about intergroup conflict, as follows:

> Hiroko: Veronica gave out the article about ethnicity and in-group and out-group theory and after I read the article I thought it was useful because I didn't realise... I realised it but I didn't think about this, because when we meet other nationalities or other ethnicities we feel fear towards them and even if we talk with them and we know each other, the article said that

still we have fear but the fear level decrease[s]. I thought it was key point of the current situation in globalised world because we feel fear and host-... feel hostile towards foreigners or other ethnicities or other religions, so, it, the article was really interesting.(Focus group 2b, p. 6)

This narrative extract displays a nascent awareness of the intricacies of globalisation, and of how the theories the students read about play out in real life. In it, we can see an example of Nussbaum's capability of critical rationality being consciously evoked as the student in question contemplates global identity ascription and development. It can be argued that Nussbaum's other two capabilities for cosmopolitan citizenship are also evoked in the classroom examples listed above, namely affiliation and narrative imagination. Throughout the module, the students showed an openness and willingness to discuss issues of social justice and social group theory and while they often professed not to know what they could do to help the situation, they acknowledged a new sense of knowledge and understanding, which is a precursor to action.

Sample peer-presentations

For the short peer-presentations, the emphasis was on working together as a group, doing a short critical piece of research on a global body in which positive, negative and interesting points were to be examined, and finally, standing up in front of the class and giving a formal presentation. It was also a chance for the students to receive formative feedback on their language and presentation skills in addition to a focus on the content being conveyed, in preparation for their longer peer-teaching sessions ahead. One group focused on the IMF, in which they gave a brief historical overview of the development of the body, together with its aims and objectives, culminating in a critical analysis of issues associated with it (Figure 3).

In the longer peer-teaching sessions, students managed to strike a deep chord in the hearts and minds of their fellow students. For example, Harumi writes of the child labour session: 'I believe this was the most shocking and unforgettable presentation given by the class' (Peer-assessment report). In their session, the child labour teachers set about creating an evocative learning experience for their peers. A centre-piece of their lesson was a critical presentation of exerpts from the film Salaam Bombay (Nair, 1988). In preparation, they drew up an activity sheet for their peers (Figure 4) in which they devised pre- and while-watching activities, followed by a set of critical questions with the intention of developing a sense of agency in their classmates.

They drew on the powers of narrative imagination in the retelling of stories of exploitation and slavery and in so doing also created opportunities for the capability of affiliation (Figure 5).

Whilst reviewing the peer-assessment reports that students wrote about the session, I was struck by the number of times the word *shock* appeared in their appraisals. Leach and Moon (2008, p.10) say that pedagogy should perform in the same way that art historian Schama (2006, cited in Leach & Moon, 2008) says good art does: get under our skin, unsettle us, and provide us with surprises and shocks that force us out of our complacent routines and habituated ways of thinking and acting. This echoes Phipps and Gonzalez' (2004) notion about pedagogy creating creative disorder as part of a positive learning process. It could be argued that the class had achieved this aim. Indeed, one of the peer-teachers of the session, Mayuko, expresses a desire on behalf of the group to deeply affect their peers with the material they presented. She writes:

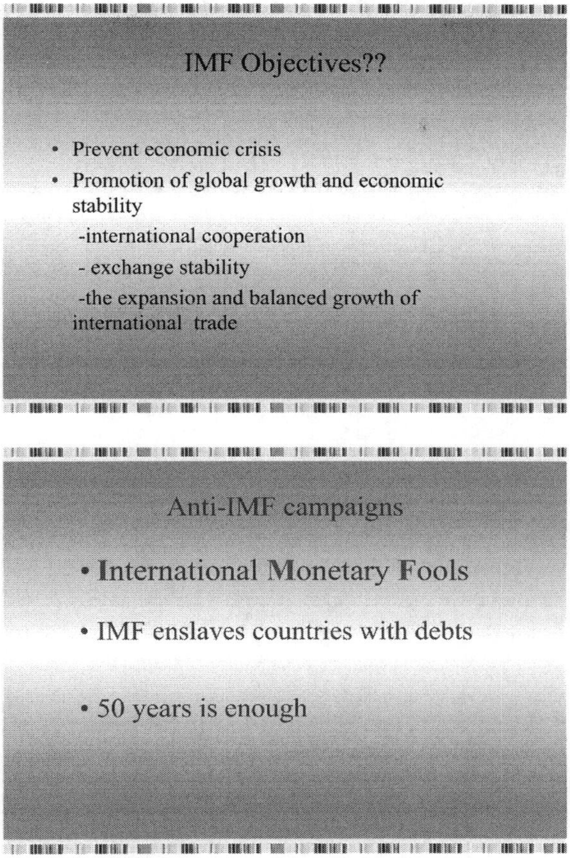

INTERCULTURAL DIALOGUE

Figure 3.   IMF peer-presentation (extract).

> I (Mayuko) wanted students to feel about child labour more realistically, because I thought most of them might think that those children are surely poor, but that's none of my concern. So I was trying to make a scratch on their heart with the video so that they wouldn't forget about the existence of child labour. (Child labour self-assessment report)

In the manner of the Stoic concentric circles, this presentation moved from inner to outer ring and back again, drawing all three together as the local and national were juxtaposed with the global. Students were invited to consider the topic of child labour in relation to their own (relatively privileged) lives; they also focused on actions carried out at national and transnational level which facilitate child labour as well as those that seek to combat it. Other peer-presentations, involving analysis of 'McDonaldisation', fairtrade and ethnicity, to mention a few, achieved similar ends in that they drew peers into the world they were describing, relating their fellow students' ways of being in the world to those who are negatively affected by globalisation and suffering from social injustice as a consequence. These peer-learning sessions also brought new insights to the students as individuals themselves with reference to ethnic identity, personal attributes and modes of behaviour, which could be equated with the innermost ring of the Stoic circles. Lola from Spain describes how the course affected her thus:

INTERCULTURAL DIALOGUE

Child labour worksheet

1. What do you know about child labour?

2. What would it be the cause of child labour?

3. How many children between the age 5 – 17 are in child labour?

4. Please write as many jobs which children are engaged as you see in this presentation.

5. Which area has child labour the most?

6. What is the name of the video, which is the story in India? What is the name of the boy? How old is he?

7. How much does he earn a day?

8. What is the name of organizations, which works against child labour?

True or False
1. More developed countries, such as the U.S., have no child labour.
2. Most child labours work in manufacturing making items like carpets or clothes.
3. Child labour won't be eliminated until poverty is eradicated.
4. I can help to eliminate child labour.

Figure 4.   Child labour activity sheet.

And it's like now I feel that one of *my* and *our* roles has to be that when I come back to Spain, I guess not only in Spain, there are people who are very closed minded, [about] for example, immigration. Because now we are having there a big problem and it's like I could …well, I could apply all I learnt about ethnicity and what I've been living all these months here, and I can apply it and see it in a very different way than people can see it. (Focus group 2a, p. 13)

Capabilities for language and intercultural learning

The findings of the case study led to the formulation of language education in a new way; through a capabilities framework. A set of twelve capabilities and functionings for human flourishing was developed, grounded in the beings and doings of the L2 classroom (Figure 6). This capabilities list offers, I would argue, a much richer way of perceiving the process of language learning than the more ubiquitous skills-based approach to be found in higher education discourse.

Three central capabilities became evident from the textual analysis of this study: (1) cosmopolitan citizenship, (2) voice and agency and (3) identity and ontological being. These emerged through the prisms of my conceptual constructs. All three can be seen as features of intercultural dialogue.

Cosmopolitan citizenship, as conceived here (and discussed above), relates to the cooperation and co-mingling of cultural others; however, a key feature of this capability, which sets it apart from some intercultural approaches, is a keen focus on the critical dimension, underpinned by social justice.

Turning to voice and agency, the next capability, according to Barnett (2007), voice has two dimensions. On the one hand, as no two voices are the same, through voice work 'one becomes oneself uniquely' (Barnett, 2007, p. 90). On the other hand, through the use of voice 'the self places itself in the world' (Barnett, 2007). In so doing, the voice looks for an audience, a response, and a means of making an impact on the world. Taken

INTERCULTURAL DIALOGUE

Child labour

- Did you know?
- -Women sewing $17.99 Disney shirts in Bangladesh are paid just 5cents for each shirt they sew, while Disney boss Michael Eisher earns about $63.000 per hour.

- Around **10,000** Nepalese girls(most between the age of **9** to **16**) are sold to brothels in India every year.

- Many of the girls are brought to India as virgins; many return to Nepal with the HIV virus.

Figure 5.   Child labour presentation (extract).

together, these two aspects of voice portray its ability to develop self-identity and at the same time to make a connection with the world and potentially change it, too.

Throughout the module, the students had many opportunities to discover and use their voice both in an embodied (through tone, pitch and range) and metaphorical (finding a unique voice) sense: at the level of pair and group work in the classroom; in group meetings to discuss the peer-teaching sessions; and on a larger scale, standing up in front of the class and voicing their opinions to the class. While both forms of voice were in evidence in the research texts and in the classroom, the metaphorical, authentic one was, understandably, the more challenging one to develop and not all students succeeded in projecting this dimension.

Sen refers to agency as 'someone who acts and brings about change, and whose achievements can be judged in terms of her own values and objectives' (Sen, 1999, p. 19). As discussed earlier, he points out, however, that such freedom to act is constrained by social, political and economic circumstances (Sen, 1999, p. xii). In the focus group interviews, both in the preliminary and final meetings, when asked about their role in the world, i.e. as cosmopolitan citizens, the responses from the students reflected a growing understanding of global issues and the kinds of actions that they might take (as discussed above).

Regarding the third capability, identity and ontological being, Barnett points out that '[k]nowing cannot be stamped in or assimilated from without; it has to come from within' (Barnett, 2007, p. 31) and the process of ontology concerns the bringing forth of this knowing from within. This process entails the bringing of the student's *being* into a new relationship with the world, thus 'coming to stand anew in the world' (Barnett, 2007). Barnett further points out that this process can only happen if the student is aware of it, has the reflexivity to understand that the epistemology has changed her, that it has become ontology. This deeper sense of knowing is one that I find resonates strongly with the texts I have drawn on, to demonstrate what I call 'ontological knowing' in the study.

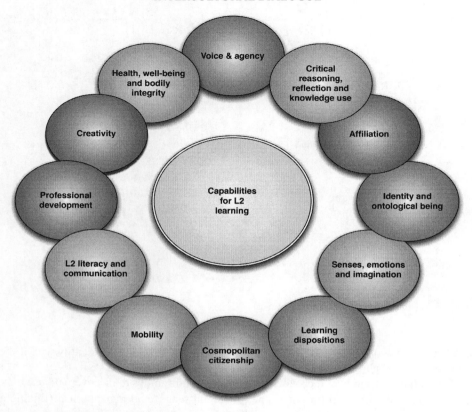

Figure 6. Capabilities for language and intercultural learning.

The remaining capabilities are named rather than discussed in full here. The following four are important for education, regardless of the discipline. They are (4) critical reason, (5) emotion, (6) creativity and imagination and (7) learning disposition. These are followed by a set of three capabilities pertaining specifically to L2 Studies, comprising: (8) L2 learning and communication, (9) affiliation (including intercultural competence) and (10) mobility. Finally, two generic capabilities are presented, that are again cross-disciplinary: (11) health, well-being, and bodily integrity; and (12) professional development (the capability my module centred on before the action research cycle had commenced).

Conclusion

Revisiting my initial research question, in which I ask 'In what ways can the language classroom be seen to contribute to the formation of learners' cosmopolitan and learning identities, which affect their capability to live and act in the world?' has led me to new ways of understanding social practice, especially those underpinned by social justice and democratic ideals. Through the capabilities approach, I discovered that notions such as agency, freedom and well-being can be employed to investigate quality of life in rich and resonant ways, including higher education contexts. One of the tenets of the approach, creating opportunities for living a life that one has reason to value, became compounded with an exploration of what these values might be, and to what extent they might be realised, leading to an actualisation of designated identities.

Having two philosophically distinct but complementary guides in Sen and Nussbaum provided for a dynamic engagement with ideas concerning human development and capabilities, including the high context approach of under specification as advocated by Sen in contrast with Nussbaum's low context propensity to spell things out in a series of lists and propositions. Rather than eschew one in favour of the other, holding the two in tension has led to inhabitual ways of reading theory that creates useful synergies, such as that a list is a useful way to begin to articulate, in a concrete fashion, what a set of valuable beings and doings might entail, thus working towards a normative approach underpinned by social justice, while at the same time, keeping in mind Sen's five instrumental freedoms as a set of fundamental principles for capability development.

Research on cosmopolitanism indicates that this is an unfinished project that has endured for centuries, with an aim to build ethically sound, sustainable communities that coexist in a principled manner based on democratic equality. Many of the tenets of this approach complement theories of interculturality, the difference here being one of a focus on civic duties and agency and on a linking of the different spheres of social influence from local, through national to global. The implications for higher education lie in a desire to have students critically engage with their social worlds, being able to critique different social discourses and practices and to envision a life of flourishing based on notions of hospitality and social translation; challenging, partial and provisional though these may be.

Acknowledgements

I would like to thank the reviewers of this paper for assisting me in making my arguments more robust. I am also indebted to the students at the heart of this study and to Prof. Melanie Walker for guidance throughout my doctoral studies on which this paper is based.

Notes

1. Names and titles are anonymised, where appropriate, throughout this study.
2. CLIL is a pedagogical approach adopted for the acquisition of a foreign language in which the target language is used to teach content (Coyle, 2007; Marsh, 2003).
3. CEFR levels were devised by the Council of Europe (2001) to create a shared approach to the teaching, learning and assessment of languages across Europe.
4. The ELP is a Council of Europe initiative aimed to assist with the development of language learners' autonomy through a set of interconnected activities designed to foster self-assessment. It allows the portfolio bearer the opportunity to showcase language and intercultural learning to language professionals, employers and peers.
5. LOLIPOP was a European Commission Socrates-funded language-learning project (2004–2007) involving a consortium of 12 partners engaged in the task of creating an interactive, online version of the ELP with an enhanced intercultural dimension: <http://lolipop-portfolio.eu/>.

References

Alkire, S., & Deneulin, S. (2009). The human development and capability approach. In S. Deneulin & L. Shahani (Eds.), *An introduction to the human development and capability approach* (pp. 22–48). London: Earthscan.

Barnett, R. (1997). *Higher education, a critical business*. Buckingham: SRHE/Open University Press.

Barnett, R. (2007). *A will to learn*. Maidenhead: McGraw-Hill, SRHE & Open University Press.

Bertram, C. (2005). Global justice, moral development, and democracy. In G. Brock & H. Brighouse (Eds.), *The political philosophy of cosmopolitanism* (pp. 75–91). Cambridge, MA: Cambridge University Press.

British Broadcasting Corporation (BBC). (2005). *Panorama:One dollar a day dress*. Retrieved from <http://news.bbc.co.uk/2/hi/programmes/panorama/4314653.stm>

Byram, M. (2008). *From foreign language education to education for intercultural citizenship*. Clevedon: Multilingual Matters.

Council of Europe. (2001). *Common European framework of reference for languages*. Cambridge, MA: Cambridge University Press.

Coyle, D. (2007). Content and language integrated learning: Towards a connected research agenda for CLIL pedagogies. *International Journal of Bilingual Education & Bilingualism, 10*, 543–562.

Crosbie, V. (2013). Capabilities and a pedagogy for global identities. In A. Boni & M. Walker (Eds.), *Human development and capabilities: Re-imagining the university of the twenty-first century* (pp. 178–191). Oxon: Routledge.

Denscombe, M. (2010). *The good research guide* (4th ed.). Maidenhead, Berks, PA: Open University Press.

Denzin, N., & Lincoln, Y. (2005). Introduction: The discipline and practice of qualitative research. In N. Denzin & Y. Lincoln (Eds.), *The sage handbook of qualitative research* (3rd ed.) (pp. 1–32). Thousand Oaks, CA: Sage.

Freire, P. (2005). *Teachers as cultural workers* (Expanded ed.). Boulder, CO: Westview Press.

Giroux, H. A. (1992). *Border crossing: Cultural workers and the politics of education*. New York, NY: Routledge.

Giroux, H. A. (2002). Neoliberalism, corporate culture, and the promise of higher education: The university as a democratic public sphere. *Harvard Educational Review, 72*, 425–463.

Guilherme, M. (2002). *Critical citizens for an intercultural world*. Clevedon: Multilingual Matters.

Guilherme, M. (2007). English as a global language and education for cosmopolitan citizenship. *Language and Intercultural Communication, 7*(1), 72–90. doi:10.2167/laic184.0

Held, D. (2005). Principles of cosmopolitan order. In G. Brock & H. Brighouse (Eds.), *The political philosophy of cosmopolitanism* (pp. 10–27). Cambridge, MA: Cambridge University Press.

Holliday, A. R. (2007). *Doing and writing qualitative research* (2nd ed.). London: Sage.

Holliday, A. R. (2010). Cultural descriptions as political cultural acts: An exploration. *Language and Intercultural Communication, 10*, 259–272. doi:10.1080/14708470903348572

Jackson, J. (2011). Cultivating cosmopolitan, intercultural citizenship through critical reflection and international, experiential learning. *Language and Intercultural Communication, 11*(2), 80–96. doi:10.1080/14708477.2011.556737

Kramsch, C. (2009). *The multilingual subject*. Oxford: Oxford University Press.

Lather, P. (1993). Fertile obsession: Validity after poststructuralism. *The Sociological Quarterly, 34*, 673–693. doi:10.1111/j.1533-8525.1993.tb00112.x

Leach, J., & Moon, B. (2008). *The power of pedagogy*. London: Sage.

Lozano, J. F., Boni, A., Peris, J., & Hueso, A. (2012). Competencies in higher education: A critical analysis from the capabilities approach. *Journal of Philosophy of Education, 46*(1), 132–147. doi:10.1111/j.1467-9752.2011.00839.x

Marsh, D. (2003). *The relevance and potential of content and language integrated learning (CLIL) for achieving MT+2 in Europe*. ELC Information Bulletin 9. Retrieved from <http://web.fu-berlin.de/elc/bulletin/9/en/marsh.html>

Nair, M. (1988). *Salaam Bombay*. Cadrage; Channel four Films, Doordarshan; Forum Films; La Sept Cinéma; Mirabai Films; National Film Development Corporation of India.

Noddings, N. (Ed.). (2005). *Educating citizens for global awareness*. New York: Columbia University, Teachers College Press.

Nussbaum, M. (1997). *Cultivating humanity*. Cambridge, MA: Harvard University Press.

INTERCULTURAL DIALOGUE

Nussbaum, M. (2000). *Women and human development*. Cambridge, MA: Cambridge University Press.

Nussbaum, M. (2002a). Introduction: Cosmopolitan emotions? In J. Cohen (Ed.), *For love of country?* (2nd ed., pp. ix–xiv). Boston, MA: Beacon Press.

Nussbaum, M. (2002b). Patriotism and Cosmopolitanism. In J. Cohen (Ed.), *For love of country?* (2nd ed., pp. 3–17). Boston, MA: Beacon Press.

Nussbaum, M. (2002c). Education for citizenship in an era of global connection. *Studies in Philosophy and Education, 21*, 289–303. doi:10.1023/A:1019837105053

Nussbaum, M. (2006a). *Frontiers of justice*. Cambridge, MA: The Belknap Press of Harvard University Press.

Nussbaum, M. (2006b). Education and democratic citizenship: Capabilities and quality education. *Journal of Human Development, 7*, 385–395. doi:10.1080/14649880600815974

Nussbaum, M. (2011). *Creating capabilities*. Cambridge, MA: The Belknap Press of Harvard University Press.

Papastergiadis, N. (2012). *Cosmopolitanism and culture*. London: Polity Press.

Parry, M. (2003). Transcultured selves under scrutiny: W(h)ither languages? *Language and Intercultural Communication, 3*(2), 101–107. doi:10.1080/14708470308668093

Pennycook, A. (2001). *Critical applied linguistics: A critical introduction*. London: Lawrence Erlbaum Associates.

Phipps, A., & Gonzalez, M. (2004). *Modern languages*. London: Sage.

Piantanida, M., Tananis, C. A., & Grubs, R. E. (2004). Generating grounded theory of/for educational practice: The journey of three epistemorphs. *International Journal of Qualitative Studies in Education, 17*, 325–346. doi:10.1080/0951839042000204661

Richardson, L., & Adams St. Pierre, E. (2005). Writing: A method of inquiry. In N. Denzin & Y. Lincoln (Eds.), *The sage handbook of qualitative research* (3rd ed., pp. 959–978). Thousand Oaks, CA: Sage.

Robeyns, I. (2003). Sen's capability approach and gender inequality: Selecting relevant capabilities. *Feminist Economics, 9*(2–3), 61–92. doi:10.1080/1354570022000078024

Ros i Solé, C. (2004). Autobiographical accounts of l2 identity construction in Chicano literature. *Language and Intercultural Communication, 4*, 229–241. doi:10.1080/14708470408668874

Sen, A. (1999). *Development as freedom*. Oxford: Oxford University Press.

Sen, A. (2005). Capabilities, lists and public reasoning. In B. Agarwal, J. Humphries, & I. Robeyns (Eds.), *Amartya Sen's work and ideas* (pp. 335–338). London: Routledge.

Sen, A. (2006). *Identity and violence*. London: Allan Lane, an imprint of Penguin Books.

Somekh, B. (2005). *Action research: A methodology for change and development*. Buckingham: Open University Press.

Starkey, H. (2011). Citizenship, education and global spaces. *Language and Intercultural Communication, 11*(2), 75–79. doi:10.1080/14708477.2011.556741

Tajfel, H., & Turner, J. (1979). An integrative theory of intergroup conflict. In W. Austin & S. Worchel (Eds.), *The social psychology of intergroup relations* (pp. 33–47). Monterey, CA: Brooks/Cole.

Walker, M. (1995). Context, critique and change: Doing action research in South Africa. *Educational Action Research, 3*(1), 9–27. doi:10.1080/0965079950030102

Walker, M., & Unterhalter, E. (2007). The capability approach: Its potential for work in education. In M. Walker & E. Unterhalter (Eds.), *Amartya Sen's capability approach and social justice in education* (pp. 1–18). New York, NY: Palgrave Macmillan.

Worchel, S. (2005). Culture's role in conflict and conflict management: Some suggestions, many questions. *International Journal of Intercultural Relations, 29*, 739–757. doi:10.1016/j.ijintrel.2005.08.011

Yeh, C. (1998). Ethnic identity development. In T. Singelis (Ed.), *Teaching about culture, ethnicity and diversity* (pp. 165–174). London: Sage.

'They are bombing now': 'Intercultural Dialogue' in times of conflict

Alison Phipps

School of Education/GRAMNET, University of Glasgow, St. Andrew's Building, Glasgow, UK

This article argues that the concept of 'Intercultural Dialogue' in its present dominant manifestation has run its course. I argue that this concept is one which may work and make sense in stable, open and equal jurisdictions where there is relative 'freedom from fear and want', but that it is at best, limited and at worst, dangerous when used in situations of conflict and aggression and under the creeping conditions of precarity which mark out the present form of globalisation. In this, I turn to field visits undertaken in the Gaza Strip in 2012 with the Life Long Learning in Palestine project. I make a connection to the work of Carolin Goerzig, with Hamas, to the conflict transformation practice of Jean Paul Lederach and to Graeber, Bigo and Scarry's theoretical and practical consideration of emergency and security conditions post-9/11. I do so in order to argue for a re-politicised concept of intercultural dialogue such that it might fit the conditions of precarity with which the field of Language and Intercultural Communication is concerned.

Dieser Artikel argumentiert, dass das Konzept des 'Interkulturellen Dialogs' in seiner gegenwärtig vorherrschenden Erscheinungsform ausgedient hat. Ich argumentiere, dass dieses Konzept möglicherweise in stabilen, offenen und gleichgestellten Rechtsystemen funktioniert und dort sinnvoll ist, wo es eine relative 'Freiheit von Angst und Not' gibt, aber im besten Falle beschränkt und im schlimmsten Falle schädlich ist, wenn es in Konflikt- und Agressionssituationen und unter der zunehmenden Prekarisierung, die die gegenwärtige Form der Globaliserung kennzeichnet, angewendet wird. Hierbei nehme ich Bezug auf Feldbesuche im Gazastreifen, unternommen mit dem 'Lebenslanges Lernen in Palästina' Projekt im Jahr 2010. Ich stelle Verbindungen zu Carolin Goerzigs Arbeit mit Hamas her, sowie zu Jean Paul Lederachs Praxis der Konflikttransformation und Graebers, Bigos und Scarrys theoretischen und praktischen Überlegungen zu den Notstands- und Sicherheitszuständen nach dem 11. September. Ich tue dies, um für ein repolitisiertes Konzept von Interkulturellem Dialog zu argumentieren, welches sich für jene Zustände des Prekarisiert-Seins eignet, mit denen der Fachbereich 'Sprache und Interkulturelle Kommunikation' sich befasst.

To clarify thought, to discredit the intrinsically meaningless words and to define the use of others by precise analysis – to do this, strange though it may appear, might be a way of saving lives. (Weil, 2005)

INTERCULTURAL DIALOGUE

Introduction

In their announcement of the award of the Nobel Prize for Peace in 2012, the Nobel Committee made the following statement:

> The Norwegian Nobel Committee has decided that the Nobel Peace Prize for 2012 is to be awarded to the European Union (EU). The union and its forerunners have for over six decades contributed to the advancement of peace and reconciliation, democracy and human rights in Europe.
>
> In the inter-war years, the Norwegian Nobel Committee made several awards to persons who were seeking reconciliation between Germany and France. Since 1945, that reconciliation has become a reality. The dreadful suffering in World War II demonstrated the need for a new Europe. Over a seventy-year period, Germany and France had fought three wars. Today war between Germany and France is unthinkable. This shows how, through well-aimed efforts and by building up mutual confidence, historical enemies can become close partners. (The Norwegian Nobel Committee, 2012)

This statement points to a history in Europe of attempts at conflict transformation and reconciliation through dialogue undertaken at the level of the individual, culture, nation state and through the union of nations. The breadth of projects undertaken is staggering, and the relationships formed, not least amongst European academics, are significant and have shaped our own field. Similar statements and definitions of Intercultural Dialogue[1] can be found on the websites of transnational agencies engaged in pursuing peace through dialogue. UNESCO understands Intercultural Dialogue as follows:

> Equitable exchange and dialogue among civilizations, cultures and peoples, based on mutual understanding and respect and the equal dignity of all cultures is the essential prerequisite for constructing social cohesion, reconciliation among peoples and peace among nations. (UNESCO, 2013)

The British Council defines Intercultural Dialogue as follows:

> Intercultural dialogue is a process that comprises an open and respectful exchange or interaction between individuals, groups and organisations with different cultural backgrounds or world views. Among its aims are: to develop a deeper understanding of diverse perspectives and practices; to increase participation and the freedom and ability to make choices; to foster equality; and to enhance creative processes. (The British Council, 2013)

The Council of Europe, which has been pivotal in the development of the field of intercultural language education worldwide, through the Common European Framework of Reference (Byram & Parmenter, 2012) developed the following definition for its White Paper in 2008 *Living together as Equals with Dignity:*

> For the purpose of this White Paper, intercultural dialogue is understood as a process that comprises an open and respectful exchange of views between individuals and groups with different ethnic, cultural, religious and linguistic backgrounds and heritage, on the basis of mutual understanding and respect. It requires the freedom and ability to express oneself, as well as the willingness and capacity to listen to the views of others. Intercultural dialogue contributes to political, social, cultural and economic integration and the cohesion of culturally diverse societies. It fosters equality, human dignity and a sense of common purpose. It aims to develop a deeper understanding of diverse world views and practices, to increase co-operation and participation (or the freedom to make choices), to allow personal growth and transformation, and to promote tolerance and respect for the other. (Council of Europe, 2008, p. 17)

INTERCULTURAL DIALOGUE

These public statements in international policy contexts demonstrate the extent of the reach of theories of intercultural communication and education. In these definitions, Intercultural Dialogue is coterminous with 'exchange'. The statements show how the now abstract values of Intercultural Dialogue point to the considerable impact of research in intercultural studies and to the development of the intercultural and dialogic concepts in the international policy arena. The award of the Nobel Peace Prize to Europe also pays testimony to the work undertaken to develop 'attitudes fostered by a democratic culture – including open-mindedness, willingness to engage in dialogue and allow others to express their point, a capacity to resolve conflicts by peaceful means and a recognition of the well-founded arguments of others' (Council of Europe, 2008, p. 17). 'Intercultural Dialogue' now acts in place of concepts such as 'multiculturalism' and 'interculturalism' offering not a fixed state of affairs, as these concepts increasingly suggest, but emphasising a conceptual fluidity and exchange. Who could possibly be against these lofty notions of Intercultural Dialogue, with their reference to Human Rights and Democracy and mutual understanding and respect?

Before congratulating ourselves too hastily as intercultural scholars on the triumph of our concepts and their impact and role in securing a peace prize, if not actual peace, we might exercise a little critical vigilance. There are two particular features of the use of Intercultural Dialogue in these arenas which I wish to highlight here.

First, the concept of intercultural dialogue, or perhaps more appropriately 'Intercultural Dialogue', is being used in what Simone Weil termed 'the middle range' in her essay[2] 'The Power of Words' – it can be easily emptied of content and manipulated for absolute ends.

> Words with content and meaning are not murderous. [...] But when empty words are given capital letters, then, on the slightest pretext, men will begin shedding blood for them and piling up ruin in their name, without effectively grasping anything to which they refer, since what they refer to can never have any reality, for the simple reason that they mean nothing. (Weil, 2005, p. 241)

Critical vigilance, for Weil, means paying attention as words are emptied of content, provisonality and nuance and become slogans for political enterprise. Words she includes in her essay (written in 1937 upon her return from the Spanish Civil War) include concepts which persist and have relevance in this first part of the twenty-first century: 'nation, security, capitalism, order authority property, democracy'. Intercultural Dialogue, as a stated international servant of particularly conservative, ideologised understandings of 'globalisation' 'democracy' and 'security', has seen at least two wars fought in which Europe has had a prominent aggressive allied role, in the last 10 years. 'Dialogue' in Iraq has been coerced and has taken the form of an illegal invasion, breaking the conventions governing war of international law and the United Nations. In Afghanistan, a protracted military struggle with the Taliban has been part of the colonising discourse of 'Intercultural Dialogue' which has arrived with a range of educational and rebuilding programmes attached to aid the occupied populations. 'Intercultural Dialogue' can now attach to anything to give it a false aura of effectiveness and importance, focusing attention away from matters of considerable injustice and concern. Just one example from the proceedings of the Association of European Schools of Planning's Annual Congress in Ankara, Turkey, in 2012 points to the ubiquity and emptiness of the concept of Intercultural Dialogue: *Planning through Intercultural Dialogue – New Perspectives for Planning Education in the Arab World*. In his paper 'Intercultural Dialogue in Afghanistan: A silver bullet?' (Karzai, 2013) traces the exponential rise in its use to the

INTERCULTURAL DIALOGUE

Huntington's thesis on clash of civilisations following 9/11. Karzai's contribution, whilst offering critical perspectives on the ubiquity of the term, concludes:

> [Intercultural] dialogue between Afghans and their international partners can help overcome many of the challenges that arise as a result of perceived differences between values, intention, and actions. (Karzai, 2013, p. 7)

Despite Karzai's concerns with Intercultural Dialogue, he slips at the end into a resigned conclusion that, because difference has been identified between Afghans and international partners, dialogue might help. However, without dialogue occurring on a ground, where the politics of the situation can be named, and there is a level playing field in a quest for just solutions, then the term simply becomes a servant of the status quo. Second, once concepts migrate into other political contexts, they lose their anchoring in the careful disciplinary rituals of the scholarship from which they were first formed. As Doreen Massey (Massey, 2008) has demonstrated in her analysis of the adoption and use of her concept of 'geometries of power' in Venezuelan political struggles, there is no such thing as an uncomplicated transfer of a concept, of evidence or of a practice from the place of its creation to a place where it is reformed for purposes not dreamt of when the concept or research or evidence was first made. 'Intercultural Dialogue' in Afghanistan will not translate simply and unproblematically from the contexts of its use in Europe in the 1990s.

> The implicit geography behind much of this form of public engagement is that the communication is one way. The term 'dissemination' makes that clear; it mirrors those projects for 'the public understanding of science'. The assumed positioning is evident, there is no need for negotiation: we tell them. (Massey, 2008, p. 493)

As evidence and concepts and ideas are made again anew they are changed. Dissemination inevitably involves interpretation and translation, and this as Derrida and Ricoeur, in particular, have shown (Derrida, 2001; Ricoeur, 2007) is an inherently messy, tricky, slippery process. It is in and of itself a new event of making, which may or may not 'stick' more generally after it has been made (Barber, 2007). It also involves an enormous effort on behalf of committees and international agencies to solidify a concept in these generic ways such that it is decontextualised. When terms become programmatic or sloganistic, when they take on capital letters, as Weil warns, then their use requires our critical vigilance because of what they can conceal, the justice they may divert and the illusion of 'good' they may foster. It is not that they cannot serve, far from it, but it is the case that they need to be nuanced and qualified. Weil suggests, 'We never use phrases such as: There is democracy *to the extent that*.... Or: There is capitalism *in so far as*....' (Weil, 2005, p. 242).

It is in this spirit of vigilance that I have come to a re-examination of the concept of intercultural dialogue which has been so central to the so-called 'peacetime' endeavours in our field. As the changes in the operations of global security eroded civil liberties in the name of safety and security (Bigo, 2006) and the presence in Europe of many migrants from contexts marked by poverty, oppression and persecution have brought a certain proximity to those for whom there has been no option of Intercultural Dialogue, there is a need for a re-examination of the fitness of the concept of Intercultural Dialogue for describing and analysing as well as engaging in the present circumstances.

I would, however, go further, and suggest that Intercultural Dialogue now actively works against intercultural dialogue in that it avoids any attempt to engage with political issues which are root causes of conflicts. If uncomfortable, political, sensitive issues are not part of Intercultural Dialogue, and the only scope for dialogue is discussion of ways

INTERCULTURAL DIALOGUE

in which people might be perceiving each other to be culturally different, then it is not possible for dialogue to achieve any change. It is possible that some content may be added to the sphere of awareness which may be mildly interesting in itself, but it does not go anywhere near the structural violence which holds inequality in place. In short, Intercultural Dialogue now serves the maintenance of a violent system of global inequality by focusing attention away from that inequality and onto perceptions of cultural difference and in such a way as to avoid political and ideological issues. Those engaging in Intercultural Dialogue are given the illusion of being part of a process of understanding when such activity merely keeps the present system, based on a belief in cultural difference and a clash of civilisations, firmly in place and further entrenched. As quoted above, Weil is correct –: 'men will begin shedding blood for them and piling up ruin in their name, without effectively grasping anything to which they refer' (Weil, 2005, p. 241).

This critical perspective on Intercultural Dialogue was brought into sharp relief for me during my work in Gaza as part of the TEMPUS funded Lifelong Learning in Palestine project. No matter how much Intercultural Dialogue enables an understanding of the differences between Palestinians and Israelis, the fact of the occupation makes any attempt at dialogue, let alone negotiation, futile in bringing about a transformation of the situation. The futility and long experience of Palestinians, from Oslo onwards, at having engaged in dialogue and diplomacy and having ended up losing more land and power in the process has sharpened my critique of Intercultural Dialogue. The Life Long Learning in Palestine project has sought to enable Palestinian tertiary institutions to think with and develop the concept of lifelong learning for their own purposes under the ever-changing and *oppressive* conditions of Israel's long occupation of Palestine. My own role, in a team of researchers, as part of this project, has been to conduct field visits and reflect on the conceptualisation of learning under the siege conditions in Non Governmental Organisations (NGOs) and universities and most especially among the more marginal groups of women, disabled people and refugees.

To the west, sea and Israeli warships lined up on the horizon about a foot apart the way my eye measures that kind of distance, 6 km out from the shore. In front, small yellow and blue fishing boats. To the east, Khan Younis refugee camp and a focus of much of the aid activity. To the south, greenhouses and olive trees, date palms and orange groves, planted on land left when the Israeli settlers left Gaza to settle more land on the West Bank. To the north, Gaza City. On the horizon, watch towers and a large air balloon watching Gaza's every move from the other side of the separation barrier. This is where leadership and hospitality occurs, between these tangible co-ordinates. We are with the vice president of administrative affairs at Al Aqsa University. This University specialises in fine art and physical education. Slowly we begin to discover campus, on foot. It is made up of new buildings generously funded by Gulf states and Turkey. Men and women are segregated, and our host is keen to explain that this is a mark of respect for women, who are honoured, he says, with the highest place in society. The line through the campus which represents this gender division is a hibiscus hedge. The lines of segregation mark our path and lead us.

The buildings we are shown used to be the villas of the Israeli settlers. This was the best land in Gaza, and the villas were spacious. We are lead to the basements of the buildings first of all and shown the bunkers and bomb shelters. It is clear that these people lived in a great deal of constant fear. Now the bunkers are prayer rooms, decorated with images of peace and rugs. They are full of the peculiar calm which soaks into the walls of places of prayer. This is a form of spiritual leadership in action, the decision taken to turn the bunkers into prayer rooms, the clear-sighted, courageous decision to refuse to live in an architecture built for fear, but to transform conflict into prayer.

INTERCULTURAL DIALOGUE

Overhead there is a buzzing noise, which I don't really register. Our host twinkles at us and nods to the sky: 'The Israeli drones'. We enter the large lecture theatre in the new block and suddenly hear the sound of bombing close by. 'They are bombing' our host says, in a matter of fact way with no sign of concern. It is reassuring and we take our cue from this reaction and continue our walk across the campus, speaking of buildings and teaching and hibiscus hedges, not bombs.

We walk over towards the faculty of fine art to an installation made in the sign of peace from the spent shells which killed and maimed many hundreds during the 2009 war. Then we begin to view the art work in the different classrooms. Everywhere the theme of the key, the return, the land, the suffering, the love of kin and family and reuse of bullet-blasted materials for expressing defiance, anger, hope and a long-sustained cry for justice. The images speak for themselves. I move among them carefully; there are no words between us. The art tells the story. Our host is bursting with pride at the extraordinary achievement and courage his students, though absent, are communicating here. A message arrives, and we learn that trees and houses to the north of Gaza have been destroyed by Israeli bulldozers. My host turns back across campus towards the point of farewell, pressing hibiscus flowers into our hands.

Questioning intercultural dialogue

What has become clear from my work on the ground in Gaza and with Palestinians is that concepts which have arisen in contexts of relative peace and stability in Europe are not suited to conditions of conflict and siege. This is true in the extreme context of Palestine, but, as I have critiqued the concept of intercultural dialogue, I have become increasingly aware that it is at best problematic and largely inoperable under present conditions of globalisation. The Nobel Prize for Peace was awarded as drones, surveillance and the export of Europe's borders by FRONTEX and Israel to prevent migrants settling have become a brutal daily practice of European and Israeli securitisation. To question it is also to suffer consequences.

Consequently, I, therefore, take a critical and contextual look at the potential of Intercultural Dialogue to serve as model under present conditions of globalisation. I understand globalisation, following Spivak (2013, p. 1) as the movement of data and capital in such a way as to create considerable damage and suffering. Whilst there are many competing definitions of globalisation from below (Santos, 2005), and from above, local forms (Appadurai, 1996) and forms embedded in social movements, it is the particular pernicious, neoliberal economics of violence which are presently on the brink of collapse but are held up by considerable vested interests, discursive practices and forms of military and state violence (Graeber, 2013). I consider in particular *to what extent* Intercultural Dialogue can function in times of conflict such as those persisting as the lines of conflict over capital and data are being drawn, globally. What happens when Intercultural Dialogue includes the threat or the reality of 'a bomb down the high street' or the experience of receiving the news that yet another boat has capsized in the Mediterranean full of refugees from Eritrea or Syria and nearly 400 have drowned? What happens to Intercultural Dialogue under conditions of mass surveillance by corporate, press and governmental bodies? Can Intercultural Dialogue coexist with practices founded on profound mistrust between states and global actors? Can the concept function in the present global insecurities *and how far*? *To what extent is* Intercultural Dialogue possible, especially when those who are its referents are subaltern, when they cannot, following Spivak, speak (Spivak, 1988)? Finally, what might be possible when Intercultural Dialogue is suspended together with the expert professional and academic activities of difference-creation and management? In the context of my own work through the TEMPUS *Life Long Learning in Palestine* project with occupied and long-term refugee populations in The Gaza Strip this has become a pressing concern. To what extent might Intercultural Dialogue be a response or simply an insult to the late Edward Said's *Question of Palestine?* (Said, 1980) who laments, echoing Weil, that:

> The terms of the debate are impoverished, for Palestinians have been known only as refugees, or as extremists, or as terrorists. A sizeable corps of Middle East 'experts' has tended to monopolize discussion, principally by using social science jargon and ideological clichés masked as knowledge. (Said, 1980, p. xiv)

Is Intercultural Dialogue, the present, tamed answer from the 'international and academic community' to Said's Question: 'What is Israel, what is the United States, and what are the Arabs going to do about Palestine?' Is Intercultural Dialogue one part of what remains after the land has been occupied and dispossessed? Is this why intercultural dialogue as a nuanced and contextualised activity took root in post-war Europe, after the land had been so thoroughly occupied and so many people dispossessed? Or is the concept only fit for purpose in times of security and peace? In the context of rising xenophobia in Europe is Intercultural Dialogue just another word for 'cohesion', or 'integration' or 'ESOL' for new refugees from sub-Saharan Africa, Syria, Iraq, Iran, Afghanistan, or is there *an extent to which* it may still serve?

The 'referent' of all this Intercultural Dialogue is not entirely clear. Is it some universal individual? Is it the citizens of Europe, the world, politicians, educators, everyone? Following Karzai (2013), is it Huntington or Muslims in general? We might gain some clarity by considering Intercultural Dialogue as a concept related to Security Studies and to the protection of Human Rights. Here the dominant referent is the state – Intercultural Dialogue protects the state by enabling conditions of respect and mutual understanding between nations. In the literature on human security, however, the referent is the individual – whether a citizen or stateless, who is to be protected through respect of their individual human rights. This raises a question for Intercultural Studies where the dominant referent is the collective created by encounters between cultural and social groups, comprising diverse individuals but manifesting corporately (for instance, in discussions of 'international student experiences' where international students become a reified group, or 'student residence abroad' where the mere fact of being abroad produces a collectivity with identifiable traits). Consistently, however, in intercultural education, there is a profound inconsistency: assessment of competence in intercultural communication takes place at the level of the individual and with an individual referent for practices which manifest culturally and collectively. Equally, Intercultural Dialogue references at least two actors in any exchange, and the referent here must also be collective – not the state, or the citizen, but social and cultural configurations, e.g. Somali women asylum seekers, Gaelic language speakers in the diaspora, belonging to the meso-level often not formally recognised as 'entities' in law.

What these questions of the referent of Intercultural Dialogue demonstrate is a considerable lack of clarity around the concept and the aim of appeals to Intercultural Dialogue. Within International Relations, the appeals appear to be diplomatic and for international representatives; within education, they seem to be concerned with enabling the development of individual competence for dialogic exchange on an equal and inclusive and respectful footing. Within The Council of Europe or UNESCO, they reflect the cultural mood of the *entente cordiale*, the post-war aspirations that the United Nations would function to secure peace between nations through dialogues and negotiations held in its chambers. Intercultural Dialogue is all well and good when there is equality structured in to the encounters. Those dialogues in the post-war era, which occurred between former enemy states and then developed across the citizenry in school exchanges and twin-town initiatives and European consortia, worked together and with an eye to equality on projects across the social and cultural spheres. Intercultural Dialogue as such is now a concept which, I would argue, has run its course and is challenged profoundly by the insecurities and precarities which now affect large numbers of people in the world. Intercultural Dialogue may work and make sense in stable, secure jurisdictions where there is relative 'freedom from fear and want' (Nussbaum, 2011), but it is at best limited and at worst dangerous when used in situations of conflict, vulnerability, insecurity and aggression.

To make this more concrete, let us consider what becomes of Intercultural Dialogue as an equal and respectful exchange where the referent is Palestinian or an asylum seeker, or a Syrian refugee in a camp in Lebanon. Here we are dealing with stateless groups, undocumented and unprotected peoples whose presence in any attempt at Intercultural Dialogue, as defined in the opening sections of this article, is anything but equal, but is marked by considerable power imbalances and by precarious existence which is the product of profound and aggressively unequal and disrespectful dialogue at a range of levels. These groups act as symbolic examples of a subaltern who are excluded from the lofty aims of Intercultural Dialogue as equal exchange in many of their encounters, thus troubling the ideal and exposing its vacuousness. It is all well and good to have educational programmes for citizens which aim to promote equality and respect towards all others, and this may, indeed, lead to some nice conversations at an individual or social level, but when groups are interacting with the law, international agencies and the military, then the playing field is far from level and to suggest Intercultural Dialogue as a remedy for injustice and aggression rings hollow and is greeted, by such groups, with incredulity. The issue is not Intercultural Dialogue for such groups, as a senior Gazan NGO official said to me in an animated interview, which echoes Karzai's example of Afghanistan, where action is focused on aid and funding for projects which cannot serve to resolve the deep, structural issues of the siege, but to give the appearance of sweetness and niceness:

> Civil society is a struggle [...] [..] the conditions for the peace process have not been built. We work in difficult conditions in civil society [in Gaza] negotiating between partners. In one night 200 NGOs were closed and attacked by the Government. What could we do? Protest, strike (but this hurts people) or dialogue. Dialogue must be based on law and responsibilities. Dialogue starts in the family, then in schools and universities, but the issue is respect. I am classified as a terrorist. Where are we in all the plans after the war? No one asked the Gazans 'what do you need?' The issue of reconstruction is not buildings; it is human beings. The siege and the occupation is there. We do not need Swiss chocolate. We need an end to the siege. (Interview in Gaza City March 2012)

Swiss chocolate is a symbol of the siege and the depoliticisation of Intercultural Dialogue, one of the bizarre and random forms taken by international aid in Gaza. It is sweet for a moment then melts away. It is where charity is, to paraphrase Augustine, no substitute for justice. At the time of my fieldwork, the small shopping mall in the heart of Gaza City is filled with Swiss chocolate which has come in, perhaps through the tunnels or perhaps after a long wait at the Raffah crossing between the Egyptian–Palestinian controlled crossing between Gaza and Egypt. Dialogue and aid take the form of consumer products. Of course, this is also an inherently 'political' action, but it belongs to the normative frame of globalised consumption, and as such, its political content is largely masked. The other signs of the siege are the regular bombing from Israeli drones and rocket fire from militias, the estimated 20,000 families needing urgent housing because the Israelis destroyed their homes and the area of desettlement in the southern end of the Gaza strip when the land was indeed returned, in exchange for more land settlement on the West Bank. For those I interview, the conditions for Intercultural Dialogue have to be built on equity and justice, but such conditions are a long way off.

In the definitions of Intercultural Dialogue laid out by the Council of Europe, or UNESCO, of 'open and respectful exchange', there is no structure for engagement with perplexing, sensitive or thorny issues. Dialogue is depoliticised into an activity of civic peace and understanding, and the trauma, anger and struggle for justice and weariness which accompanies these is to be left out with its operations. Therefore, quite simply, it becomes meaningless for any genuine pursuit of openness, respect or equality.

In her astute study of the potential for dialogue between Hamas and the Israeli forces 'Mediating Identity Conflicts: Potential and Challenges of Engaging with Hamas', Carolin Goerzig (2010) considers what might enable dialogue or mediation in the context of protracted conflict. She works with scenario interviews in order to shift the ground from the present situation to one of imaginary conditions, with a technique of asking 'would, should and could questions'; 'What would make you recognise Israel? What would make a major change in the situation possible?' The first interviewee cited demonstrates that peace and dialogue have become equated with loss and surrender – the opposite of the stated aims of Intercultural Dialogue:

> Don't ask me to recognise those who killed my father, my son, the tree…! I cannot give you my house. People come, steal my house and make it into an internet café. And then you ask me to sit at the same table and talk with you. Would you do it? Could you do it? Could you? (Goerzig, 2010, p. 8)

Intercultural Dialogue for mutual understanding has become meaningless. The prerequisite for any dialogue with Hamas is the renunciation of armed struggle. The group is characterised as a 'terror' group in many states, and this categorisation clashes with Hamas's own belief in its right, under UN Security Council and international law, to resist unlawful siege and occupation. Dialogue with those who besiege, occupy and kill is impossible:

> It is Friday, the weekend here and the day of prayer. Our hosts have arranged a day, to take us the length and breadth of the Gaza strip. A day to see and experience it all. From the gold market to the meat market, the fruit and vegetable market, the mules, rabbits, chickens, foals, the overwhelming stench of the slaughtered halal meat into the peace and tranquillity of the mosque before prayers. Gaza is 45 km by between 12 and 6 km. It is bordered all around by fences and buffer zones, by the wall, and by the exclusion zone out to sea. We are given, as guests and researchers, a deliberate, careful, generous and tactical sharing of this landscape of suffering and hope so that we might understand and appreciate something of the way in which life goes on despite the atrocities.

> The sun shines here. There is blue sky. All distances are short. Our host speaks to us as he leads us through the Strip and tells us what we are seeing. 'Here, there was heavy fighting'; 'This area was bombed two years ago in the war'; 'They bombed the prison'; 'People living here are bombed'. We drive north from the sea to the fence. This is perhaps the most dangerous area in the world, constantly under threat, constant attacks and barbed wire stretching across the buffer zone. To the west, UNWRA food stores, clinics, services for the disabled, rehabilitation ventures for the wounded, an old people's home, light industry and the rubbish tip. To the north east we see the golden domes of a small and isolated mosque. 'There is a cemetery here'; 'My father is buried in the cemetery'; 'The Israelis have bulldozed the cemetery'. Cautiously we are driven a little way along the dusty rutted track

INTERCULTURAL DIALOGUE

towards the border. 'This used to be full of orange groves and olive trees but they destroyed everything'. We turn back as we reach the cemetery 'Here is everyone you love.' Quiet. Quiet, not peace, but quiet, and bird song. Eyes fill with tears of sadness and rage.

During my meetings with Gazans, some of whom were no doubt members or supporters of Hamas and all of whom had strong Gazan and Palestinian identities, it was clear that Intercultural Dialogue was a suspended concept, something for future generations to consider perhaps, but not one for the present. The present was to be endured, survived and for 'the justice of the cause' to stay alive. News reports of bombing and assassinations would be reported in matter of fact tones, not with panic but with weariness and understanding, and another one, and another one. The regularity of the news of violence brought an accommodation, not an acceptance, but a facility for living with a reality that those experiencing it were powerless to change. Goaerzig's work with Hamas demonstrated that 'Complex dynamics and the need to regain control and simplify the world into clear friend-enemy structures go hand in hand.' (Goerzig, 2010, p. 10). There were few attempts to nuance the complex dynamics, which we find in scholarly discussions of complexity in intercultural dialogue, but rather flattened statements: 'The Israelis … they …' which are precisely the kinds of relations Martin Buber (Buber, 1983) defined as the Ich:Es/I:It domain where humans cease to be human one to another, differentiated from Ich:Du/I:Thou. The I:It relations stripping the 'enemy' on both sides of all but the characteristics which, for those affected, determine their state of being an enemy. For there to be intercultural dialogue, the relations would need to shift into an acknowledgement of the humanity of the enemy – an I: thou relationship and this requires levelling and an equality of relationship (Lederach, 2005).

Whilst Goerzig's work with Hamas echoes my own in Gaza it also describes, aptly, the post-9/11 conditions which have emerged in the security era of globalisation. The leader, for example, of the English Defence League, has repeatedly used the phrase in his quest for racial purity in England which begins 'Muslims … they …' or 'Muslims are …' in an I:It mode. In the new law on migration, the State of Israel no longer refers to Africans arriving through the treacherous Sinai as 'refugees' but as 'Infiltrators.' And there are many examples in public discourse where the Palestinians are referred to using subhuman discourse. In detention facilities for Asylum Seekers in Australia, there is a prohibition on staff using the name of the detainee. Numbers are to be used in place of names. These are not groups with which dialogue is desired by those using the I:It conventions. Again, these are extreme examples, but they are another illustration of the creation of friend–enemy structures which make dialogue both impossible and meaningless.

Critical intercultural literature is full of examples of attempts to break with such overtly controlling simplifications as 'The Germans … they' or 'The Americans … they'. The de-centering of self, the work to think ethnographically about the experiences and nature of different ways of living or understanding the world, meeting with people in such a way that relationships may be formed and where intercultural dialogue is possible have all enabled complex dynamics to be acknowledged. Goerzig's work demonstrates how the urge for a single identity, and the imposition of a single identity on the other, or the enemy, is a result of the loss of multiple identities. She sees this as part of a process of radicalisation:

> Radicalisation can be defined as this process of losing identities. While I am not only a sister, but also a daughter, neighbour etc., identity conflicts are characterised by a loss of multiple roles, such that I turn into a resistance fighter and the identities I build up through relations around me are categorised into those who resist with me and those who I have to resist

INTERCULTURAL DIALOGUE

against. Each identity I lose or subordinate to the identity of friend or foe is one step further on the radicalisation ladder. (Goerzig, 2010, p. 12)

This is a fascinating and crucial insight for understanding how it is that Intercultural Dialogue is rendered meaningless by conflict and loss of control and identity. The insight may well be of immediate value to mediators in international conflict situations such as those between Israel and Palestine, or the civil war in Syria, but it is also pertinent for the present conditions of eroded identity and mistrust which govern the collapse of the neoliberal state and the precariousness of individuals experiencing the sharp end of globalisation and the new security state.

The work of dialogue for mutual understanding and respect requires an agile imagination, the ability to not so much empathise as to see things from multiple perspectives, through multiple language frames, to suspend one's own identity or beliefs, to imagine a different future. Fear, lack of control over decision-making and what Butler (2004) calls the 'precarious life' of the large global underclass and the newly insecure middle classes, creates conditions of continual loss and erosion of identity. This is the fertile ground for xenophobia and the development of a politics of fear such as we are presently witnessing in the guise of 'Go Home' vans and posters targeting immigrants in the UK, the setting aside of the Refugee Convention and mass deportations of refugees in Australia and the surveillance wars being conducted between security agencies, governments, global corporations and those who whistle blow and leak:

> Nothing is safe, my keystrokes are being monitored, someone somewhere is listening to my conversations, reading my text messages, in some far distant land. I am no longer who I was. I am data for the security state. I live in an emergency and need control.

Emergency conditions and their implications for Intercultural Dialogue

The discursive injunctions of 'emergency' post 9/11 have created conditions in which those who believe they are elected to maintain global positions of power, rather than the freedom and justice and well-being of people, have created a post-democratic context where citizens 'stop thinking' (Scarry, 2011, p. 3) and have, unwittingly, ceded control of thought to 'experts' and those in power under a variety of regimes of special powers:

> A recent report by the Geneva Center for the democratic Control of Armed Forces reviews the governance structures of the earth's eight nuclear states: the United States, the United Kingdom, France, The Russian Federation, China, Israel, India, and Pakistan. All eight have ceded control of nuclear weapons to their presidents or prime ministers; all eight have permitted their legislative assemblies and their citizenry to disappear. (Scarry, 2011, p. 3)

Goerzig sees the erosion of identities and loss of control in the face of overwhelming threat to life as implicated in the formation of a single identity which accompanies the process of radicalisation, and which I also trace to the creation of I:It forms of relation. However, radicalisation, whilst now primarily used to refer to the process of radicalisation of Muslims, is also a process which can be traced along similar structures and processes to any group under threat or perceiving its dominant identity as under threat. Where the thinking of the citizenry and also of those the state charges to think on its behalf are suspended or neutralised, academic freedom begins to be endangered, as we have seen post 9/11. There is then an urgent need for scholars to practice their thought and vigilance vis-à-vis their concepts. Intercultural Dialogue will no longer do in such circumstances, where the possibility of dialogue has been suspended and in its place eight men have their own decision-making fingers on the nuclear triggers, in the name of safety and security

118

and with the state remaining as the referent. Intercultural Dialogue – mutuality and trust and openness and respect – are not possible for a citizenry under surveillance – the literature on the operations of the Secret Police – Stasi – in the former German Democratic Republic – demonstrates the extent to which this is the case. Intercultural Dialogue does not work for the people of Malta and Lampadusa, as their islands are turned into morgues for the bodies of asylum seekers to whom Europe did not grant safe passage or a humanitarian corridor.

Emergency conditions, such as those into which global citizenry and Europe, in particular, are now newly interpellated (Bigo, 2006) and have both collective and physiological effects. They numb the possibility for dialogue without structured scaffolding and commitment. Intercultural dialogue does not happen by assertion or through repetition and exhortation in policy documents. It happens because spaces and structures are created and principles laid down which will enable it to be practiced. It does not happen because experts generate content based on difference. It requires spaces of equitable relations, imagination and where multiple identities and frames can be held together. Grief, fear and betrayal do not foster such conditions. It is usual, we know from medical research into the effects of trauma, for the effects of emergency situations to be registered in the limbic stem of the brain and provoke instinctual action (Lederach, 2003; Schirch, 2004). This is the fight or flight instinct, and it is overcome, as Scarry argues (2011), and as Bourdieu (1984) has also shown, by force of habit. It matters that the habits of imagination, dialogue and debate, physical safety [such as, in Scarry's examples, fire safety drills or first aid/cardiopulmonary resuscitation (CPR)], which are practiced for emergency conditions and which serve in peacetime, are preserved in ways which are practically helpful during emergency conditions.

This means that at the very least, the concept of Intercultural Dialogue needs to be supplemented with further concepts such as creative practice, trauma healing and conflict transformation. Without attention to the damage created by exposure to the multiple pervasive varieties of conflict, trauma and mistrust which are part of the present global conditions or to the loss of identities caused by present circumstances, there can be no movement into practices which transform and could create, anew, conditions for intercultural dialogue. These are all habits of mind-in-body, enabling the recognition of the phases of feeling and thought which accompany injustice, fear and panic, of learning not always to speak too easily on behalf of others but to find ways of bringing multiple words, alternatives or images to bear (Sontag, 2004).

Creative practice and conflict transformation

How do we teach people to think and to act under emergency conditions and to prepare for life in such situations? How do we get beyond an ethic of dialogic 'balance' or 'neutrality' in conditions of precarity and insecurity? I conclude by considering some practices, which I believe can shift language and intercultural communication from the 'middle ground' and 'middle range' concepts and can enable a move into practices of conflict transformation and creative practice for intercultural dialogue. Kramsch (2009) maintains that:

> Foreign language education has been characterized up to now by the search for a 'middle landscape'. It has usually tried to solve conflicts quantitatively by taking a little bit of this and a little bit of that from several, often opposing view points. By refusing to be ideological, this approach has in fact espoused a middle-ground conservative ideology, recognizable by its positivistic, pragmatic bend, intent on assimilating conflicts by minimizing them.

INTERCULTURAL DIALOGUE

First, it is the refusal of the ideological which has led to the flattening out of intercultural dialogue into Intercultural Dialogue, the eradication of any political logic to proceedings, the avoidance of difficult issues and above all, I would argue, a resolute resistance to learning to engage with conflict and work for its transformation.

It is here that the work of Jean Paul Lederach (2003) and Lisa Schirch (2004), from the field of Peace and Security Studies, can offer frameworks and practices which may enable language and intercultural studies to move away from its insistence on Intercultural Dialogue and offer ways of working with acknowledged and inevitable identity loss and precarity. For Lederach, the problem with models of intercultural dialogue which ignore or seek to resolve conflict 'quantitatively', i.e. by enumerating reparations or focusing on body counts, is that they take away the possibility of advocacy and imagination and carry the danger of co-option because the political elements are not part of any encounter and are not brought into the light. Any intercultural dialogue attempts which seek to avoid conflict bring false hope and are bound to fail. Lederach maintains that this is simply because conflict is normal and continuous in human relationships, peace is not a static, end state but evolving and dynamic. Conflict avoidance and resolution through dialogue, he says, asks the question, 'How do we end something not desired?' and it does so by (1) a focus on content (in Intercultural Dialogue this has often been content based on description of difference and aimed at promoting awareness of difference). (2) It aims to achieve agreement and solution to any crisis (in Intercultural Dialogue this has been present through a transcendentalism, critiqued by MacDonald & O'Regan, [2012]). (3) It focuses on immediate present relationships and on symptoms of 'feeling better' in the present and bringing relief to discomfort in dialogue. (4) Its horizon of action is relatively short term for bringing relief to anxiety and pain of distress, and it is therefore focused on de-escalating conflict, not on its analysis (Lederach, 2003).

The inadequacy of models of Intercultural Dialogue which presume openness and respect and equality of sharing, the depoliticisation of Intercultural Dialogue and creation of an industry of difference-creation, difference management and difference training as 'solutions' to problems in intercultural dialogue can be seen through the lens Lederach presents for the analytical and practical inadequacy of conflict resolution. Conflict resolution models, he says, also depoliticise conflict and seek relief before analysis, de-escalation rather than critical analysis and transformation. Lederach's use of 'transformation' may appear problematic in the context of an argument relating to terms that inhabit the 'middle range' and are easily emptied of meaning. This is certainly a risk with a term such as 'transformation', particularly in educational contexts. However, Lederach's use of the term is quite precise.

Transformation, he sees going beyond the question: How can I end this conflict?' to add new frames which seek to imaginatively fuse two seemingly incompatible desires. Transformation works to move beyond absolute answers of *either this or that*. As such this approach resonates with Weil's suggestions in her nuancing of terms such as democracy *to the extent that*, or we might add dialogue *to the extent that*, which I presented in the initial critique of Intercultural Dialogue at the start of this paper. Lederach asks 'How do we end something destructive *and* build something desired?' and thus shifts the focus to relationships, from content to purpose and change, from immediate solutions, from a focus on 'presenting issues' – i.e. issues which are superficial outbreaks and placeholders for an enduring conflict – to one of structural change. The horizon moves from short-term to medium-long range so that the work of dialogue can be 'crisis responsive, not crisis-driven'. Significantly, Lederach's understandings mesh with those of van Lier in the field of applied linguistics, (van Lier, 2004) as 'an ecology of dynamic relationships'. The idea of conflict transformation focuses on both the immediate situation and the underlying patterns and context, and it works not with models of competence such of these which have dominated the field of intercultural language education, but with models of capacity or capability building. It is here that Vernoica Crosbie's (2012) excellent work (see this special issue) on developing a capabilities framework for languages and intercultural communication has much to offer but discussion of this is beyond the scope of this paper. The focus in capacity building is described by Lederach as follows (paraphrased to facilitate the connections to intercultural dialogue):

(1) Capacity to see presenting issues as part of wider patterns (cultural, historical, structural, personal, social, global).
(2) Capacity to integrate multiple time frames.
(3) Capacity to pose the energies of conflict as dilemmas.
(4) Capacity to embrace complexity.
(5) Capacity to hear and engage multiple identities.

Each of these five aspects require imagination, discussed by Lederach (2005) at length in *The Moral Imagination*, and when applied, shift Intercultural Dialogue into a re-politicised terrain and also require not 'a little bit of this and a little bit of that' to cite Kramsch (2009) again, but continuous creative practice. Creative practice was defined in the 1970s by Raymond Williams:

> It is already and actively our practical consciousness. When it becomes struggle - the active struggle for new consciousness through new relationships [...] it can take many forms. It can be the long and difficult remaking of an inherited (determined) practical consciousness: a process often described as development but in practice a struggle at the roots of the mind - not casting off an ideology, or learning phrases about it, but confronting a hegemony in the fibres of the self and in the hard practical substance of effective and continuing relationships. (Williams, 1977)

Creative practice is the critical work of considering concepts in Weil's middle range and identifying their limits or the moments when historical conditions mean they become semantically unstable or flattened of meaning. It is the long road back from the kinds of us–them/I: It understandings which arise from precarity and identity loss, from persecution and trauma and from surveillance and mistrust. It is a prerequisite for intercultural dialogue, and without it, the concept remains meaningless for such conditions. It requires the multiple perspectives on intercultural dialogue's derivative concepts of mutuality, equality, respect and openness to be understood from the perspective of those who bring their experiences of inequality, disrespect, closure and surveillance into new relationships. It also requires attention to alternatives. Deconstruction can take us a fair way in vigilance and discursive creative practice, but where Intercultural Dialogue is devoid of meaning under present conditions, it is also worth attending to those social movements and societies where new forms of intercultural dialogue are attempted and form their own creative and experimental practice. The Occupy Movement, with its strong statements of diversity and reclaiming of multiple identities – 'We are the 99%' – offers a compelling example of emergent dialogic practice, which works creatively and critically (Graeber, 2013). Anthropology, as a newly confessional discipline, may offer a range of alternatives for enabling human beings to relate through different structures designed to create open, respectful relationships between diverse groups. In the field of Language and Intercultural Communication, there is ample potential

INTERCULTURAL DIALOGUE

for creative practice and conflict transformation, but this will require the following, at the very least:

(1) The abandoning of de-politicised notions of Intercultural Dialogue.
(2) A willingness to consider the work of mediation as a core element in politicised intercultural dialogue in contexts where there has been considerable identity erosion.
(3) Astute, continuous, critical appraisal of contexts – the extent to which dialogue now takes place in 'unbalanced' and precious situations, the risk of identity attrition, the presence of mistrust.
(4) A shift from a focus on content and competence in dialogue to relationships and capability for dialogue, grounded in ethics.
(5) Imagination and creative practice such that multiple identities may be recovered and flourish, which are prerequisites for any dialogic process.

These are not small matters, but they are necessary for the regaining of a political and transformation potential in intercultural dialogue for the precarious conditions of the present. Viable alternatives to the models designed for depoliticised and normatively conservative conditions do exist, and they exist within our own field see (Corbett, 2010; Crosbie, 2012; Guilherme, 2002; Guilherme, Glaser, & Méndez-Garcia, 2010; Holliday, 2009; Kramsch, 2009; Nair-Venugopal, 2012; O'Dowd, 2007) to name but a small selection of critical, engaged intercultural scholars who contribute to this journal. David Graeber maintains that the identification of such alternatives can indeed be the work of a radical intellectual:

> One obvious role for a radical intellectual is to do precisely that: to look at those who are creating viable alternatives, try to figure out what might be the larger implications of what they are (already) doing, and then offer those ideas back, not as prescriptions, but as contributions, possibilities – as gifts. (Graeber, 2004, p. 12)

Finally, and in conclusion, I would offer a final element for a renewed, repoliticised approach to intercultural dialogue: silence.

Intercultural Dialogue is full of words and concepts that cloud and obscure with their jargon from the middle range. The experiences of precarity, of persecution and of violence and mass surveillance all have the effect of also rending mute and voiceless. They take us into the place where the subaltern, indeed, cannot speak (Spivak, 1988). They, therefore, also take us as academics into places of advocacy, speaking with and even, of necessity for, places of problematic, messy contexts of dialogue, politics, engagement and dispute. These are contexts where certainly my regular experience has been of having nothing to say that is of any immediate relief and needing time with my books and screen. Time to settle and muse – time in the medium-term horizon (Lederach, 2003) – makes it possible to analyse and work towards political transformation and participatory approaches to democracy, to struggle 'in the roots of the mind' (Williams, 1977). Perhaps attending to silence, first, and then perhaps to multiple forms of expression and identity, can enable an act of resistance against the various politics of control and identity eradication and the concepts which mask or promote this control and insecurity.

'A narrative seems likely to be more effective than an image. Partly it is a question of the length of time one is obliged to look, to feel' (Sontag, 2004, p. 110). But is this the case when dialogue is the normative medium and would a practice which includes silence and image, and aesthetic and multimodality enable intercultural scholarship to reach

INTERCULTURAL DIALOGUE

beyond its own vast discursive space: its codified transcripts, corpus linguistics, machine translation, crowd sourcing, foreign language pedagogy and communicative competence. Is what helps in these times a break, what (Benjamin, 1973), in his discussions of Brecht's theatre practice of *Verfremdung*, termed a 'halt' – a pause, a break in the flow of the dialogue onstage for a different perspective, a critical stance or a new aesthetic moment to rupture the flow and help create a new understanding of the way things are.

Writing is only writing, says Mary Oliver in *Long Life*, bringing me back to my senses as I work away at the screen with the words I have, 'The accomplishments of courage and tenderness are not to be measured by paragraphs' (Oliver, 2004). If they can ever be measured at all.

'When it is very quiet we don't say Sabbath, we say curfew'

It is very quiet.

'They are bombing.'

Silence.

Notes

1. I differentiate between 'Intercultural Dialogue' and intercultural dialogue by means of capitalisation and inverted commas throughout this paper following the insights of Simone Weil, discussed in this paper, relating to concepts of the 'middle range'.
2. Inverted commas in Weil's writing refer to new coinages and ways of describing identified phenomena. Capitalisation is used by Weil to signal the emptying of words of content such that they come to mask complex nuances or violent actions.

References

Appadurai, A. (1996). *Modernity at large: Cultural dimensions of globalization*. Minneapolis: University of Minnesota Press.

Barber, K. (2007). Improvisation and the art of making things stick. In E. Hallam & T. Ingold (Eds.), *Creativity and cultural improvisation* (pp. 25–45). Oxford: Berg.

Benjamin, W. (1973). *Illuminations*. London: Fontana.

Bigo, D. (2006). Globalized-in-security: The field of the ban-opticon. In N. S. Sakal & J. Solomon (Eds.), *Translation, biopolitics, colonial difference* (pp. 109–156). Hong Kong: Hong Kong University Press.

Bourdieu, P. (1984). *Distinction: A social critique of the judgement of taste*. London: Routledge.

Buber, M. (1983). *Ich und Du* [Ich und Du]. Stuttgart: Reclam.

Butler, J. (2004). *Precarious life: The powers of mourning and violence*. London and New York: Verso.

Byram, M., & Parmenter, L. (2012). *The common European framework of reference: The globalisation of language education policy*. Bristol: Multilingual Matters.

Corbett, J. (2010). *Intercultural language activities*. Cambridge: Cambridge University Press.

Crosbie, V. (2012). *New pedagogies for the cosmopolitan undergraduate: Generating a critical space for capability development in the HE ESOL language class room*. Dublin: University of Sheffield EdD.

Derrida, J. (2001). *Deconstruction engaged: The Sydney seminars*. Sydney: Power.

Goerzig, C. (2010). *Mediating identity conflicts: Potential and challenges of engaging with hamas*. Berlin: Bergh of Occasional Papers.

Graeber, D. (2004). *Fragments of an anarchist anthropology*. Chicago, IL: Prickly Paradigm Press.

Graeber, D. (2013). *The democracy project: A history, a crisis, a movement*. London: Penguin.

Guilherme, M. (2002). *Critical citizens for an intercultural world*. Clevedon: Multilingual Matters.

INTERCULTURAL DIALOGUE

Guilherme, M., Glaser, E., & Méndez-Garcia, M. C. (2010). *The intercultural dynamics of multicultural working*. Bristol: Multilingual Matters.

Holliday, A. (2009). The role of culture in English language education: Key challenges, Language and Intercultural Communication. *Language and Intercultural Communication, 9*(3), 144–155. doi:10.1080/14708470902748814

Karzai, H. J. (2013). Intercultural dialogue in Afghanistan: A silver bullet? In *13th International Likhachov Scientific Conference*, St Petersburg, May 16–17.

Kramsch, C. (2009). *The multilingual subject*. Oxford: Oxford University Press.

Lederach, J. P. (2003). *Conflict transformation*. Intercourse, PA: Good Books.

Lederach, J. P. (2005). *The moral imagination: The art and soul of peace building*. Oxford: Oxford University Press. doi:10.1093/0195174542.001.0001

MacDonald, M., & O'Regan, J. P. (2012). The ethics of intercultural communication. *Educational Philosophy & Theory, 12*(1), 1–5. doi:10.1080/14708477.2012.638106

Massey, D. (2008). When theory meets politics. *Antipode, 40*, 492–497. doi:10.1111/j.1467-8330.2008.00619.x

Nair-Venugopal, S. (2012). *The gaze of the west and framings of the east*. New York, NY: Palgrave Macmillan. doi:10.1057/9781137009289

Nussbaum, M. C. (2011). *Creating capabilities: The human development approach*. Cambridge, MA: Belknap Press. doi:10.4159/harvard.9780674061200

O'Dowd, R. (2007). *Online intercultural learning*. Clevedon: Multilingual Matters.

Oliver, M. (2004). *Long life: Essays and other writings*. Cambridge, MA: Da Capo Press.

Ricoeur, P. (2007). *Reflections on the just*. Chicago: University of Chicago Press.

Said, E. (1980). *A question of palestine*. New York: vintage.

Santos, B. D. S. (2005). The future of the world social forum: The work of translation. *Development, 48*(2), 15–22. doi:10.1057/palgrave.development.1100131

Scarry, E. (2011). *Thinking in an emergency*. New York, NY: W.W. Norton & Company.

Schirch, L. (2004). *Strategic peacebuilding*. Intercourse, PA: Good Books.

Sontag, S. (2004). *Regarding the pain of others*. London: Penguin.

Spivak, G. (1988). Can the subaltern speak? In C. Nelson & L. Grossberg (Eds.), *Marxism and the interpretation of culture* (pp. 271–313). Chicago: University of Illinois Press.

Spivak, G. (2013). *An aesthetic education in the era of glabalization*. Cambridge, MA: Harvard University Press.

van Lier, L. (2004). *The ecology and semiotics of language learning: A sociocultural perspective*. Boston and Dordrecht: Kluwer Academic.

Weil, S. (2005). *Simone Weil: An anthology*. London: Penguin.

Williams, R. (1977). *Marxism and literature*. Oxford: Oxford University Press.

Reports

Council of Europe. (2008). White paper on intercultural dialogue: Living together as equals with dignity. Retrieved from http://www.coe.int/t/dg4/intercultural/source/white%20paper_final_revised_en.pdf.

The British Council. (2013). Intercultural dialogue. Retrieved from http://activecitizens.britishcouncil.org/content/intercultural-dialogue-icd.

The Norwegian Nobel Committee. (2012). The Nobel Peace Prize for 2012. Retrieved from http://www.nobelprize.org/nobel_prizes/peace/laureates/2012/press.html.

UNESCO. (2013). Intercultural dialogue. Retrieved from http://www.unesco.org/new/en/culture/themes/dialogue/intercultural-dialogue/.

The application of general education and intercultural communication in a 'news-listening' class

Tiao Wang

School of Foreign Languages, Harbin Institute of Technology, Nangang District, Harbin, China

General education (GE) is a new fashion in Chinese university courses, as can be seen by the fact that a GE curriculum has been set in several high-ranking universities in China recently. These courses include knowledge of history, arts, science, society, law and medicine, etc., and require English as the bridge between Chinese cultures and English cultures. English departments (or schools) are responsible for introducing foreign civilization within the framework of GE, resulting in the increasingly crucial role of English teachers in China in helping students to develop their intercultural knowledge, skills and awareness. In this new curriculum, teachers and students must acquire the skills for English reading, news listening, academic writing, and conference presenting. This changing scenario means that intercultural competence will need to be a new goal for all English teachers and students in China. In this paper, the development of GE in China is discussed, along with the setting of core courses for GE, and the relationship of GE and Intercultural Communication based on a 'news-listening' class analysis.

摘要: 中国几所知名高校最近纷纷开设了通识教育课程, 从而掀起了通识教育在国内的高潮。通识教育一般包括国内外历史、艺术、科学、社会、法律和医学等学科知识, 要求英语作为重要的语言工具成为沟通中外知识的桥梁。于是, 各高校的英语学院及英语教师在通识教育框架下肩负起帮助学生发展其跨文化知识、跨文化技能和跨文化意识的重要职责。在通识教育课程设置中, 英语教师和大学生们必须掌握英语阅读、英语新闻听力、学术写作及国际会议报告等基本技能。这种新变化意味着跨文化能力将成为中国高校师生新的教学目标。本文简述了中国的通识教育发展过程, 介绍了中国通识教育的核心课程, 并基于"新闻听力"课程阐述了通识教育和跨文化交际的关系。

Development and implementation of general education (GE)

Previously, most Chinese universities followed models of Russian universities from the 1950s and focused on very specific education instead of GE. In the mid 1990s, Chinese higher education began to carry out the 'Culture Quality Education Reform,' which aimed to enhance college students' quality of education in all areas. Culture Quality Education can be regarded as the predecessor of GE in China, or as it is known, 'General Education' (in capital letters), because they shared the same philosophical notions of education. In recent years (roughly around 2005), GE was proposed and implemented in some top universities. It aims to provide students with a new curriculum that breaks from the clear boundary of arts and sciences existent in traditional Chinese universities. Since then, GE has become a new fashion in Chinese universities, while it is not at all new to American or British universities. Harvard University is famous for its 'General Education in a Free Society,' initiated in 1945, and Oxford University has had GE since its foundation in 1167 (Zhu, 2005).

As an Internet search will show, the GE curriculum setting is quite new and is currently being implemented in a few top universities in China in order to foster students' adaptation to the international world. Fudan University (in Shanghai) was the forerunner in China to undertake GE in 2005. This university founded Fudan College (which is separate from the rest of the University) for the experimental development of GE. University officials established a '1-year GE plus 3-year specific education' model for Fudan College students. Its GE includes six curriculum modules, i.e., 'classic literature and culture,' 'philosophy and critical thinking,' 'civilization dialogue and the world view,' 'science and technology,' 'ecology and environment,' and 'art and aesthetics.' They had developed 107 subjects for GE by the end of 2007 (see http://www.fudan. edu.cn).

Peking University set up Yuanpei College in 2007, and started their GE in 2008. Their GE curriculum is organized in five modules: 'mathematics and natural science,' 'social science,' 'history and culture,' 'philosophy and psychology,' and 'literature and art.' They have developed 92 subjects within the five modules (Wang, 2006; see also http://hexin. fudan.edu.cn/edu/www.web.magazine.php?id=51).

Zhongshan University (in Guangzhou) opened their GE curriculum in 2009 and set 16 credits for all the subjects in four modules, i.e., 'Chinese civilization', 'global civilization', 'science, economics and society', and 'arts and humanities' (http://www.comsci.sysu. edu.cn).

Shanghai International Studies University (in Shanghai) set 10 GE curriculum modules in 2012, which are 'world civilization and international view,' 'Chinese civilization and development,' 'arts and aesthetic appreciation,' 'mathematics, philosophy and creativity,' 'scientific development and spirit,' 'law and fairness,' 'business administration and social services,' 'news media and social ethics,' 'language skills and communication,' and 'psychological, physical and health education' (http://news.shisu.edu.cn/mediashisu). As it can be observed, all the courses of GE require intercultural knowledge within aspects of humanities, arts and natural science. All the universities seek to improve their students' intercultural communication competence by providing these courses.

Intercultural communication and GE: aims, challenges, and proposals

Intercultural knowledge is a goal of education, a goal whereby students learn to construct, act upon, use, and communicate their disciplinary knowledge across diverse linguistic and cultural contexts. In the educational domain, Byram (1997) developed a definition of intercultural competence containing five dimensions, namely, *savoirs, savoir apprendre, savoir comprendre, savoir etre*, and *savoir s'engager*. Byram defines *savoirs* as 'knowledge of social groups and their products and practices in one's own and in one's interlocutor's country, and of the general processes of societal and individual interaction' (Byram, 1997, p. 58). *Savoir comprendre* is defined as 'the ability to interpret a document or event from another culture, to explain it and relate it to documents or events from one's own' (Byram, 1997, p. 61). *Savoir apprendre* is the 'skill of discovery and interaction: ability to acquire new knowledge of a culture and cultural practices and the ability to operate knowledge, attitudes and skills under the constraints of real-time communication and interaction' (Byram, 1997, p. 61). *Savoir s'engager* is described as 'critical cultural awareness/political education: an ability to evaluate, critically and on the basis of explicit criteria, perspectives, practices and products in one's own and other cultures and countries' (Byram, 1997, p. 63). Finally, *savoir-etre* is defined as 'curiosity and openness, readiness to suspend disbelief about other cultures and belief about one's own' (Byram, 1997, p. 57).

In intercultural communication practice, these five dimensions can be divided into three aspects. *Savoirs* and *savoir comprendre* are about intercultural knowledge. *Savoir apprendre* and *savoir s'engager* are about intercultural skills and *savoir-etre* is about intercultural awareness. These aspects are also the three main teaching goals in GE courses. In addition, the curriculum recognizes that all communication in a foreign language is intercultural and that, therefore, teaching and learning of languages should promote the acquisition of intercultural competence.

In order to successfully implement the GE curriculum, it is necessary to ask 'what is the challenge for teachers and students in intercultural communication?' As Olson and Kraeger (2001, p. 116) state:

> Time and space have shrunk; we are no longer insulated from cultural differences as we have been in the past. Today, we encounter people of different culture in every realm of our lives. When we meet each other, we discover differences in perspectives, behaviors, and communication styles. As we interact, we are engaged in an intercultural communication. Yet, intercultural sensitivity does not come naturally; unfortunately, we are more likely to ignore, copy, or destroy the difference.

In the broader context of teaching and learning, Paige (1993) articulates the challenge posed by intercultural education for both educators and learners. For educators the challenge is that:

> Intercultural education, if it is to be effective, must help learners develop these culture-learning skills and enable them to manage their emotional responses. It must therefore incorporate cognitive, behavioral, and affective forms of learning into its structure. (Paige, 1993, p. 1)

As we know intercultural education is a highly specialized form of instruction, the purpose of which is to prepare persons to live and work effectively in cultures different from their own. At the same time, the learners come to the courses with different personalities and different individual experiences, and the curricular contents and instructional methodologies must be developed over the years in response to the needs of learners. This means that there is a huge challenge for educators. And for learners, the challenge is:

> Learners must study the impact that culture, race, ethnicity, gender, politics, economics, and other factors have on the perceptions of the world which individuals and groups come to hold in another culture. (Paige, 1993, p. 3)

A first difficulty is that it requires learners to reflect upon matters with which they have had little first-hand experience. Second, 'unlike more conventional approaches to education, which tend to emphasize depersonalized forms of cognitive learning and knowledge acquisition, intercultural education includes highly personalized behavioral and affective learning, self-reflection, and direct experience with cultural differences' (Paige, 1993, p. 3).

INTERCULTURAL DIALOGUE

This same author goes on to point out how 'learning-how-to-learn,' which is a process-oriented pedagogy, becomes the goal of the course, replacing 'learning facts, a product-oriented pedagogy' (Paige, 1993, p. 3). For students who are not used to these outcomes and expectations, this can be disorienting. Paige points out further challenges for the learning where intercultural communication is concerned:

> Intercultural education involves epistemological explorations regarding alternative ways of knowing and validating what we know, i.e. the meaning of truth and reality. In the intercultural framework, human reality is viewed as socially constructed, a function of perception and of culture-group memberships, and something which varies considerably across human communities. Finally, these inquiries lead logically to the idea that cultures are social inventions which address, in vastly different ways, how basic human needs are met and how meaning in life is derived. Cultures possess their own internal logic and coherence for their members and hence, their own validity. Making judgments about them is hazardous when the criteria for evaluation come solely form another culture. Inevitably, learners struggle with these ideas. (Paige, 1993, p. 3)

So the focus on effective intercultural communication should be placed on the 'interculturality' of each communicator and how this feature contributes to intercultural teaching and learning. Furthermore, in view of the fact that in a teaching and learning context a learner's 'non-native speaker' status and identity is an inseparable part of their position and identity within a given 'native' educational community, this status and identity needs to be recognized and valued by teachers and learners as an integral part of intercultural competence, which the learner is constantly developing and negotiating (Byram & Risinger, 1999). These considerations of interculturality and teaching contents mean that for intercultural teaching, learning, and assessing, educators should seek a specifically intercultural understanding of the status and acquisition of knowledge in their particular disciplines.

Another question which must be considered is 'how do teachers bring interculturality into teaching and learning?' Aspects of interculturality can be brought into teaching and learning by considering the learner's intercultural development and making content and process decisions accordingly. In its own way, each discipline provides opportunities for academic staff to support the students' intercultural development. Every discipline, for example, can introduce students to knowledge that originated in a particular cultural context, to new and sometimes contradictory theories, and to alternative methodologies. By making the cultural elements of disciplinary learning explicit, students can acquire understandings that are directly or indirectly related to their intercultural development. For example, they can search for the cultural context and origins of particular concepts, propositions/hypotheses, theories, and methods. They can develop their critical and comparative learning skills, such as critically analyzing phenomena from multiple perspectives and comparing ideas across cultures.

Sample of intercultural teaching and assessing for GE: intercultural teaching for the news-listening class

Teachers have a significant role in intercultural teaching and learning. Teachers make course content decisions, select learning activities, determine the activity sequence for the course, and give assignments to students. All of these decisions can be meaningfully informed by a model of intercultural development. As those curriculum decisions are increasingly made with intercultural learning in mind, teaching and learning that follow this model will more effectively promote students' intercultural development.

INTERCULTURAL DIALOGUE

An example of how this has been done within a GE curriculum is through a 'News-listening' class (one of the core courses for GE at Harbin Institute of Technology, based on the book *Listen to News*, edited by Yang, 2007). The teachers first prepared news items under a specific topic unit to be used as the listening materials in the classroom. News in the textbook served as one source, and abundant news items from the Internet were supplements. The teachers introduced a piece of the recent news as a warming up exercise at the beginning of each class. By doing this, students were alerted to what was currently happening in the world and became interested in learning more news vocabulary and relevant knowledge on the topic for the following news piece. Between the listening exercise and explanations in the class, teachers highlighted cultural points. For instance, at specific cultural points teachers stopped to explain them for a few minutes, while at some other points teachers just mentioned them to students and encouraged the learners to look for more details after class.

Teachers also had strategies to deal with vocabulary and intercultural knowledge. One example is the use of the word 'highway' in a piece of news. The teachers compared 'highway' and 'expressway' in China and UK, and then gave a more accurate definition for the two words. Teachers also extended learning by giving the students the word 'highwayman' (Yang, 2007, p. 43). Students were asked to guess its meaning and to check it in their dictionary, and then they laughed at the meaning of 'highwayman.' (Despite – or because of this moment of humor – no one will ever forget the meaning of those learnt words.) The teachers gave the students the historical point of view, explaining when 'highways' first appeared in the UK or the USA and when 'expressways' appeared in those countries. At the time highways first appeared, horses and carts were used. No wonder 'highwayman' means the robbers who ride on a horse with arms and rob people on highways. Using this approach may encourage some students to become interested in road history and designing in other parts of the world; some may be interested in reading more about robbers and heroes in literature stories. In short, teachers can bring intercultural knowledge and intercultural understanding to students through the creative introduction of vocabulary.

Another aspect that can be explored is geography and intercultural knowledge. In the aforementioned textbook, there is a piece of news that reports 'The bodies of ten New Jersey senior citizens were killed in a tour bus crash in North Chile and flown home' (Yang, 2007, p. 43). Students are asked to choose the correct interpretation of the news, as 'Ten Americans were killed in a car accident' (Yang, 2007, p. 44). If students do not know that New Jersey is a state in the USA, they will not get the correct answer. This is very simple knowledge of geography. Teachers can prepare a USA map and show students where New Jersey is to give them a visual idea. The teachers can encourage students to find out more about the fifty state names in the USA, or encourage students to search for some basic geographical knowledge on the UK, New Zealand, Canada, France, Germany, Israel, Iran, Iraq, or whichever geographical context emerges from the news article. Even if students cannot remember all of the information, they have the increased intercultural awareness of how to look for more information to equip themselves with more background knowledge. Next time they listen to news, when they encounter the names of foreign cities, states, areas or countries, they will know where they are and what general topics will be concerned with these names mentioned. For example, when the news mentioned Iraq, students knew the capital city of Iraq is Baghdad, and the most popular topics dealing with it are terrorism, Iraqi war, US–Iraq relations, etc.

A further area that can be explored through interculturally is politics and intercultural knowledge. When listening to news, we often hear information about politics, such as the

129

new election of national leaders, or the comments and talks from a leader on international problems. Teachers ask students to remember all the major leaders' names and their general political views, and the English titles for all the leaders. For example, in China we use President or Chairman to address Xi Jinping, but President Obama, and Prime Minister Cameron. The students learn that the Secretary of State of the USA is equal to Foreign Minister, not Prime Minister, in China.

Intercultural assessment of students

Nowadays, in the optional curricula system, most students choose to study 'live English' (versus traditional grammar) with the aim of using English in real life situations. Students demonstrate a preference for classes that teach intercultural knowledge and intercultural communication skills over classes that offer factual knowledge they can find by themselves. The news-listening class is one of these choices to learn some 'live' English. While it may be more challenging, the course offers more real and authentic English content.

As a credit course, interests and rote learning are not enough to keep students motivated, especially in China where students often only learn what will be assessed. So assessment is always a very important guideline for students to learn. Since news-listening, as one of the GE courses, aims to build up students' intercultural competence through listening comprehension of news items, all means of assessment are closely related to news-listening. First of all, students are required to use English in classrooms for their discussion, reporting and presentation and these activities are part of the assessment. Student presentations are an efficient way to assess students' intercultural communication skills as well as their target language use. Students can be judged on whether they express themselves clearly, have correct pronunciation, whether they have prepared the speech content, and their speaking manners –in this sense, intercultural aspects can be brought in. Presentations can be evaluated by teachers and peers. (I sometimes ask students to give comments to their classmates' presentation, and they talk about points as if they were the teacher).

Since the class time is limited, teachers must give assignment to students, and give feedback to students in real time. In the news-listening class, students are required to video-record themselves broadcasting a piece of 3-minute news. The tasks, ranging from news choice to video-recording, imply that students must read a lot of news and choose one item suitable to broadcast, and know some basic news-broadcasting rules and knowledge of acceptable dress as well. In other words, it is a full-scale testing of their intercultural competence. Students also have examinations with news-listening compre-hension exercises and background cultural exercises too. Teachers include background cultural knowledge for the listening class examinations in order to check students' understanding of intercultural knowledge.

Final words

GE in universities means all college students should know interdisciplinary knowledge, along with intercultural perspectives. Intercultural communication knowledge, skills, and awareness are important in ensuring that students can carry out a critical dialog with others, regardless of who they are. This is a life skill that does not end with a course or a program of study, although an emphasis on intercultural competence within a GE curriculum, offers students the opportunity to begin to develop this competence through authentic intercultural communication activities.

References

Byram, M. (1997). *Teaching and assessing intercultural communicative competence.* Clevedon: Multilingual Matters.

Byram, M. S., & Risager, K. (1999). *Language teachers, politics and cultures.* Clevedon: Multilingual Matters.

Olson, C. L., & Kroeger, K. R. (2001). Global competency and intercultural sensitivity. *Journal of Studies in International Education, 5*(2), 116–137. doi:10.1177/102831530152003

Paige, R. M. (Ed.). (1993). *Education for the intercultural experience.* Yarmouth, ME: Intercultural Press.

Wang, Y. (2006). University general education and culture quality education. *Peking University Education Review, 4*(3), 2–8.

Yang, S. (2007). *Listen to news.* Beijing: Foreign Language Teaching and Research Press.

Zhu, X. (2005). The notions of general education in American universities. *Inner-Mongolia Normal University Transactions, 18*(1), 5–8.

Websites

http://www.fudan.edu.cn.

http://hexin.fudan.edu.cn/edu/www.web.magazine.php?id=51.

http://www.comsci.sysu.edu.cn.

http://news.shisu.edu.cn/mediashisu.

How pedagogical blogging helps prepare students for intercultural communication in the global workplace

Radhika Jaidev

Centre for English Language Communication, National University of Singapore, Singapore, Singapore

Employees in the global workplace must be able to communicate effectively with interlocutors from different cultural backgrounds. To do this, they must be aware of the similarities and differences between their own and other cultures and of cultural biases that they and other people may have. This paper reports on the use of pedagogical blogging in a professional communication module to encourage students to reflect on their awareness and application of intercultural communication skills when working on group assignments inside and outside the classroom. The elective module attracted mostly second- and third-year Science and Engineering undergraduate students, and a few other students from first and honours years and other degree programmes such as Business and Computer Science. Also, although the majority of the students were Singaporeans, the module also attracted Malaysian, Indonesian, Indian, Chinese, western European and Korean students. As the module aimed to help students hone their verbal and written communication for the professional arena, it incorporated intercultural communication, a subset of professional communication competence and skills necessary for the global workplace today. This paper discusses students' reflective blog posts on their own as well as their peers' intercultural interactions in group learning tasks and assignments.

简介: 在全球性的工作场所,
员工们必须与来自不同文化背景的人们进行有效的交流。要达到有效交流,
他们必须熟悉自己的文化和其他文化之间的异同之处
及其他们自己或他人可能抱有的文化偏见。
本文论述了一门专业交流课程上使用教学博客鼓励学生反思他们的文化意识和
在课堂
内外做小组课题时跨文化交流技巧的使用。这门选修课程主要吸引的学生群体
为二三
年级的科学和工程系本科生, 一小部分一年级或四年纪的学生,
和来自其他学科系如商科和电脑科技的学生。虽然大部分的学生是新加坡人,
但也有部分来自马来西亚, 印尼, 印度, 中国,
西欧和韩国。由于此课程的目的为帮助学生培养他们职场所需的口头与写作技
能,
课程也融入了跨文化交流,这一属于专业交流能力的,
为今日职场所需的技能。本文分析讨论了学生独立完成的反思博客和他们与同
学在完
成小组课题过程中的跨文化交流。

INTERCULTURAL DIALOGUE

Introduction

What constitutes a 'global workplace' could be perceived in two ways. It could be in the form of a job that requires the employee to work virtually with a diverse range of people in different parts of the world that he or she may never meet in person, or it could be a physical office context in which the employee works among colleagues with a wide range of cultural backgrounds. Both of these situations are common in today's context and although on the surface they are different in terms of the communication medium, the need to craft the message to fit the purpose, context and audience is of utmost importance in both situations (Benoit & Benoit, 2008; Hartley, 1999; Ruddock, 2007). The challenges encountered in intercultural communication may be similar in both scenarios of a global workplace. However, for the most part, the difficulties encountered by people with a common cultural background (Kramsch, 2001, p. 201) tend to reside in the fact that 'language is ambiguous' (Scollon & Scollon, 2001, p. 21), whereas people from different cultures bring with them their varied cultural experiences which influence the way they encode and decode messages (Scollon & Scollon, 2001), making intercultural communication that much more complex in the global workplace.

Real communication in any situation involves much more than giving and receiving information: 'it is focused on establishing and maintaining relationships' (Byram, 1997, p. 3). This is true in professional contexts as well. Holmes and Meyerhoff (1999) explain that when an individual 'join[s] a new workplace', they enter into a process of socialisation that involves 'many aspects of behaviour, including global or specific aspects of language structure, discourse, and interaction patterns' (p. 175). Kramsch (2007) states that working relationships, even in fairly homogeneous cultural contexts, for example, in some organisations in Singapore where the employees are mostly ethnic Chinese Singaporeans or in other organisations where the employees are Singaporeans of mixed ethnic origins but homogeneous by way of their Singaporean nationality, are built when people engage in a variety of 'procedural strategies' (p. 61) such as taking turns to speak when conversing with others, asking questions, discussing and debating with colleagues, and working in teams to satisfy both personal and common goals. In addition, group members use language to do more than just communicate specific information; they make meaning of their roles in that particular social circle based on their shared assumptions (Liddicoat, 2009). In short, the way a homogeneous group uses language gives them the advantage of membership to a community of practice that 'grow[s] out of mutual engagement' (Eckert & McConnell-Ginet, 1992, p. 464). In culturally heterogeneous contexts such as the global workplace, however, interlocutors bring their varied cultural experiences and world views, products of 'complex interactions' (Hill & Mannheim, 1992, p. 400) with other communities of practice and 'everyday practices below the threshold of awareness' (p. 381) that have come to bear upon the way they communicate. These complexities can cause breakdowns in communication even if all members of that community speak the same lingua franca. In short, in the global workplace interactions among colleagues inevitably carry additional cultural overlay and this demands closer attention from the interlocutors.

Nevertheless, this attention to the 'additional cultural overlay' must be approached with caution. For instance, the way people speak, write or work with others cannot be pigeonholed based on the external symbols or indicators of their cultural origins. For example, Chinese from mainland China and Indians from India may speak English or dress differently from people from other parts of the world, or even from Chinese and Indians in their own countries. But 'stereotyping' does not help build real working relationships. Instead, what helps a person's 'socialization' (Scollon & Scollon, 2001, pp. 162, 168) process with culturally diverse colleagues at the workplace is self-awareness of the factors that have influenced her own cultural make-up and of the way she communicates with respect to her sensitivities towards and biases against people with different cultural backgrounds. This self-awareness, though difficult to achieve and come to terms with, when nurtured can serve as a first step towards understanding that every individual's cultural make-up has been and will continue to evolve based on the influence of the whole range of cultures, people and experiences that the individual has been exposed to. Such an understanding may enable a person to set aside or manage her own sensitivities and biases and adapt to the communication and working styles of colleagues who do not share her own cultural background, which, in turn, may aid her communication with them in work-related situations.

In academic curricula in the last two decades there has been a 'general shift toward seeing knowledge operationally, in terms of competence... and towards seeing education as training in skills' (Fairclough, 1995, p. 239). This is implicit acknowledgement of the need to keep education at every level relevant to the 'economic future' by linking learning to 'socio-economic achievement' (Bills, 2004, p. 14). The teaching of intercultural communication skills in universities could be viewed as a manifestation of this shift since intercultural communication skills, though not necessarily overtly stated as a requirement in job descriptions, are certainly an asset to the new graduate looking to secure a position in a large organisation. Intercultural communication skills would be especially important if the position sought by the new graduate is one that involves travel or relocation. For example, increasingly, employers seek candidates with not only the content knowledge that they need for particular functions, but also the ability to engage with the people they work for and with. Hence, it is not uncommon today that candidates are tested on their communication skills through hypothetical questions as well as hands-on, group interviews where they are expected to work with other candidates from diverse cultural backgrounds, discuss problem scenarios with them, brainstorm possible solutions, arrive at a consensus and present their findings.

However, economic motives are not the only reason why students in higher education need to learn intercultural communication skills. More importantly, the exposure that students receive in such intercultural communication contexts at university helps raise their awareness to the fact that, in order to be able to work with people over a period of time, a relationship of trust has to be nurtured which, in turn, requires investment of time and effort. Presumably, this is necessary in any working relationship, even those in which the people can be considered principally, culturally homogeneous. Thus, this just means that in culturally heterogeneous work contexts, over and above the time and effort required to nurture working relationships, people have to keep an open mind and be willing to learn about the other culture(s). They should also reserve judgement on a colleague's words or actions that is based on their own experience until they know enough about that person's culture. For these reasons, adequate attention needs to be given to the teaching and practice of intercultural communication within the curriculum in university.

In this paper, I describe the use of blogging as a pedagogical tool and platform in a professional communication module to enable students to reflect on their own perceptions of people with different cultural backgrounds than theirs, their biases, sensitivities and their perceptions of how they could manage some of those biases better so that they may prepare themselves for the global workplace. Pedagogical blogging has been incorporated into the curriculum in higher education to encourage collaboration, creativity and critical thinking (Duffy & Bruns, 2006), facilitate reflection on learning (Hourigan & Murray, 2010), cultural competence (Oikonomidoy, 2009) and encourage peer feedback on writing in a second-language classroom (Dippold, 2009).

In this module, blogs served as a platform for students to encourage students to think, write about and reflect on their learning. Although their posts were assessed, the weighting was capped at 15%. To this end, students were also provided with a set of rubrics that outlined the content and language requirements of their blog posts right from the beginning. The same rubrics also facilitated tutors when assessing the posts. Students were encouraged to be creative and innovative in their reflection on the content by incorporating examples, anecdotes, links to relevant YouTube clips and Technology, Entertainment, Design (TED) lectures, as well as other published material. At the same time, they were also advised to revise and edit writing for grammaticality, cohesiveness and coherence. Additionally, students were reminded that both their own reflective blog posts and their responses to their blogging buddies' posts would be assessed for their depth of discussion and evaluation. Their blogging buddies were one or more of their classmates. With the help of this framework, students were able to explore and identify their own views on intercultural communication as well as gain deeper insights into their peers' perspectives on this topic. In short, blogging about the topic with their buddies enabled students to forge reflective dialogue groups akin to Lave & Wenger's (1991) 'communities of practice'. When assessed for content, the posts of these reflective dialogue groups demonstrated evidence of deep learning by way of questioning and re-evaluating students' perspectives on intercultural communication as well as enhancing their existing knowledge of it.

The professional communication module

The module, the focus of this article, was entitled Professional Communication and it comprised both oral and written communication. However, the assessment was structured such that 55% was allocated to oral communication, for example, oral presentation skills, peer teaching of some topics, group project discussion and oral interaction in class, while 45% was devoted to written communication comprising a job application letter, the group project proposal and pedagogical blogging. These macro skills incorporated a range of micro skills such as active listening, questioning, instructing, checking understanding, working in groups made up of members from different disciplines and cultural backgrounds, leading group discussions and projects, persuasive speaking and writing techniques as well as reflection and self-assessment. Students had to apply these micro skills in order to complete their larger tasks.

Pedagogical blogging

Blog post following peer-teaching on intercultural communication

One of the peer-teaching topics was intercultural communication. The peer-teaching element in this course was structured so that students formed groups and drew lots on five topics for peer-teaching at the start of the course. When their turn came up, the group members taught their classmates the particular topic that they had drawn. The group members had to read their notes and prepare an interactive seminar for their peers as well as provide hands-on tasks for them for a period of 30–40 minutes. At the end of the seminar, the tutor summed up what had been taught and then introduced Deardorff's

INTERCULTURAL DIALOGUE

(2006) Process Model of Intercultural Competence to the students. A class discussion ensued and students were asked to share their knowledge of their own cultures and what they knew of at least one other culture with the group.

At the end of that week, students posted a blog on what they had learnt and discussed intercultural communication in class. In the week that followed, they read their blogging buddies' posts and commented on them. The tutor participated in the discussions by responding to their comments and since it had been established at the outset of the course that students' posts would be open for comments from any member of the class and the tutor, the tutor highlighted noteworthy comments from students in class. In their blogs, students commented on their attitudes on respect (valuing other cultures), openness (withholding judgement), and curiosity and discovery (tolerating ambiguity). They also reflected on their own knowledge of and attitudes towards other cultures (valuing other cultures), openness (withholding judgement), curiosity and discovery (tolerating ambiguity) (Deardorff, 2009, p. 480). Here are some excerpts from students' blog posts on intercultural communication and their experiences:

> We live in Singapore, a land of many cultures but I think we assume we know the Asian culture very well. But I realise that the individual racial culture in Singapore is very diluted and it isn't a very accurate representation of a certain race. Perhaps it is so because people in Singapore have given up parts of their individual culture in favour of the collective homogeneous Singaporean culture. (Student 6)

> I feel that one's culture is constantly evolving as we are subconsciously adapting to changes. We ourselves embody the culture that we have grown up in, and there is no need to doubt yourself, or question if you are leading the 'Chinese' way of life correctly or not. (Student 9)

As can be observed, Student 6, as did many others in this module, questions his knowledge of his own as well as other cultures, while others, like Student 9, acknowledges that one's culture is inevitably influenced by all the experiences, cultures and interactions he or she has been exposed to while growing up so it would be futile to measure one's 'cultural purity'. Student 10's post gives a further example of cultural evolution:

> I am Mexican, but right now I am asking myself what I know about Mexico? How other cultures impact on me? What are the festivals I celebrate? I think we are adopting some things of the American culture. For example, in Mexico we celebrate the 1st and the 2nd of November like the day of dead ('Día de muertos'), to remember the person who is dead. However, we are forgetting this tradition because in U.S.A. Halloween falls on the 31st of October, so many people in Mexico celebrate Halloween and forget to celebrate the day of dead. (Student 10)

Kramsch's (2011) reference to the symbolic dimension of the intercultural can be observed in this post where native and non-native speakers of a language construct social reality and influence each other's culture 'in persistent and subtle ways' (p. 365).

A further observation was that even those students who were usually too self-conscious to express their views in class 'found their voices' through blogging, not so much because of the anonymity the platform allowed them, because they all knew one another by name in class and their blog posts showed their names, but because the delayed response time between bloggers and their readers in this asynchronous medium gave the author of the post time and space for deeper reflection and more incisive reflections. For example, Student 8 who had written about his difficulty in communicating face-to-face at the start of his post said:

INTERCULTURAL DIALOGUE

I have always been a hesitant speaker and awkward communicator. People quite often tend to misunderstand what I meant to say, are misguided by the tone I use or the facial expressions I showed. This creates barriers to effective communication, even more so when you are trying to talk across cultures. Nevertheless, I am very curious about other cultures. (Student 8)

This same student later wrote:

We tend to view the world through our own colored lens. Looking at a white piece of paper through our red lens we assume that the paper is red. Along the way, another person looks at the same piece of paper through a yellow lens and inevitably a scuffle ensues between both parties. Who is right? Well, neither is because the paper is white. Similarly our perspectives on world issues are tainted with an invisible coloured lens - depending on the way you are brought up, and largely in part, influenced by your culture. What we should do then is to step into the other party's shoes and try to think from his/her perspective. Perhaps we might even see the white paper in the end. (Student 8)

In short, blogs provided students with a communication medium that was in keeping with their generation but, and also created a non-threatening, low-stress environment for them to express their thoughts on intercultural communication freely, even though they knew their posts were being assessed. It can be inferred that the sharing and exchanging of perspectives on intercultural communication on their blogs, in a sense, simulated what would be required of students when working and interacting with people from diverse cultural backgrounds in the global workplace.

Final blog post upon completion of the group assignment

During this time, students were simultaneously working on their group research assignment at the end of which they wrote a final blog reflecting on their experience of working with their groups. One student reflected as follows:

I was the only local in this group. I felt that I could have been a little more sensitive to some differences in our working styles. I edited my group mates' proposal section on Google Doc without seeking his permission and I think it upset him because I had assumed that it would be 'okay'. I later realized my folly and apologized to him when I met him in person. The valuable point I've taken away from this is not to assume and always respect another member's work no matter the circumstances. (Student 11)

Through their observations and reflections in their blogs and the responses from their 'blogging buddies', students demonstrated some understanding about communicating with individuals whose communication styles are not only influenced by their own cultures, but also by the myriad of other people and experiences that they have been exposed to in their past. The students acknowledged that they needed to be aware of their own communication styles first before evaluating another person's way of interacting. Furthermore, they seemed to recognise that an individual's efficiency of working with others was closely linked to how that person communicates with others at the workplace.

Final words

At the cognitive level, theory and class discussions are useful for provoking thought about intercultural issues, but for more experiential learning, active participation in group assignments that bring together culturally diverse people is useful. This type of hands-on participation (in this case, communicating through blogs and in-class discussions) forces students to think about the way they might communicate in a real world workplace. By providing adequate opportunity for students to reflect on the hands-on group assignment experience and receive feedback from their peers about their reflections, deep learning took place. The experience outlined here demonstrates that pedagogical blogging facilitates this kind of interactive reflection between peers in a non-threatening, low-stress environment, while using technology that this current generation of students is comfortable with. The blogging experience provided a concrete intercultural 'takeaway' which could potentially inform their intercultural communication practices in increasingly globalised workplaces.

Acknowledgement

I wish to thank my dear friend and colleague, Yang Ying, Senior Lecturer at the Centre for English Language Communication, National University of Singapore for helping me with the Mandarin translation despite her busy schedule.

References

Benoit, W. L., & Benoit, P. J. (2008). *Persuasive messages: The process of influence*. Malden, MA: Blackwell.

Bills, D. B. (2004). *The sociology of education & work*. Oxford: Blackwell.

Byram, M. (1997). *Teaching & assessing intercultural communicative competence*. Clevedon: Philadelphia Multilingual Matters.

Deardorff, D. K. (2006). Identification and assessment of intercultural competence as a student outcome of internationalization. *Journal of Studies in International Education, 10*, 241–266. doi:10.1177/1028315306287002

Deardorff, D. (2009). *The Sage handbook of intercultural competence*. Thousand Oaks, CA: Sage.

Dippold, D. (2009). Peer feedback through blogs: Student and teacher perceptions in an advanced German class. *ReCALL, 21*(1), 18–36. Retrieved from http://www.journals.cambridge.org/REC

Duffy, P., & Bruns, A. (2006). The use of blogs, wikis and RSS in education: A conversation of possibilities. In *Online learning and teaching conference 2006* (pp. 31–38). Brisbane: QUT. Retrieved from http://www.eprints.qut.edu.au

Eckert, P., & McConnell-Ginet, S. (1992). Think practically and look locally: Language and gender as community-based practice. *Annual Review of Anthropology, 21*, 461–488. doi:10.1146/annurev.an.21.100192.002333

Fairclough, N. (1995). *Critical discourse analysis*. London: Longman.

Hartley, P. (1999). *Interpersonal communication* (2nd ed.). London: Routledge.

Hill, J. H., & Mannheim, B. (1992). Language and world view. *Annual Review of Anthropology, 21*, 381–404. doi:10.1146/annurev.an.21.100192.002121

Holmes, J., & Meyerhoff, M. (1999). The community of practice: Theories and methodologies in language and gender research. *Language in Society, 28*, 173–183. doi:10.1017/S004740459900 202X

Hourigan, T., & Murray, L. (2010). Using blogs to help language students to develop reflective learning strategies: Towards a pedagogical framework. *Australasian Journal of Educational Technology, 26*, 209–225.

Kramsch, C. (2001). Intercultural communication. In R. Carter & D. Nunan (Eds.), *The Cambridge guide to teaching English to speakers of other languages* (1st ed., pp. 201–206). Cambridge: Cambridge University Press.

INTERCULTURAL DIALOGUE

Kramsch, C. (2007). The uses of communicative competence in a global world. In J. Liu (Ed.), *English language teaching in China: New approaches, perspectives and standards* (pp. 56–74). London: Continuum International.

Kramsch, C. (2011). The symbolic dimensions of the intercultural. *Language Teaching, 44*, 354–367. doi:10.1017/S0261444810000431

Lave, J., & Wenger, E. (1991). *Situated learning: Legitimate peripheral participation*. Cambridge: Cambridge University Press.

Liddicoat, A. J. (2009). Communication as culturally contexted practice: A view from intercultural communication. *Australian Journal of Linguistics, 29*, 115–133. doi:10.1080/0726860080 2516400

Oikonomidoy, E. (2009). Conceptual collective online reflection in multicultural education classes. *Multicultural Education & Technology Journal, 3*: 130–143. doi:10.1108/17504970910967564

Ruddock, A. (2007). *Investigating audiences*. London: Sage.

Scollon, R., & Scollon, S. W. (2001). *Intercultural communication: A discourse approach* (2nd ed.). Oxford: Blackwell.

Intercultural education in primary school: a collaborative project

Marta Santos, Maria Helena Araújo e Sá and Ana Raquel Simões

Departamento de Educação, Universidade de Aveiro, Campus Universitário de Santiago, Aveiro, Portugal

In this article, we present and discuss a collaborative project on intercultural education developed by a group of educational partners. The group was made up of 12 people representing different institutions in the community, namely primary schools, cultural and social associations and the local council. The project takes an intercultural approach to diversity by focusing on strategies aimed at: (1) increasing language awareness through intercultural education in primary school, (2) promoting intercultural dialogue and (3) enhanced development of intercultural competence of all participants. Data were collected through a 30-minute interview, carried out individually with each of the partners at the end of the project. Participants' responses showed that the activities carried out during the project were an important way to promote the development of their intercultural competence. They also mentioned that working in partnership was a successful method to promote reflection and to improve their working practices concerning intercultural education.

Neste artigo pretendemos apresentar e discutir um projeto colaborativo sobre educação intercultural desenvolvido por um grupo de parceiros educativos. O grupo era composto por 12 representantes de diferentes instituições da comunidade, tais como escolas do 1° Ciclo do Ensino Básico, associações culturais e sociais e a Câmara Municipal. O projeto partiu de uma abordagem intercultural da diversidade, focando-se em estratégias com os seguintes objetivos: (1) sensibilizar para a diversidade linguística no 1° CEB através da educação intercultural; (2) promover o diálogo intercultural e (3) desenvolver a competência intercultural de todos os participantes. Os dados foram recolhidos por meio de uma entrevista de 30 minutos a cada um dos parceiros do projeto. As suas respostas mostraram que as atividades desenvolvidas no âmbito do mesmo desempenharam um papel importante no desenvolvimento da sua competência intercultural. Referiram ainda que o trabalho em parceria foi permitiu a reflexão crítica de todos os participantes e a melhoria das suas práticas de trabalho em educação intercultural.

Introduction

This article is grounded in the study 'Intercultural education in primary school: partnerships involving schools and community'[1] currently being developed at the University of Aveiro (UA) in Portugal. The broader study investigates how a group of educational partners representing cultural, social and political institutions within a specific local/regional community design, implement and evaluate a joint project on intercultural education in Primary Schools (with children between the ages of 6 and 10).

INTERCULTURAL DIALOGUE

The article intends to (1) present some of the activities developed within this project; (2) outline the partners' point of view on the opportunities for intercultural dialogue provided by the project; (3) identify the partners' point of view on the role of those activities for the development of the intercultural competence of all participants; and (4) highlight the ways in which participation in the project influenced their professional practices.

We begin this article by presenting the theoretical framework on which our study is based (namely the concepts of intercultural education, intercultural competence and intercultural dialogue), followed by an explanation of the methodology used to collect data, a brief presentation of the work plan of the partners involved and the presentation and discussion of the results. Finally, we will make some final considerations about the impact of the project on the development of intercultural competence of all the participants and on the implications of this type of approach for strategies for developing and promoting intercultural education, namely those involving network partnerships.

The need for intercultural dialogue

The increasing cultural, religious, social and economic diversity in European societies raises issues about human rights and social cohesion, and emphasises the need to ensure the welfare of all members of a society by minimising disparities and avoiding polarisation (Beacco, Byram, Coste, & Fleming, 2009). At this level, attitudes must be shaped by promoting intercultural dialogue, which can be understood as 'a process that comprises an open and respectful exchange of views between individuals and groups with different ethnic, cultural, religious and linguistic backgrounds and heritage, on the basis of mutual understanding and respect' (Council of Europe, 2008, p. 15).

Dialogue and contacts can occur in two different modes: they can be real and direct (face-to-face), with possibilities for interaction (behavioural adaptations, verbal and emotional responses); or virtual and indirect (via email, forums, chats or blogs), producing also possibilities for textual and visual responses (Beacco, 2011). In either case mutual understanding, openness, tolerance and respect are necessary for effective intercultural dialogue to take place. It involves a positive attitude towards diversity, seeing the meeting between different people as enriching for all, and seeing one's individuality as being developed through meeting that diversity (Beacco et al., 2009). Because diversity exists both in the classroom and out of it, situations of intercultural dialogue should be promoted not only in society, but also included in intercultural classroom activities, allowing students to be aware of the richness of diversity (Beacco, 2011).

Developing intercultural competence

As we mentioned, the role of intercultural dialogue is essential in creating and maintaining social cohesion. In this sense, intercultural competence can be considered as its practical foundation, since intercultural dialogue requires the acquisition of intercultural competences, including multiperspectivity and the ability to see oneself and familiar situations and events from perspectives of 'others' (Beacco et al., 2009).

The development of intercultural competence, usually described as a 'lifelong process' (Deardorff, 2010, p. 1), involves the ability to interact effectively and appropriately with people from other cultures and is related to four dimensions: knowledge, attitudes, skills and behaviours, in a pyramidal model (Deardorff, 2009).

The author places attitudes at the base of the pyramid, as a fundamental starting point, on which knowledge and comprehension of cultures and the development of skills, such as analysing and relating, are developed. The next level is an informed frame of reference which includes flexibility and empathy. Finally at the top of the pyramid lies the level of the desired external outcomes (behaving and communicating effectively and appropriately).

The development of intercultural competence departs from situations of intercultural dialogue which occur in daily life and should be learned, practiced and maintained. This is why the *White Paper on Intercultural Dialogue* (Council of Europe, 2008) highlights the importance of working on its development in all institutional contexts and at all levels (such as public authorities, education professionals, civil-society organisations, religious communities, the media and all other educational stakeholders). Although the development of intercultural competence is relatively independent of educational content (it can also occur outside of the school), the school contact with communities in which individuals from different cultural backgrounds move may help to modify students' cultural perceptions and promote the contact with foreign languages (Coste, Moore, & Zarate, 2009). Thus, it is essential to prepare teachers to develop theoretical and practical tools for the promotion of intercultural competencies (Beacco et al., 2010), including methods to interpret and value diversity, to overcome their own stereotypes and prejudices and to raise awareness for the complexity of intercultural contact (Rey-von Allmen, 2004). So, teacher training should be considered essential in the initial and continuous formation of these professionals (Permisán, 2008), preparing them to manage new situations arising from diversity and to resolve conflicts peacefully, as well as to foster a global approach to institutional life on the basis of democracy and human rights (Council of Europe, 2008).

Intercultural education: a key to the third millennium

The global and pluralistic society, deeply affected by social and economical changes, reveals a great polyphony of values and a strong fragmentation of life. The education system is deeply affected by these changes and is witnessing a serious pedagogical crisis, which brings out the need for clear, bold educational goals (Portera, 2011). In this sense, we share the opinion that intercultural education constitutes the most appropriate way to answer these questions.

Currently, there are several definitions of intercultural education reported in literature. The context in which we theorize this perspective follows a European guideline that makes the distinction between multiculturalism – 'a peaceful coexistence of cultures' (Portera, 2011, p. 19) and interculturalism emphasising the (inter)relations, interaction, exchange and dialogue provided by the *inter* prefix (Abdallah-Pretceille, 1990; Portera, 2011). Thus, intercultural education can be understood as a holistic educational approach, based on respect and appreciation for cultural diversity, which aims at giving equal opportunities for all, promoting dialogue, communication and intercultural competence, and overcoming racism, discrimination and exclusion (Aguado & Malik, 2006). It promotes values of citizenship and interculturality in the students and allows them to develop their critical thinking about the way they interact with other individuals or groups, while acknowledging and understanding their characteristics within universal human values (Alred, Byram, & Fleming, 2002).

Intercultural education is indispensable for all students, even in monocultural contexts, and should not be seen simply as a way to integrate migrant students or to

INTERCULTURAL DIALOGUE

deal with multi-cultural contexts, because all students should have the opportunity to see diversity as normal and as a means for personal development (Alred et al., 2002; Gil-Jaurena & Ballesteros, 2009). Education is a powerful tool for maintaining and valuing ethnic, linguistic and cultural diversity and achieving social inclusion, equity and intercultural understanding. Because identities, cultures and societies are dynamic, not static, and values are not genetically transmitted to foster democratic culture, it is necessary to reinforce and invest more in the field of education (Portera, 2011). Thus, teacher training in intercultural education should be a concern of all teacher training institutions, both in their initial and continuing training (Angelides, Stylianou, & Leigh, 2007).

Furthermore, this understanding of the demands of living in a diverse society suggest that the educational process should involve other educational partners and be understood as a continuous process, not as a single action or intervention, that takes into consideration the context of implementation, the needs and the resources available (Beacco et al., 2010). Teamwork should be encouraged, promoting collaboration and solidarity between school, parents and the whole community, thereby enabling closer links within these institutions (Gil-Jaurena & Ballesteros, 2009).

Method

As part of a study currently being developed at the Research Centre 'Didactics and Technology in Education of Trainers' (CIDTFF) of the University of Aveiro (UA), Portugal, a group of educational partners was created. Twelve participants were involved, all representing different institutions within the municipality of Aveiro: two primary schools, an immigrants' association, a cultural association, an institution working with disabled people, the City Hall and Library belonging to the City Hall. Their aim was to design, implement and evaluate a joint project on intercultural education to be implemented in primary schools (with children between the ages of 6 and 10). Almost every student had Portuguese nationality. There were only two students with different nationalities (Moroccan and Capeverdian), both in the same class. The partners of the group are described in Table 1.

During the academic year 2010/2011, the group had the opportunity to participate in several meetings and undergo training on interculturality and intercultural education; activities were:

Fourteen work meetings for training on the themes of intercultural education, intercultural competence and intercultural dialogue. Different types of materials were

Table 1. Description of the partners.

Partners	Partners' functions
P1, P2, P3, P4, P5 and P6	Primary school teachers (working with children from 6 to 10 years old). Only P2 had two foreign students in her classroom
P7	Music teacher (immigrant from east Europe)
P8	Music teacher
P9	Socio-cultural animator. Represents a cultural association
P10	Immigrant from east Europe and coordinator of an immigrant' association
P11	Speech therapist. Works with physically or mentally disabled people
P12	Librarian. Represents the Municipal Library and the Council

presented and discussed by all the members, such as some guidelines and materials of the European Commission, for instance 'The Autobiography of Intercultural Encounters' (http://www.coe.int/t/dg4/autobiography/). There were also workshops on language and cultural awareness developed by the Open Laboratory for Foreign Languages Learning (http://www.ua.pt/cidtff/lale/) of the University of Aveiro. In these sessions they also had the opportunity to share experiences, ideas and (re)constructed knowledge and to design a set of activities on intercultural education, aimed at the students and the school community (also involving parents and staff working in schools).

Ten classroom sessions where the planned activities were implemented, some of which are described in the following section. These sessions took place throughout the entire school year and were carried out by the teachers in collaboration with some of the other partners of the project.

Two final sessions (closing parties of the first and third school terms) aiming to disseminate the results of the activities were developed during the project. These sessions involved all the school community (partners, other teachers, staff, students and parents) and took place in public spaces of the community (one City Hall Social Centre and the playground of one of the participant schools).

Summary description of the intervention plan

The project on intercultural education allowed the development of a large set of activities. As an example of that work, we will here present some of those activities, their aims, dates of implementation and partners involved in their execution.

(1) Musical orchestra – in November 2010, organised by the Socio-cultural animator (P9) together with the primary school teachers (P1, P2, P3, P4, P5 and P6). The musical orchestra was composed of instruments made from daily life materials, such as pails, plastic tubes and cookware. The aim of this activity was to explore the meaning of *diversity*, applied not only to people and cultures but also to different aspects of life, such as the sounds we hear in our everyday life. All the students of both schools had the opportunity to explore all the instruments and to play musical pieces in small groups.

(2) Arabic session – in November 2010, a P1 teacher invited a native Arabic teacher from the University of Aveiro to come to her class. The aim of the activity was to develop openness, interest, curiosity and empathy towards other cultures and languages, in this case, Arabic. The students learned how to write and pronounce some words in Arabic, compared the characters of both Arabic and Latin writing systems and identified common lexicon. They also talked with the Arabic teacher and asked him about some aspects of his culture, country, traditions and family.

(3) Intercultural Christmas Party – at the end of the first school term (December 2010), all the partners organised a party at the City Hall Social Centre which was open to the entire community, where the students could show some of the work on interculturality they had done during the previous months, as well as the understanding they had developed on values, relationships between people, aspects of different cultures, knowledge on their own culture, etc. They presented plays imagining intercultural encounters between people from countries they had studied in class, performed dances they had learned with natives from other cultures (namely those from P10, from the Immigrants'

INTERCULTURAL DIALOGUE

Association, and the P7 music teacher and also an immigrant from eastern Europe) and interpreted a song in sign language. By interpreting this song, the students tried to explain that the concept of diversity goes far beyond the difference between cultures, but also referred to differences between people that make every individual different from each other. There was also an exhibition of posters, drawings, stories and flyers they had made during the planned activities on issues such as diversity and interculturality. Accordingly, this party also had the aim to encourage a harmonious relation between the school, the families and the community, making them aware of the need for intercultural understanding and the implementation of intercultural education. A short video of this activity can be accessed at http://www.youtube.com/watch?v=DJbEg9v64rU.

(4) Intercultural stories – in February 2011, P12 classes prepared a reading session for all the students and teachers of the two schools. They heard stories on intercultural issues, telling about children of different countries, and were asked to reflect on characteristics, traditions, religions and languages included in the stories. With this activity, the partners tried to encourage the students' critical thinking with regard to other countries' traditions and values.

(5) Ukrainian session – in March 2011, P1, P2, P3, P4, P5 and P6, along with P12 classes, developed a session to promote openness, interest, curiosity and empathy towards the Ukrainian culture and language. P10 students presented a puppet show called 'The Giant Turnip', where the other children were invited to listen to the story spoken entirely in Ukrainian. Through the gestures of the characters, the situations presented and a few words that the P10 students had taught them previously (both in written and spoken forms), the children tried to understand the meaning of the story. After that, the story was discussed together so that everyone could understand the plot, indicate the words they found more different or difficult to understand and give their opinion about the similarity between the Ukrainian and Portuguese languages. They also had the chance to talk to the Ukrainian native and ask a few questions about Ukraine, its location on the map, its traditions, the way people live there and some materials that Ukrainian students use in their classes.

(6) Imaginary people – from February 2011 to June 2011, all the partners developed with the children an activity which aimed to discover the value of unity in diversity and to develop a joint activity to achieve common goals. It consisted in inventing an imaginary people with its own language, writing system, values, clothing, games and traditional dances. This was developed by taking into account all the previous research about other countries and cultures they had undertaken during other activities of the project. The new people was named the *Unis*, meaning the *union*, because the children wanted to transmit the message that every people of each and every culture should live together in peace, knowing, accepting, respecting and valuing each other. At the end of the school year, the *Unis* people were presented to all the community, in an open party where everybody was welcome to take part. The parents of the students helped them by making the costumes/clothes and other accessories; some local associations provided food and a sound system to the party and, at the end, the children sang in chorus the hymn of the *Unis*, which had been previously prepared with the help of P7 and P8.

Data collection

After the completion of the project, 30-minute semi-structured interviews of the 11 partners were carried out by the researcher with the purpose of finding out the partners' representations regarding: (1) the opportunities of intercultural dialogue promoted by the activities of the project; (2) the impact of the project on the development of the intercultural competence of the group of partners, students and the community; (3) the impact of the project on their future professional practices.

This interview was recorded, transcribed and analysed, using the content analysis technique (Bardin, 2013). The data collected were organised into three main categories. Two of them were created according to the theoretical background of this research project: (1) opportunities for intercultural dialogue; (2) development of intercultural competence; a third category resulted from the interview guide and data collection; (3) impact of the project. In the next section, we will present and discuss those categories.

Findings

Opportunities for intercultural dialogue

According to the partners' answers, the participation in the project on intercultural education furthered several opportunities for intercultural dialogue and allowed the students contact with other languages, and interaction with people from other countries. As an example, referring to the Ukrainian session promoted by P10 classes, a P7 teacher recalled that:

> at first/the students found the language very different and could not understand anything. But then/with gestures and pictures/they were able to understand a few things. I think it was a good moment of learning and interaction between people from different cultures. (P7_EF:08[2])

This partner highlights the importance of the experience of meeting and talking with a person from another country and getting into contact with a different language and writing system. In the same way, a P1 teacher tells us that in the Arabic class students had a very rich intercultural experience because 'they had contact with a writing system and a language different from their own/they interacted with the Arabic teacher/they loved this class and the experience provided/they had never had an opportunity like this' (P1_EF:036).

From these statements, we can infer that the partners perceive that the contact with people from other countries or cultures causes great excitement in students and curiosity about these people's language. In fact, interaction between learners and native speakers of a language is a strategy often used to enhance both language learning and cultural awareness and understanding (Byram & Feng, 2004). As the partners tell us, according to its specific aim, the strategy was successful.

Development of intercultural competence

Regarding the partners' voices about the development of intercultural competence, the data were organised into three sub-categories, according to the development of intercultural competence in the: (1) partners, (2) students; and (3) community.

In the first place, partners considered that the intercultural competence of the other partners was developed. A P6 teacher believes that the impact of the project was very positive because:

INTERCULTURAL DIALOGUE

all partners had to broaden their way of thinking. By participating in the activities we reflect on them and there was an exchange of knowledge. We found that there are differences and similarities between people and that this diversity enriches us. (P6_EF:04)

A P7 teacher reinforces this idea saying that 'We all learned to respect other people and realized that contact with others is also a way of learning new things' (P7_EF:08). The statements of these partners highlight three major points related to intercultural competence: the development of critical thinking (which leads them to reflect on values such as respect for other people), the exchange of knowledge and the valorisation of diversity (given that diversity allows them to learn new things).

Secondly, according to the respondents, also the students had an opportunity to develop their intercultural competence. As a P3 teacher states '(…) students showed more solidarity, were more aware of the need to share and learn from what their colleagues have to give. This project made us all (teachers and students) reflect on the subject' (P3_EF:04). A P1 teacher also tells us that this work allowed the students to acquire 'new knowledge and deepen reflection on what means to be different/accept diversity/live with it and appreciate the inner qualities of each person/ more than the physical characteristics/ the different cultures/ the different countries/ the different languages' (P1_EF:046). To this partner, it does not matter if people are different but they have to know how to communicate, how to socialize and how to live together. These answers allow us to infer that the students developed competences that can improve their interaction with people from different origins, and with different characteristics and personalities. Those competencies are: learning to give more value to diversity (not only to cultural diversity but to the diversity that makes each one of us a unique person), the acquisition of new knowledge about people from different countries and showing more solidarity and respect for the views of their colleagues.

Finally, this project was also a means for the community to become more aware of the need of intercultural education. A P4 teacher thinks that 'it was well accepted by all/the whole community/ and I think we were able to call the attention to the importance of diversity/ how it enriches us. We managed to raise awareness to the values/ to the respect.' This partner adds that 'our goal has been achieved' (P4_EF:04). A P2 teacher tells us that 'The project also had an indirect public. We organized parties/ both for families and for the community itself/ the room was open and everyone could join us/ even if it was just to see what was happening' (P2_EF:08).

By these statements, we may suppose that the activities undertaken by the students made some terms more familiar to them, such as *diversity, interculturality, intercultural competence* and *dialogue*, which might have been unknown by many people. To listen to their children or neighbours talking about this project might have contributed to curiosity about the topic, prompting them to search for more knowledge about it and to get them to understand the message it tries to communicate.

In general, the perspective of the partners related to the development of the intercultural competence of all participants (partners, students and community) corresponds to the 'requisite attitudes' level of Deardorff's (2009) pyramid, explained above in the theoretical framework of this article. At this level, which should be the basis of the development of intercultural competence, people develop respect and learn to value cultural diversity, acquire the openness needed to embrace cultural learning, accept people from other cultures, and develop a sense of curiosity and discovery related to other peoples' characteristics, traditions, ways of living, languages, etc. (Deardorff, 2009). So, in our opinion, supported by the partners' statements, the activities carried out within the project seemed to have contributed to an initial development of intercultural competence in all participants.

Impact of the project

The partners' voices about the project's impact on their future professional practices tell us that the experience gave them many ideas to be developed that involve schools and other institutions. They highlighted two important issues: valuing diversity; and working in partnership.

Regarding the first issue, a P10 teacher states that:

> We learned that we can do a lot of things with schools and other associations/ I had never realised that we could have so much to show and share with others. This project gave us many ideas and showed us how we can do things. (P10_EF:30)

This partner tells us that working with others made her realise that she can learn a lot from each other's life experiences, opinions and ideas and so, in the future, she expects to adopt this way of working.

Regarding the second issue, a P12 teacher says that '(…) teamwork was important because everyone contributed to the activities. That helped us give more value to others, to their opinion. I always worked in partnership and intend to work always like that' (P12_EF:021). Therefore, and as we stated in a previous article, we believe that this project contributed positively to these partners' training on intercultural education, making them aware of the need to disseminate the knowledge and the strategies developed (Santos, Araújo e Sá, & Simões, 2012). In many cases, the initial formation of these professionals is not enough to prepare them to develop this particular subject. It should always be complemented with continuous teacher training education (Permisán, 2008), which may include participation in specific training on this subject (McNeal, 2005) like the research project presented in this article. Also the fact of having worked in partnership was an important way to rethink and improve their working practices. Thus, according to the participants, it made them more conscious of the need to work collaboratively, respect the opinions and ideas of other people, which is a principle that they should transmit to the students in their everyday classes (Díaz-Aguado, 2000).

Final considerations

Throughout this article, we have attempted to present a project on intercultural education developed in partnership involving two primary schools and different institutions from the surrounding community. We have argued that intercultural education is a necessary educational approach in both mono- and multi-cultural schools and communities, and also for all people in general. We believe that the participation in the project on intercultural education, providing contact and dialogue with different people, from different schools, institutions and countries, was a positive contribution towards the development of the intercultural competence of all participants. According to the data collected via the interviews of the partners, children and adults, the participants had the opportunity to increase their knowledge of different countries and cultures, to develop their critical thinking and to develop attitudes such as increased curiosity and awareness of linguistic and cultural diversity, respect for the others and working in partnership.

Thus, the project presented herein might be one of many feasible proposals to introduce intercultural education into the curriculum and to disseminate educational practices of collaborative work within a community, after having been adapted to each particular context. The project gave us the possibility of developing new materials and ideas, gathering research data, and carrying out analysis for new projects which can be

INTERCULTURAL DIALOGUE

presented to other schools and institutions, thus promoting the development of future projects and partnerships.

Notes

1. Project co-funded by the FCT (Foundation for Science and Technology) under the programme QREN – POPH – Typology 4.1 – Advanced Training (subsidized by the European Social Fund and the MCTES (Ministry of Science, Technology and Higher Education).
2. All of the extracts have been translated into English by the authors.

References

Abdallah-Pretceille, M. (1990). *Vers une pédagogie interculturelle* [Towards an intercultural pedagogy]. Paris: INRP Sorbonne.

Aguado, T., & Malik, B. (2006). Intercultural education: Teacher training and school practice. *Intercultural Education, 17*(5), 447–456. doi:10.1080/14675980601060401

Alred, G., Byram, M., & Fleming, M. (2002). *Intercultural experience and education*. Clevedon: Multilingual Matters.

Angelides, P., Stylianou, T., & Leigh, J. (2007). The efficacy of collaborative networks in preparing teachers. *European Journal of Teacher Education, 30*(2), 135–149. doi:10.1080/0261976070 1273953

Bardin, L. (2013). *Análise de conteúdo* [Content analysis]. Lisboa: Edições 70.

Beacco, J.-C. (2011). *The cultural and intercultural dimensions of language teaching: Current practice and prospects*. Seminar on "Curriculum convergences for plurilingual and intercultural education", Strasbourg.

Beacco, J.-C., Byram, M., Cavalli, M., Coste, D., Cuenat, M. E., Goullier, F., & Panthier, J. (2010). *Guide for the development and implementation of curricula for plurilingual and intercultural education*. Strasbourg: Council of Europe.

Beacco, J.-C., Byram, M., Coste, D., & Fleming, M. (2009). *Multicultural societies, pluricultural people and the project of intercultural education*. Strasbourg: Council of Europe.

INTERCULTURAL DIALOGUE

Byram, M., & Feng, A. (2004). Culture and language learning: Teaching, research and scholarship. *Language Teaching, 37*(3): 149–168. doi:10.1017/S0261444804002289

Coste, D., Moore, D., & Zarate, G. (2009). *Plurilingual and pluricultural competence – Studies towards a common European framework of reference for language learning and teaching.* Strasbourg: Council of Europe.

Council of Europe. (2008). *White paper on intercultural education.* Strasbourg: Author.

Deardorff, D. (2009). *The Sage handbook of intercultural competence.* Thousand Oaks, CA: Sage.

Deardorff, D. (2010, September). *Intercultural competence in the classroom.* 22nd EAIE conference: Making knowledge work, Nantes International Congress Centre, Nantes.

Díaz-Aguado, M. (2000). *Educação intercultural e aprendizagem cooperativa* [Intercultural education and cooperative learning]. Porto: Porto Editora.

Gil-Jaurena, I., & Ballesteros, B. (2009). Resources for teacher training in intercultural education. Report on INTER research group activities and products. In E. Czerka & M. Mechlińska-Pauli (Eds.), *Teaching and learning in different cultures – An adult education perspective* (pp. 147–159). Gdańsk: Gdańsk Higher School of Humanities Press.

McNeal, K. (2005). The influence of a multicultural teacher education program on teachers' multicultural practices. *Intercultural Education, 16*(4), 405–419. doi:10.1080/14675980500304405

Permisán, G. (2008). Es la formación del profesorado la clave de la educación intercultural? [Is teacher education the key to intercultural education?] *Revista Española de Pedagogia, LXVI*(239), 119–136.

Portera, A. (2011). Intercultural and multicultural education – Epistemological and semantic aspects. In A. Grant & A. Portera (Eds.), *Intercultural and multicultural education – Enhancing global interconnectedness* (pp. 12–32). New York, NY: Routledge.

Rey-von Allmen, M. (2004). Towards an intercultural education. In M. Mesić (Ed.), *Perspectives of multiculturalism: Western and transitional countries* (pp. 103–112). Zagreb: Faculty of Philosophy, Croatian Commission for UNESCO.

Santos, M., Araújo e Sá, M. H., & Simões, A. R. (2012). Interculturality and intercultural education – Representations and practices of a group of educational partners. In M. Byram, M. Fleming, & I. Pieper (Eds.), *L1-educational studies in language and literature, 12*, (pp. 1–22). Amsterdam: Universiteit van Amsterdam, Instituut voor de Lerarenopleiding. Retrieved from http://l1.publication-archive.com/public?fn=enter&repository=1&article=141

Index

acculturation theory 60
additive bilingualism 60
Adorno, T.W. 14
affiliation 93, 94
Afghanistan 110–11
agency 92, 94, 102–3, 104
Al Aqsa University 112–13
Alvesson, M. 43
ambiguous *we* 48–55
Arabic class 144, 146
Aramin, B. 4–5
Archer, M. 71–2
Argentina 34
Arthur, J. 87
assessment, intercultural 130
asymmetrical obligation 14–15
asymmetry 76–90
attitudes 141–2, 147
audiolingual methods 60–1
audiovisual methods 60–1
Australia 117
autonomy 14–15, 16, 64, 79, 80–1, 83–4
Aveiro, Portugal 4, 140–50

Baker, P. 55
Bakhtin, M.M. 68, 71
Bargiela-Chiappini, F. 49
Barnett, R. 102, 103
Beacco, J.-C. 141
behaviours 141–2
Beijing Olympic Games student volunteers
    69–70
Bertral, R. 35, 39
Biesa, V. 35
Bildung 12
bilingualism 60
blogging 4, 132–9
Blommaert, J. 10, 63–4, 66
Boni, A. 92
Bourdieu, P. 64
bridge design project meeting 47, 49, 50–3,
    54
British Council 1, 109
Bruner, J.S. 27

Buber, M. 117
Bucholtz, M. 45, 48, 70
Bulgaria 2–3, 24–40
Business English 11
Byram, M. 11, 70, 126–7

CANBEC corpus (CCC) 44
Canetti, E. 25
Cao, Q. 66–7
capabilities approach 3, 91–107; central tenets
    92–5
capability lists 93–4; language and intercultural
    learning 102–4
capacity building 121
categorisation: interreligious dialogue under
    76–90; problematising categories 84–5; of
    we 47–9
Center for Intercultural Dialogue 1
child labour 100–1, 102, 103
Chile 34
China 2; Culture Quality Education Reform
    125; general education and intercultural
    communication 4, 125–31; English learners'
    identity prototypes 3, 59–75
China Central Television (CCTV) 65
China English 65
Chinese cultural aphasia 64
choice 79, 80–1, 92–3
Christmas party, intercultural 144–5
civil rights movement 64
Clandinin, D.J. 27
clash of civilisations 71, 111
clothing 79
Cohen, D. 40
coherence 13
collaborative project on intercultural education
    4, 140–50
collectivism 9
collectivist identities 42
colonialism 61
communicative competence 17, 63; and
    intercultural responsibility 12–14
communities of practice 133, 135
community, as educational partner 143–9

INDEX

competence 2, 3, 92, 134; communicative
12–14, 17, 63; intercultural *see* intercultural
competence; intercultural responsibility and
2, 7–23; symbolic 12, 63
concordance lines 43–4, 47
conflict 3–4, 108–24
conflict avoidance 120
conflict resolution 120
conflict transformation 119–23
Connelly, F.M. 27
constraints on identity prototypes 61–2, 65,
67–8, 72, 73
contexts 122; identity prototypes 61, 64, 67,
71–2, 73
corpora: and intercultural studies 43–4;
professional 44–5
corpus-informed discourse analysis 3, 41–58
cosmopolitanism 92, 95–105
Council of Europe 1, 87, 109, 114, 141,
142
creative practice 119–23
creoles 65–6
Creswell, J.W. 27
critical examination 94, 100
critical intercultural language pedagogy
11–12
critical participatory action research (CPAR)
97–104
critical theory 14
Crosbie, V. 121
Cuba 34
cultural difference 9
cultural evolution 136
cultural identities 3, 41–58
Curtin, M.L. 10

Damelin, R. 4–5
Deardorff, D. 9–10, 135–6, 141–2, 147
democratic citizenship 91, 92, 94
Derrida, J. 15
Dervin, F. 11
Descartes, R. 15
diachrony 15–16
dialogical communicator 3, 59, 68–73
'Dialogue Among Civilizations' 71
diaspora zone 29, 33–4
Ding, J.X. 67
Diogenes 95
discursive practices 42
dissemination 111
diversity 141, 144; valuing 148
Dollar a Day Dress, The 98
domestic zone 29, 30–1
Du Fu, 'Deng Gao' 68–9
Dulce Canto choir 32

educational partnerships 4, 143–9
Ehteshami, A. 2
emergency conditions 118–19

empathy 13
endangered languages 25–6; *see also*
Ladino
English 11; identity prototypes for English
learners 3, 59–75
English Defence League 117
English as a Foreign Language (EFL) 60
English and Globalisation module 98–9
English as Lingua Franca (ELF) 63
English as Second Language (ESL) 60
English to Speakers of Other Languages
(ESOL) teaching 97–104
entente cordiale 114–15
essentialism 9–10, 42
ethical communication 2, 7–23
ethical individualism 92
ethnic identity development exercise 99
European Framework of Reference for
Languages 11, 109
European Union (EU) 1, 109
exclusion 31
exclusive *we* 48–55

faithful imitator 59, 60–2, 72–3
Finland 3, 76–90
Flizzow, J. 65–6
fluidity 67
France 33
freedom 79, 80–1, 92–3, 94
frequency lists 44
Fudan College 126
functioning 92–3

Gao, Y.H. 69–70
Gaza 3, 112–13, 115–17
Gee, J.P. 45
general education 4, 125–31
geography 129
'Giant Turnip' puppet show 145
Gillespie, A. 84
Giroux, H.A. 91
Global People project 10
globalisation 67, 113; capabilities approach in
English learning and 98–104;
sociolinguistics of 63–4; workplace 4,
132–9
Goerzig, C. 116–18
Gonzalez, M. 11, 100
Graeber, D. 122
Greece 33
group assignments 137–8
Guilherme, M. 11, 12–13, 96

Habermas, J. 14
Hall, K. 45, 48, 70
Hall, S. 42
Hall, W. 9
Hamas 116–17
Haq, M. ul 93

INDEX

Harbin Institute of Technology 128–30
Harvard University 126
hegemonic interculturalism 9
Herakova, L.L. 2
heterogeneity 95
highways 129
hip-hop 65–6
Hofstede, G. 9, 42
Holliday, A. 10, 70–1
Holmes, J. 133
Horkheimer, M. 14
Hueso, A. 92
Hüllen, W. 11
Human Development Index (HDI) 93
human rights 114
Huntington, S. 71, 111
hybridity 66, 67

Ich:Es/I:It domain 117
identity 42; cultural identities in international, inter-organisational meetings 3, 41–58; imagined 63; loss of 61–2, 117–18; and ontological being 102, 103–4
identity-performances 29–36
identity prototypes 3, 59–75
ideology, religion as 85
imaginary people activity 145
imagination 121, 122; narrative 94
imagined identity 63
in-groups 99–100
inclusion 31
inclusive *we* 48–55
indexical *we* 3, 41–58
individualism 9
integrativeness 60
intercultural competence 9–10; development of 141–2, 146–7; dimensions of 126–7
intercultural education: collaborative project 4, 140–50; Deardorff model 9–10, 136, 141–2, 147; general education and 4, 125–31; importance of 142–3; pedagogical blogging 4, 132–9
intercultural responsibility 2, 7–23
intercultural stories 145
interculturalism, origins of 8–11
internal conversation 71–2
International Association of Languages and Intercultural Communication (IALIC) conference 1
international community of Spanish-speakers 29, 34–6
international, inter-organisational meetings 3, 41–58
International Monetary Fund (IMF) 100, 101
interreligious dialogue 3, 76–90
(intra-)personal zone 29, 30
Iraq 110, 129
Islam 80–1, 82, 86
Israel 33

Israeli–Palestinian conflict 4–5, 112–13, 114, 115–17

Jack, G. 9
Jehovah's Witnesses 86
Jenkins, J. 63
Jones, A. 83

Kachru, B.B. 63
Kantian ethics 14–15
Karzai, H.J. 110–11
kerygmatic proclamations 15–16
keyword in context (KWIC) concordance lines 43–4
keyword lists 44
Khatami, M. 71
knowledge 141–2
Koester, A.J. 53
Kramsch, C. 12, 63, 70, 119, 133, 136
Kroeger, K.R. 127
Kuala Lumpur 65–6
Kushner, A. 25

L2 investment 63
Ladino 2–3, 24–40
Lambert, W.E. 60
languaging 11
Leach, J. 100
Lederach, J.P. 120–1
Leeds-Hurwitz, W. 1
legitimate speaker 59, 62–5, 72–3
Levinas, E. 2, 8, 15–18
Lidgi, R. 35–6, 39–40
Life Long Learning in Palestine project 112, 114
life stories 27, 28–36
linguistic capital 64
'live' English 130
local identity 54–5
local *we* 48–55
local zone 29, 31–3
loss of identity 61–2, 117–18
Lozano, J.F. 92

Martin, J.N. 9
Massey, D. 111
Mautner, G. 55
mediation 122
meetings, international inter-organisational 3, 41–58
Mexico 34, 136
Meyerhoff, M. 133
Mignolo, W. 81
Monceri, F. 11
Moon, B. 100
Moon, D.G. 8–9
Mulderrig, J. 52
multilingual research 27–8
multi-perspective approach 96

INDEX

musical orchestra 144
Muslims 80–1, 82, 86

Nakayama, T.K. 9
Nandy, A. 85
narrative imagination 94
narrative research 26–7; Ladino-focused
    narratives 2–3, 24–40
Näss, H.E. 1–2
nation state 12; religion and 85
National Communication Association 1
national identity 54–5
national *we* 48–55
native speakers 60–1, 62
Navon, Y. 33
negotiation with the other 81–2
New Zealand 83
news-listening class 4, 128–30
Nobel Peace Prize 1, 109, 110, 113
Noddings, N. 96
non-participation 63
Norton, B. 63
nuclear states 118–19
Nussbaum, M. 92, 95–6, 105; capability lists
    93–4; central capabilities for education 94

Occupy Movement 121
Oliver, M. 123
Olson, C.L. 127
ontological being 102, 103–4
ontological thinking 15
opportunities for intercultural dialogue 146
organisational identity 54–5
organisational *we* 48–55
other 2; negotiating with the other 81–2;
    othering the other 78–81; self and 15, 17–18,
    76–90
othering 13–14, 77–81
out-groups 99–100
Oxford University 126

Paige, R.M. 127–8
Palestinian–Israeli conflict 4–5, 112–13, 114,
    115–17
Parents' Circle 5
partnership working 148
partnerships, educational 4, 143–9
peace work 3–4, 108–24
pedagogical blogging 4, 132–9
peer-presentations 100–2, 103, 130
peer-teaching 135–7
Peking University 126
Pennycook, A. 65–6
performativity 29
Peris, J. 92
pharmaceutical meeting 47, 48–9, 49–53
Phipps, A. 10–11, 100
playful creator 59, 65–8, 72–3
Plovdiv 32–3

politics: of fear 118; general education and
    129–30
Poncini, G. 46, 48, 49, 50
Popkewitz, T. 83–4
Portugal 4, 140–50
postmodern turn 14–15
power 64; relations in interreligious dialogue
    and educational space 82–4
practical reason 93, 94
precarity, conditions of 3–4, 108–24
primary schools 4, 140–50
procedural strategies 133
process model of intercultural competence
    9–10, 136, 141–2
productive bilingualism 68
professional communication module 135–7
professional corpora 44–5
prototypes, identity 3, 59–75
psychological development 72, 73
puppet show 145
pyramidal model of intercultural competence
    development 141–2, 147

radical intellectual 122
radicalisation 117–18, 118–19
'real' other 80–1
regimes of special powers 118–19
relational sequences 53
relationships 121–2; working 133–4
religion 77–8, 85; *see also* interreligious
    dialogue
researcher narratives technique 28
responsibility, intercultural 2, 7–23
restorying of narratives 28–9, 39–40
Rodriguez, R. 62
Roma people 2
Roy, A. 10

Said, E. 114
said, the 8, 15–18
Salaam Bombay 100
same-other 80–1
savoir apprendre 126–7
savoir comprendre 126–7
savoir-etre 126–7
savoir s'engager 126–7
savoirs 11, 126–7
saying, the 8, 15–18
Scarry, E. 118
Schirch, L. 120
Schumann, J. 60, 62
second language acquisition 96; capabilities
    approach 98–105; identity prototypes 3, 59–75
secularism 83
self 2; decentering of 12; and other 15, 17–18,
    76–90
self-awareness 134
Sen, A. 92–3, 94–5, 103, 105
Sephardic Jews 24–40

INDEX

Shalom Jewish Centre Ladino Club 28
Shanghai International Studies University 126
Shen, W.J. 67
Shi-xu 64
siege conditions 112–13, 115–17
silence 122–3
Singapore 4, 132–9
situated meanings 45
skills 141–2
social identity theory 61
SOCINT corpus 44
sociolinguistics of globalisation 63–4
solidarity 13
space of dialogue 82–4
Spain 34, 35
Spanish-speakers, international community of
    29, 34–6
Spencer-Oatey, H. 10
Spinzi, C. 44
Spivak, G. 113
Stadler, S. 10
Starosta, W.J. 10
state, the 114
stateless groups 115
Stoics 95–6
stories, intercultural 145
subaltern other 80–2
subhuman discourse 117
subtractive bilingualism 60
surveillance 118, 119
Swiss chocolate 115
symbolic competence 12, 63
synchrony 15–16

Tajfel, H. 61
teacher-led lessons 99–100
temporality 15–16
TEMPUS Life Long Learning in Palestine
    project 112, 114
third place 70
Tian, H.L. 66–7
totalisation of meaning 17
transcultural flows 66
transformation, conflict 119–23

trauma healing 119
trousers 79
Turkey 33

Ukrainian class 145, 146
UNESCO 1, 109, 114
Unis people 145
United Nations 114–15
United Nations Alliance of Civilizations
    (UNAOC) 71
University of Aveiro, Portugal 140, 143

vague *we* 48–55
valuing diversity 148
vehicle manufacturer meeting 47, 49, 50–3
veil 80–1
viable alternatives 122
vocabulary 129
voice 102–3, 104
von Humboldt, W.F. 12

we, indexical 3, 41–58; categorisation of 47–9
Weil, S. 108, 110, 111, 112, 120
Whiteside, A. 63
Williams, R. 121
Wilson, J. 52
Wiseman, R.L. 9
Witteborn, S. 2
Worchel, S. 99–100
working in partnership 148
working relationships 133–4
workplace, globalised 4, 132–9
world Englishes 63
worldview 87
Wu, D. 66
Wu Zongjie 71

xenophobia 118

Yang, S. 129
Yuanpei College 126

Zhongshan University 126
zones of interculturality 3, 24–40